Inside-Out

Inside-Out

A Journal Out of a Spiritual Journey

SMANU

PARTRIDGE
A Penguin Random House Company

To order additional copies of this book, contact
Partridge India
000 800 10062 62
orders.india@partridgepublishing.com

www.partridgepublishing.com/india

Dedicated to The Cosmic Family of

Shiva, Shakti, Skanda, Ganesha and Manikanta…

Acknowledgements

First and foremost, though I dislike sounding formal, I extend my deepest gratitude to my parents – Sri *Bose Salakapurapu and* Srimati *Sita Maha Lakshmi.* To say the least, I owe a lot to them for the person I am today. Especially my father has had a profound impact on my personality and thoughts as a kid. Thanks to my brothers Shravan and Raghavendra (The S Kumars! – Kumar is their middle name) for all the love, care, laughs and annoyances we share. If not for my family, which has been with me and stood by me through my thick and thin times, I would not have reached this point of being able to share my experiences with you.

Thanks to my Physics Teacher Sri *Narasimha Gowda* for becoming my other family member through his valuable words and timely advice. Thanks to all my friends, real and virtual – my fellow blog authors @Twilight Musings, @flawsophy and @vramya (my friend off the blogging too) – who prodded my inquisitiveness constantly during this journey. Thanks to Betsy Rabyor for her efforts in reviewing the manuscript. She has been my companion in the process of Awakening since late 2013.

Special thanks to the South-Indian Newspaper *The Hindu* (and ofcourse the people behind it who make it happen!) which shaped my perspectives and ideologies ever since my childhood. And thanks to every person who touched and impacted my life so far and helped me grow, with or without my knowledge…

Foreword

The world today is suffering with unbalanced mind power growing expeditiously at the cost of spiritual strength. The human evolution so far is the expression of a whole, a Trinity of body, mind and soul.

A powerful mind requires a 'more' (or let's just say 'an equally') powerful spirit to guide it. The deficit of it, is the manifestation of destructive science instead of a constructive science (a science with a heart), we are more or less seeing today.

In such times of imbalance, the Cosmic Spirit finds a necessity to express itself through humans and that is the reason for rising Kundalini/Cosmic Awakenings within thousands of people today. It's an expression to reinstate balance in the world, to usher in Spiritual Power tantamount to the Mind Power.

This author too had one such Awakening in 2012, but in hindsight she sees that the journey started in 2008 itself. She would like to share her spiritual journey with people, for the Cosmic Wisdom feels a necessity to express itself and be propagated for a collective benefit.

This book *Inside-Out* is a journal of her personal notes presented in the same time sequence of the journey - of how her pain culminated in peace. There is no story in it. The notes are not connected in any intentional manner. It is a discrete set of analyses of things that happened around her, as she made this journey. It is a set of many small stories, very similar to the way we live in this world. We are all part of a bigger story, have been spawned out of it and are weaving our own stories. And living in the little bubble worlds of our own stories, we are weaving the bigger story back.

The intention of this book is to facilitate the readers to explore their part and role in this Grand Design that is Universe, through their own soul journey spanning this vast history of human evolution. Because that is what her journey enabled her to find out - her role and part as a little cog in this grand schema. In exploring your own self, you never know, you might just bump into the deepest human mysteries of all times. Irrespective of what she gained or lost, discovered or got demystified of, this journey has reinforced this author's long-held conviction that – *Happiness is the default state of a being...*

"We have no more right to consume happiness without producing it than to consume wealth without producing it."

— George Bernard Shaw.

"We are not rich by what we possess but by what we can do without."

— Immanuel Kant.

"The most terrible poverty is loneliness and the feeling of being unloved. One of the greatest diseases is to be nobody to anybody."

— Mother Teresa.

The Awakening has already started Inside You. And on the Outside, the sublime plot unleashes itself as Tapestry and Serendipity intertwine in Destiny Divine ...

Contents

Images

Your Inception into this Journey

Sometimes, what we think is our inside is outside and vice versa. We hurt our inside to see some benefits on the outside, just for temporary gains, while they might not be of any worth in the long run. On the other hand, they might hamper the 'Long Run'. But it is our inside that is ours, that has been with us, not just in this life-time but every time we assumed life. It is our soul! It is the only thing that is ours. It is precious, it needs to be handled with care for IT is us - WE ARE THE SOUL, we are not the bodies and minds we think we are. Nevertheless, we are a sum-total of all - body, mind and soul - a whole, if that awareness of the soul has to manifest.

Nothing gauges today's sorry state of the world more than the fact that many amongst us don't believe in the existence of soul. That tells me the seriousness of the problem we as a world are facing today, it tells me about the chaotic lives we are leading today and thus the chaos we have put the Earth and the Humanity in - at the anti-thesis of the Cosmic Wisdom. As a dialogue in an English movie "Lucky You" goes - *"We are leading our lives as we should play cards and we are playing our cards as we should lead our lives"*.

The Earth and The Humanity that we often refer to in our day-to-day lives are not mere terms, they are living entities - cosmic beings who ARE bearing the burden of the earth as a planet and Karma of mankind, respectively. What they are bearing becomes a 'burden' when the Karma is not manageable here and it becomes a 'responsibility' of contributing to the evolution of Universe, if the Karma is manageable. This means our deeds are very important. Each and every one of us is contributing and impacting the course of the Universe in a good or a bad way. We all have an inside-out relationship with Gods. As Gods are working there, we are working here and as we are working here, they are working there - they make us and we make them, there is no other magic. In that sense God is both inside of us and outside of us.

When we deplete Earth of its resources and energy to make money for our temporary lives, we are making Her unusable as a planet for future generations, we are depleting her of her capacity to bear life! Sure we NEED to use resources to perpetuate life, but as the famous saying by the Mahatma goes - *"Earth provides enough to satisfy every man's needs, but not every man's greed"*. Science is a way of life for us. Let's shed the meaning we generally tend to attribute to Science. But is Science anything more than man's introspection and passion of the mystery of the nature around him? Science must NOT be seen as a sheer modern tool which advocates rationality and disproves our so-called belief in God. Rationality sometimes is being seen by some, as synonymous with atheism, which is so untrue. Science as an instrument, no doubt, has achieved fantastic things so far. But we are now almost at crossroads of devising destructive Science instead of a constructive Science by forgetting our roots, our awareness of our souls. Let this truth be known, Gods too have been with us, in our journey of Science. And they are struggling to stop our plunge on to the destructive side of Science and its impact on us! We all need to act on this - how? You might ask! For now, I'll defer this answer, for you are more capable of finding it on your own, when that time comes when you have to act.

While many things can turn a person inside-out, it is said love or the denial of it, is the most powerful way. Fortunately or unfortunately it wasn't the love for a guy that did this for me. But what did turn me inside-out is the devotional fervour and love towards my Cosmic Father, Lord Shiva. Yes, there was a Cosmic/Kundalini Awakening in me ever since 2012. And I'm so glad to come out and voice this out in public today. My journey of these 2 years has been steered by the Cosmic Guidance. Having been through it, I've become an even stronger defender of free-will of human being, than I was before. I understand the scope of free-will in human life more because of a better understanding of God. Because, if there was no free-will, there would not have been so many sins here just as there are merits!

I'm mesmerized by the diligent care The Father takes of this Universe. I can see His Protection in my doting father here especially, as also in my mother and brothers, teachers, doctors, good preceptors, many men and women who are passionate to know things, specialize in various aspects to serve or contribute to the society while they are making a living, those who are working day and night to keep things going on in the society and many more, it's such a long list. And last but not the least, as any other girl would, I'd love to see such fatherly protection in my husband too, when he enters my life. God is truly in the intricate and subtle details around us. While there is good, there is bad too because of our deeds and that is how society distributes itself.

The absolute truth of human life is that this Universe is expanding through the periodic fission and fusion of masculine and feminine aspects of Universe. I call these forces - Shiva and Shakti. You might call them with whatever name you want. The ultimate realization of human life is not just the mere awareness of this fact but reaching a state where we can believe this FACT. I do not expect everybody here on Earth to experience this realization - for it depends on their own soul journey - their past merits, demerits and purpose of lives. One's purpose of life could be to save a life through medicine, another's to teach and somebody else's could be to just collect this information I wrote. All are equally important whether or not you believe it.

I literally lost myself when I started this journey. It is a tough one, no doubt. But having been through it, I would not mind losing my identity one more time, get absolved in the vast eternity of Universe - that is the beautiful Shiva-Shakti intertwining - redeem myself and come out pure! The journey is worth the journey, for there is no destination, since the Universe is Continuous. But as it is said, it all ends where it starts, so I give back and dedicate all my writing ever since 2012 till now, to Lord Shiva for it all started there.

The experience of God is beyond words, yet I tried... I tried to put this experience in words. It starts with a naive "me" musing about the world and the events around. So, as you go through this book you see all the facets – grief, comedy, enquiry, helplessness, arrogance, philosophy - of a person confronted with such a challenge and the acceptance of such exploration. Such is the all-encompassing nature of the process of Realization of God. It is an aggregate of different perspectives and different ways of looking at the world. It is not a guide, not a self-help book for Kundalini/Cosmic Awakening within a person, not a compilation of some ancient wisdom that can be part of a scripture. It's only a write-up of the journey as guided by the Gods; it has their love, their criticism, their diligence and care towards human beings as also my response to this experience - my pain and exhilaration. This journey is open to anybody who senses a need or even curiosity and has time to know this. So check it out if it strikes with you at all, if it interests you, leave me your feedback, it matters.

Watch out! We are extremely lucky to be in one of the rarest of rare transition periods that marks an important milestone in human evolution. While death can gift one, redemption, experiencing redemption while one is alive can be chaotically fascinating. Rudolf Otto uses the phrase *mysterium tremendum et fascinans* to describe it. Kabir Das described it differently -

यह तन्न विष कि भेल है, गुरु अमृत कि खान,
शीश दिएः जोह गुरु मेलः, तोह भी सस्ता जान!

(*This Body is a pot of Poison; God is reservoir full of nectar.
If I cut my head for God, it would still be a cheap bargain.*)

And this author has written quite many pages on it, with some purpose behind it. And that purpose is most probably fulfilled today. But if she too has to come up with a phrase, it's - "Inside-Out"...

With all due reverence and fond love towards The Father,

- A daughter.
(smanu,
S. Mamata Anurag.
Contact:
mamata.anurag@gmail.com)

- Feb 13, 2014, 11:33 PM.

. . . . .

This book is majorly compiled out of my blog posts and few Facebook notes. Hence I refer to each chapter as 'blog post' in this book. And since I have with me the time-stamps for each post (all of them as per Indian Standard Time, despite them being written in different countries in different time zones), I just retained them in the book. They are not intended to add any additional information. Yet, *Time* is the only connecting thread that connects all these notes. And in that sense, yes, may be it does add some information. Also I used certain non-English terms and phrases in Telugu, Hindi or Sanskrit as they occurred to me. For the convenience and understandability of the readers, the terms or phrases which are either Non-English or Indian colloquial or specifically technical jargon or not-so-generally used English content (say for instance Kundalini) are differentiated using this font. These terms are explained as Footnotes at the end of respective pages. Some terms are explained multiple times as per their occurrence for the convenience of those readers who might not read the content sequentially. In fact a suggestion for reading this book is that this need not be read sequentially, as will be evident once you start reading it and in fact it makes a better reading that way to pick up a random piece any time that strikes with you better for a given situation.

Also, the tone of the content might sound preachy at some places as though I am offering some advice to the readers. But let it be known that it was not my original intention. In fact all the content was written for myself for future reference and for few readers of my blog. It never occurred to me that I might make a book out of it...not until towards the end of it. In fact, through this book, I am sharing more or less a diary of mine. When statements like "This is profound", "This is ridculous" are made, they inherently mean - "This feels profound to me", "This sounds ridiculous to me". Ofcourse this is evidently implied and I am aware that this is understood by the readers too. But when talking about sensitive subjects, there is a possibility that such sentences might offend the views of the readers and I have thus tried, wherever possible, to make it explicit that such views are personal. But, wherever such qualifying is missed out, please read them as my personal views.

And another thing is, many statements in the book are generalized observations, unless otherwise mentioned, for a given context and I understand there will always be exceptions or the other side of the argument. So, when a statement like *"The over-protective woman treats her son like a kid and never allows him to be a man"* is made, read it as a generalized statement made for a given context. It does not in anyway imply that a mother never gives her son the liberty to be a man, nor is it aimed to belittle the attributes and strengths of a mother. Another important note for the readers is that I'm not trying to advocate any particular religion through this book. Though, I have vastly spoken about Hinduism for that is the religion of greater acquaintance to me. I'm sure it would be possible to talk about the most of those, if not all concepts through other religions as well. Any advice – spiritual or otherwise – may be taken only as per the reader's discretion. Finally, the content of this book is restricted by my purview of awareness and knowledge levels. If it offends the feelings, opinions or views of anybody, I am open to receive corrections, suggestions, criticism or feedback.

A *Disclaimer* I would like to make is - I do not own any responsibility of coincidence of the content and thoughts written in this book in case these experiences and thoughts occurred to other people at almost about the same time. That is purely coincidental. I cannot rule out a high incidence of probability of such coincidence because, I thoroughly believe, we are all after all a part of and at the same time inherently guided by The Absolute Consciouness and hence ONE.

Part I: 2007-08

BACKGROUND:

2007-08 was the period when I was in Sweden as the Onsite Coordinator from TCS for a Telecom project with Ericsson in Linkoping. This period of about more than a year was a period of self-discovery for me. It was that time when I had to manage residing all alone in a vast apartment provided by TCS, in a very sparsely populated country that is Sweden (which I fondly call "The Icy Desert"), quite contrary to the crowd culture I'm pretty much used to, back in India. Except for few brief intermittent periods when some girls of my Company joined me during their brief assignments in Sweden, I resided more or less alone there.

It was during May 2008 just as I returned back to India, that the Cosmic Awakening first started within me. It is Awakening only in hindsight, but back then all I sensed was that something strange was happening inside me. What was more strange was, something of that sort to happen when I was home, no more alone.

After about five months of enduring it and coming to terms with the fact that something strange was indeed happening (I read it "abnormal" back then!), I tried to seek medical help. But within 10 days of medication, I put on 15 kgs of weight and realized that the medication was proving more counter-productive. I immediately stopped taking medicine and resorted to Yoga for *healing. It worked well and soon by mid-2009 I was able to lead life normally again. Sure, this phase was a mystery and left many unanswered questions for me, but little did I know then that this phase was to recur again to answer all those questions…*

. . . . .

1. What keeps a person going?

Had been wondering what it is, that everybody is after, in this life.….

Went to a library and behind the scores of books saw the varied perspectives peeping. Different people see life in different perspectives, yet each of them is so true and appeals, well, if you 'listen' to the writer's voice. Reasoning doesn't always work, but accepting does, being receptive does!

Sat in the bus and saw people had different ways to keep themselves busy. Some play Sudoku, some read newspaper, some stare into the vacuum, some stare into the future, some cherish the past, very few think of the present. Huhh! The present is not all that interesting, is it? Because you need to act immediately! I consider the driver the luckiest of all, he takes us to our destination! What greater act can a person do than to help one reach where one is destined to be?

Switched on the TV…the journalists and reporters are busy putting their best show forward, gather news, edit it well, present it in an appealing way, use their best English. The news channels are always filled with some or the other news, that's always Flash Flash news, each of them claims they are the best news channel in the country. Doesn't matter! They are spending every minute to be the best, so it doesn't matter even if they are bluffing. It's interesting in fact, to see so many competitors on field! Everyone wants to give one's best. The actors and actresses are busy with all the feats they can do to sustain longer in the field...

Opened a newspaper...the Science and Technology column had various articles that hardly interested me. People do research for so many years, with such a lot of patience but that's not of interest to everybody, it's only to some people belonging to an elite group, akin to the authors themselves. Where do they derive all the energy from? The Page 3 articles are different though, it has a larger section of audience. It's both fun and easy to be bothered about what you don't usually have to bother yourself of.....

What keeps each of us motivated? Well the answer isn't that easy! The search to answer this question is what keeps us busy. You got to do everything to justify your existence and at the end of day, you need to keep yourself happy, that is all what matters. But that is what, is the toughest thing on earth - To be happy with one self! You be happy with yourself, the next moment the world is in all harmony with you!

- Nov 10, 2007, 4:07 AM.

2. Break the ice

Today walked in the grass, breaking the ice!!! Not really ice, snow! Yep, it's time for some snowfall. It started snowing yesterday, the 9th of November. Hmm! Linkoping did host me already with snowfall when I came here first on March 24th. But that was when I was quite oblivious to the surroundings around me!

It was Diwali yesterday, left office early at about 5:15 in the evening, just to discover that snowfall has started this winter! Deepthi my room-mate left for Germany to visit her brother and other relatives. I was left with Rajani, my other room-mate. On the way back home in the bus, I was thinking of how great a Diwali night would be back home in India. Ok, enough of missing things, I really wanted to pep up myself then. May be we can't burn crackers, but we can at least decorate home with some lights right, ok we thought let's go buy some candles. Rajani and I bought a pack of 100 candles and decorated our home.

Ok, by the way how many of us try to break the ice when it is time to? Do that when you have to, it might cost you a good friend!

- Nov 11, 2007, 3:36 AM.

3. When the going gets tough, the tough get going!!!

Well it's definitely not about me. And I don't want to be one of those tough people. Well, I don't want to get into tough times actually, but life is so cruel *and I'm so foolish* that I mistake even the best opportune times as the toughest :-)

Tough times!!! Well there are a variety of them, but my tough times were when I was getting incapable of things I love to do. Yes! When you are disinterested in doing something and you don't do it, that's absolutely fine. But if you have to be a silent incapable spectator of things you love, then that's really terrible.

When does that happen? When you lose confidence in yourself. Never think low of yourself, self -respect is quite important and give it the due respect and most of the times you are lucky if you don't have to get into this kind of thinking....

- Nov 18, 2007, 4:09 AM.

4. When the going gets tough, the tough get going?!?!?

The previous post was the Part-I alright :-) and was written when I thought I really was in tough times...

Not that, things are much better now, just that I realized - tough times are but a part of life. Yes turbulence is good! If that's not there, where's the place for "change" in life. Hmmm, 'disturbance' is not really disturbing, interesting aint't it?

For instance, just take the Second law of Thermodynamics which states that - The *entropy* of an *isolated* system not in *equilibrium* will tend to increase *over time*, approaching a maximum value at equilibrium. When I read the statement somewhere that - All things in the observable universe are affected by and abide by the laws of Thermodynamics - I didn't quite agree with it, thought it's only for the material objects. But no, I was wrong, this law is so well applicable to the 'living species' too! I'd restate it for you - the homo sapiens - The frustration of a *lonely* being *untouched* by the rest of the world will tend to increase *over time*, approaching a maximum value when he could almost go mad, but since he can't (you know why), he attains *equilibrium* or the so called *peace of mind* :-)

Yeah so you know why one can't go mad, yeah everybody knows it. The strongest force in the world is the will to survive. Yes you need to survive!!! You can let go things only until you realize that they intimidate your survival, you can't let them go beyond that! That is when you get back to your usual self or that is when you realize that all this analysis is a mere non-sense and only 'living normally' makes sense. Then all that you want to do is 'live', nothing else. The past shall no more be a barrier, the future shall no more be a daunting challenge.....

Yes, too much of analysis spoils things, when you are in tough times or rather when you think you are in tough times, keep silent. Just keep silent and do not give your brain too much of a job...it isn't good aid at all! All the logic in the world seems to defy your comprehension...just keep silent...easier said than done??? Well, this was said only after that 'too much' analysis and then loads of silence ;-)

Yeah I did try analyzing why I get so much unequipped during insecure times, but it only added to that insecurity. You see, the burgeoning complexity of mind is mind boggling and it's beyond human comprehension. So it's better to stay away from this thing. Well, let me conclude it by saying - when you start analyzing yourself, when you start being too critical about your flaws, you cease being yourself...

Ok fine let's go back to the interesting Second law of Thermodynamics, the law of increased entropy, stated in a different form - The 'quality' of matter/energy deteriorates gradually over time - how? - Since the usable energy is inevitably and irretrievably lost in the form of unusable energy for productivity, growth and repair. Let's not 'let go' the usable energy...tap it...create disturbances to vibe in the maximum amplitude every now and then...

You can have 'order' in place for a long time, but the order that comes after disorder/chaos is very valuable and more stable since you know what destruction that disorder has created...

There's hope after despair and it is more 'hopeful'... :-)

When the going gets tough, the tough get going...the weak get tougher too...

- Dec 13, 2007, 2:48 AM.

<u>*Note left by Lakshmi Suma:*</u>

Mams... I could read your mind as is with each and every sentence you have written. I agree with every word you said.

You are so good at presenting the emotional picture to the readers, which is quite often so difficult, that I could almost feel, just with your blog, the intellectual storm in the mind and also the silence that comes after it's gone.

I am glad that you have penned this wisdom you gained through your experiences, for others also to gain from it.

- Dec 15, 2007, 09:32 PM.

5. The year that was 2007!!!

Well - All's well that ends well, what we remember of a thing is mostly from what happened with it last. Though 2007 was an important one for me for more reasons than one, let me capture the last days of this year.

We girls (Soujanya, Neelima, Deepthi and myself) went on a short Euro trip - covering the bordering countries of Sweden. Our trip started at 1:30 am, 30th Jan 2007 and our first destination was Malmo on bus. We reached there at about 7:00 am, visited Turning Torso, our only place of interest there since we allocated very less time for Malmo, had breakfast at about 9:00, roamed again and then started for Copenhagen. Actually our tryst with the Inter-Rail Pass started at Malmo. We first enquired the Information Personnel there if we have to pay anything extra, since we were warned enough that we'll have to shell out lot of money towards the reservation charges. But fortunately, that wasn't the case. Later we got into a train, but we got into a first class compartment by mistake, while our passes were those of second class. We soon found ourselves crossing the Oresund Bridge on train. Well, Oresund connects Sweden and Denmark.

.... To be continued

- Jan 15, 2008, 2:26 AM.

6. I often wonder...

Today I was reading an article on the experiences of a theatre-artist, settled in Perth, during her trip to India. I was truly amazed by her versatility, energy and passion for various things. But what caught my notice was this part...

"This time, her home country made her realize that she has changed. Inevitably for those who live abroad, there comes a time where they seek a place to call home, to set roots. She came home with the idea that India could be a place that she could retire to, during her final years. "Could I possibly go back and live there?""

Yes, the longing to be back home was clearly there. Not just with her, apparently 90 out of 100 people settled abroad would want to get back home at some point in life. Ahahh! Not some point, let me be clearer, I personally believe, they want to get back when they can't earn anymore, when their presence abroad doesn't fetch them any money and above all when they can't find any peace, when there's no one to care for them, when there's no helping hand, that is when they would like to get back. I might sound very harsh when I say this, but I believe that's the fact, I have seen it happen with many...

I'm no patriot in any sense and I'm not against the idea of one staying abroad or settling abroad, but why does one like to get back to homeland??? Because it's home and home is the 'place to be' finally! Yeah, it's the place to be, but isn't it also a place you build and make, filling it with stuff truly worth cherishing...

I had asked some of my friends staying abroad this question - "When do you prefer to get back?". The common answer is - definitely not now, may be after 5-10 years. When asked - "What's the right time to be abroad", most of them said 20 - 30, but I said 25-30 was the time when you start a family and don't you think India is the right place to be??? Their immediate answer was - that's the time when you can earn the most, so logically that's the best time.....

No doubt I completely agree with the answer. It is absolutely true, more so logically. But I'm not quite happy with the idea that most of them see their homeland as the best place to retire. You need your homeland to be reared up, to be educated, to make friends, to build yourself, you go abroad to make money, but you again need homeland to retire? Aren't you being selfish? You leave your country, when you can best serve it? You leave it, when it needs you the most? Why can't you find the same solace and peace that you find in your homeland, in the so called "foreign" country, during your days of incapability? You definitely lack the "warmth", because it's "foreign"...

- Jan 21, 2008, 3:54 AM.

. . . . .

In Hindsight:

Life, faith, aspirations and destiny takes people to different places while emotional attachment and craving for roots might sometimes bring some people back home. Some are well capable of finding a home away from home. Who am I anyway, to question these evolutionary human tendencies? :-)

7. All is well, that begins well...

Sarvadharinama Samvatsara Subhakankshalu[1]...

(Wishes for this new year by name *Sarvadharinama*)

My day began with the greetings from home :-) It was really special to get them from much loved ones staying miles away...

The day before, my Mom was reminding me, *You didn't eat* Ugadi Pachadi[2] *the last year too...* Hey I was already trapped in Linkoping by that time and there rang the bells.... Okkkkk!!! That's the reason the year that was past wasn't all that good!!! ;-) *Ok what good is it Mom, reminding me this late, I got to prepare well ahead to be able to eat Pachadi the next morning aint it???* I was cursing myself.

Ok, today the new year started and I don't know how, but new energy started flowing in. At least I believed so. It was reflecting in my workspace and mind space too :-) I started feeling pleasant, went to office late and left early and I was feeling great!

---

[1]   Sarvadharinama Samvatsara Subhakankshalu: *(Telugu)* It means *"New Year Wishes for this year of Sarvadharinama"*. The Telugu New Year is not the same as English New Year. And as per Telugu Calendar, years repeat with a periodicity of 60, each of them assuming different names. The year 2008 assumed the name *Sarvadharinama*. (*Samvatsara*: year's; *Subhakankshalu*: wishes)

[2]   Ugadi Pachadi: (Telugu) The eve of the Telugu New Year is reckoned using the term *Ugadi*. To be more precise, as per Sanskrit, it is *Yugadi - adi* means beginning, *Yugadi* literally means the beginning of a *Yuga* (age). *Pachadi* in Telugu means pickle. The Pachadi is usually made of six ingredients offering it six tastes synonymous with six facets of life.

I hurried to the so called *Irani Shop* to fetch Jaggery and Tamarind, the two main ingredients of the Pachadi. Actually a sign board 'closed' was hung by the time I went (It was 10 mins past 6:00 and the shops close by 6:00), but who cares? I'm always late and I never mind :-)

And by the way I just sneaked into the shop as they were just winding up and managed getting the ingredients.

After that, went to the neighboring *Hemkop* to buy Mango. I allowed myself to pamper myself, go exotic and buy some 'Exotic Snacks'...came home, called home and finally felt home almost a year after coming to Linkoping. Yes, this day was special... bringing new air into my life... I started loving it...the very thought of going home filled me with more and more energy. Hmmm! Ate Pachadi as I intended, shared it with my dear friends Manasa and Rajesh. They invited me for dinner and it was real yummy. It was an apt beginning for a new year...

I'm just looking forward to go home and I'm already feeling better.

After all, all's well, that begins well. Keeping fingers crossed for a fun-filled year ahead for me and my loved ones. Happy Ugadi to all the readers too...

- Apr 08, 2008, 4:35 AM.

8. Do surprises only surprise you?

Pleasant surprises are those things which we would always look forward to. On your birthday if you wake up to see a loved one wish you with a flower it might well be a pleasant surprise, but if that loved one has built a home with a few years spent on it, not with a slightest hint to you, then it might be little too hard to take. What would be really good is, if the loved one lets you be a part of that pleasantness and could give you an equal part in bringing out the cherished surprise...

- May 06, 2008, 12:18 AM.

9. The Year that was 2007!!! - Part II

Well where were we? Yeah near the Oresund Bridge... It connects Sweden and Denmark. I was actually thinking of some good number of snaps capturing the catwalks of my friends. But alas! All my dreams came shattering! We just could pass by it, not on walk unfortunately...passed by it in a jiffy...how good photographs can you get from a moving train, tell me?... So those were Oresund reminiscences...

And then we were already in Denmark. The first thing we were actually doing is...enquiring @ the counters - *When is the next train to Germany please?* We were cross checking if it is at the same time we thought it is, so that our plan is not spoilt. Well, even if it is spoilt, nothing worse can happen. All we would have done perhaps was to have a better trip in Denmark and find our way back to Sweden.

But we were not very unlucky, so the trains were timed as we thought. I mean we had the right time table with us. Ok *cool, let's trip Denmark in a record time of about just 3 hours!* So what did we trip, wait did we trip Kopenhagen? Yeah, we were on roads and what ever were located on roads were our destination favourites...

All that I could remember is some photos on a stream side, few at a famous market square and few before the palaces, museums located strictly in the heart of the city. We only had glimpses of Thivoli Gardens which is credited to have inspired Walt Disney towards his magical creative Land - The one and only Disney Land.

And then we hurried to have our grab of Chips. And back to the Railway Station, there came steaming our train to Germany. The train to Germany was fortunately not the train to Berlin. First to Hamberg and then to Berlin. I guess the beauty of Europe started revealing itself only then... The Euphoria was just setting in!

- Jun 23, 2008, 10:18 PM.

* * * * * * * * * *

"Every child comes with the message that God is not yet discouraged of man."

"Everything comes to us; that belongs to us if we create the capacity to receive it."

— Rabindranath Tagore.

* * * * * * * * * *

Part II: 2009

T his was the period during which Yoga healed me quite well and I was getting on with my life as before. I did not write much during this period.

. . . . .

10. What's in a Rashee?

Heyyy, I write this in the context of the much talked about 'yet to be released' Hindi film - *What's your Rashee?*

This was one of my favourite topics for browsing at one point in life. It was so intriguing to me back then, that I might have laid my hands on almost all the legible websites that describe the 12 zodiac signs.

If you ask somebody whether they really believe in zodiac signs, I'm sure it's a tough question to answer. As for me, I should say I believe in them to the extent that - "Yes, there are certain traits which are indicative of a sign, which are usually seen in most of the people falling under that sign", but not to the extent that - "You behave the way you do because you fall under that sign". Well I believe, we are prone to certain traits because we belong to a particular sign but whether we nurture/hone/suppress them depends on our attitude and a multitude of other factors of reality in the world.

There are two sets of people - those who believe in astrology and the others who don't.

Those who believe in astrology also must admit that everything is destined, so there is little one can do to change it - so why bother? Those who do not believe in it need not anyway bother about it!

The bottom line is there's no point being bothered about horoscopes.

Again coming to me, I started it off just for fun and I hope I submit my thesis on it someday! (and you know that I'm kidding...)

I'm sure there's something about the zodiac signs, a scientific explanation must surely exist, if there is research in that direction - but the research might not be worth it - because I doubt if anybody would benefit from its results, if there is a use case at all!

Well here's my hypothesis for those interested to do a thesis on it ;-)

- ❖ Different vegetables and fruits grow in different seasons, rather different seasons are suitable for the growth of different plants - why? Because factors like sunlight, water, soil play a great role for a plant to survive. So isn't that the case for human beings as well? The season or rather the period in which a life is conceived and nurtured – wouldn't that have a direct bearing on how that being evolves?

❖ There is a force of attraction or repulsion between any two bodies in the universe. And that holds good for as huge a body as Jupiter and as small an organism as amoeba. So definitely the way in which a planet orbits has a direct impact on a person's behaviour.

❖ Why we behave the way we do, is all because of hormones. In short, hormones and genes dictate our attitude. And who knows the "season" factor might well influnce the hormonal constitution of a living being...

That goes to say atleast sun signs are worthy of practical belief. Our ancestors might have based their astrological predictions on some valid theory and research, we never know!

Ok, what's my rashee? Keep guessing..... (Hint: The very fact that I'm interested to write this post on Sun Signs!☺)

- Sep 23, 2009, 10:16 PM.

. . . . .

In Hindsight:

Firstly, a disclaimer is that this post might be relevant for a very narrow set of audience as checking Horoscopes to understand future predictions is a practice followed by a very narrow proportion of world population. As I already voiced out my opinion here in this post, I do not see much point in people checking horoscope compatibility before getting married. This (relying upon and considering horoscope match as essential criteria) usually has been happening in the arranged-marriage setup in India. It perhaps happens in other parts of Asia and also perhaps (I'm not much aware) in very few parts of West too, in different forms though – Indians might call it a horoscope *(Kundali)* match, Westerners might simply call it Sun Sign compatibility.

The point is simple. If fate has already been written and if fate is to be believed – it is unchangeable. Why check something that can't be changed? Isn't it like trying to know the road ahead when you know that a road has already been carved? So it is like wanting to change that pre-destined road! In short checking horoscopes defies the faith in horoscopes and fate and contradicts the basic logic behind them.

Anyway, the fundamental expectation out of all this is to beget some good out of the future. And there, lies the fundamental flaw too, I guess. That, one always expects good to happen. And in that expectation, we sometimes forget that we might not always know what is good for us and that both good and bad are part of life and future. Furthermore, though Astrology started off as a branch of Science, the current day astrologers base their analysis on very old astronomical charts, data and theories; they do not really take into account the dynamic nature of the Universe and its changing influence on Earth and its constituents. Anyday, it's easy and better to accept life as it comes than trying to plot against it in vain.

11. Mysore-Coorg Trip - Mysore!

When I look back at my life, I have many fond memories to cherish about. Of them, some entertained me and some challenged me. Rather than the trips headed for far-off places I have many occasions spent at my very home memorable. Trips might not be major sources of entertainment for a family, but I guess they start assuming importance as the family grows and progresses.

Trips with family are those few occasions when a family re-unites not in the literal sense of it actually. It's that time when you get out of your temporary entrapments of life which you seemingly spent for an eternity in the recent times. It's that time when you switch back to your default state - your default state of happiness.

Kolkata, Annavaram, Tirupathi, Vizag, Rajahmundry, mark a few major spots that I tripped with my family and relatives. It was Mysore-Coorg trip during this Oct 01 - Oct 04th. It was such an unplanned trip that we thought about it on Sep 30 morning, booked the tickets online and set on for the trip that very night. I might be wrong when I said 'unplanned', it was rather sudden, but we did plan it well...gathered all the possible information from Mr. Google, so it turned to be actually well planned. The only exception being the cyclone that havocked the states of Andhra Pradesh and Karnataka during exactly the same time. The week before the travel, my Dad somehow happened to hear this weather forecast of this cyclone on TV. But it was something I rubbed off saying it was another forecast that always goes wrong and more importantly as just another reason that my Dad was trying to cite to avoid this trip. But this time it actually happened but fortunately we were never directly hit by the cyclone. Of the four days, it rained only once, that too in Coorg, where it almost rains everyday during the May - October period.

We knew this but we hoped to be lucky. We were lucky indeed since rain never managed to dampen Coorg's beauty. And now when I think of it, I can't help but write the wonderful reminiscences of the trip. And I write this not for the mere beauty of writing, I mean it in every sense of it, more so because I was desperate for a break at that moment.

Our bus was damn late to Mysore, we reached Mysore at 12:30 noon as against 10:00 AM, the expected time, on Oct 01st. After refreshing ourselves, we quickly made it to the Zoo (only because it was the nearest spot) and Brindavan Gardens. That was the only combination possible since Chamundi Hills were far off and Brindavan Gardens was not something to be missed and we had limited time. Brindavan Gardens was absolutely beautiful during the night with its color fountains and all, but honestly I did not find it as amazing as it was described, they seemed to be just other color fountains. May be it would have been even better had we visited it during the day. The gigantic Krishna Raja Sagar Dam adorned by the Gardens was also good. The sheer engineering brilliance of Sir Mokshagundam Vishweshariah stands out.

The next day on Oct 02nd, we dedicated the first half to Srirangapatnam, located 26 km off Mysore. It has two tourist wings on either sides of Mysore Highway. One wing covers Nimishamba Temple, Sangam, Gumbaz, Daria Daulat Bagh Gardens and the other wing comprises of Sri Ranganathaswamy Temple, Dungeon and gives a bird's eyeview of Mysore City and Tippu's fort.

Nimishamba Temple was a good place to start the day with. It stood serene on the banks of River Cauvery and we just started realizing how it feels to be getting pampered in the lap of nature. Nimishamba Temple derives its name from the faith that Goddess Parvathi blesses her devotees here every nimisha[1]. The weather too was too pleasant - it was neither very hot nor was it raining. It was an apt sunny day that's many a tourist's dream. Sangam was just an extension of this beauty where the tributaries of Cauvery meet, apart from that nothing worth mentioning. You might enjoy the "theppa[2] ride" there (we avoided it with the cyclone dominant during that time in Karnataka). Gumbaz is Tippu's tomb. Not just his', it's the place where his parents and his soldiers too were laid to peace. Daria Daulat Bagh Gardens is Tippu's Summer Palace and Museum. Here you can see his and his family portraits sketched by foreigners after his kingdom was taken over.

And later we went to the other wing. Ranganathaswamy temple was closed by then and we could not wait until 4:00 PM in the evening when it would be opened again. So we had to be satisified with just an outer glimpse. Dungeon is the place where Tippu jailed his British Prisoners, gives you a

---

[1]   Nimisha: *(Telugu)* Minute, the unit of time.
[2]   Theppa: *(Telugu/Kannada)* Wave.

good view of the city interlaced with Cauvery. *This part of the city you can cover on foot and surely you get the feel of dwelling in some 18th Century. This one's not to be missed.* We now started off to Mysore city on bus. The journey on bus from Srirangapatnam to Mysore City was very soothing. It took a longer route covering the countryside of Mysore unlike the Mysore Highway route our Hyd bus took the previous day.

Maybe our royal senses were pampered by the royal fort, but our human senses were reminding us that it was already late for lunch. We had our lunch in Gupha Restaurant as per my friend Bindu's suggestion. If not for the food which did not taste too different from Kannada food as elsewhere in the state, the ambience of the restaurant was worth visiting surely! And then after lunch we went to Philomena's Church, an ancient Roman church. Good one. It was weather that played the hero all the while. It was so damn pleasant that I can't stop thanking it now. And to add to it, there was minimal, rather no pollution at all.....need I say more?

The biggest attraction and the finale of Mysore trip was still awaiting.... Mysore Palace! We passed by it quite many times already but never bothered to take a glance even. Yes Mysore Palace in all its astounding beauty needs to be watched during the night with all its 37000 odd lights on! So we intentionally managed to keep it last on Oct 02 nd night. Mysore Palace is adorned that way on Sundays and national holidays. Needless to mention, it's a tourist's delight! I've not felt the way I felt there, even when I viewed the gigantic Eifel tower..... Awesome! Maybe my patriotic side makes me feel so. No, no! No biases, no prejudices whatsoever, Mysore Palace is much much beautiful than Eiffel Tower. And now my diplomatic side takes over, sorry sorry, no comparison at all..they are completely two different things.

Mysore! Be there during Dussehra[1]...and it would be a festival with an experience of lifetime!

- Oct 07, 2009, 12:08 AM.

---

[1] Dussehra: is an Indian festival celebrated for nine days (called Navratris in India, nav – Nine, ratri - night) symbolic of the victory of good over bad, a victory established by the Supreme Goddess Shakti (*Durga, Parvati and Kali* being Her usual celebrated forms during the festival).

* * * * * * * * * *

"The reasonable man adapts himself to the world; the unreasonable one persists in trying to adapt the world to himself. Therefore all progress depends on the unreasonable man."

— *George Bernard Shaw.*

* * * * * * * * * *

Part III: 2012

BACKGROUND:

*A*s I said in Part I, I had no clue back in 2008 that the symptoms of Awakening shall recur again in my life. What I considered 'abnormal' back in my past soon was to become a 'normal necessity' in the path of realization of my self and my purpose of life.

I came to Delhi during August, 2011 after working for Quantum (an American based organization that works on devising efficient Storage Backup and Retrieval methodologies), Australia, to take coaching for UPSC (the coveted entrance test by Union Public Service Commission which facilitates, among other jobs, entry into Indian Administration giving one a place in Indian Bureacracy and hence Indian Governance, Decision and Policy Formulation) preparation.

But UPSC preparation took a huge setback with the Awakening symptoms recurring, since a huge share of my mind was demanded by the process of Realization. To begin with, I started experiencing the phenomenon of Synchronicity. This process has been explained already elsewhere by many, but I define it for you here, my way... the way I perceive it. It is the ability one gets, when raised to a higher dimension through an external intervention, in all the possibility, through the process of Cosmic/Kundalini Awakening, to see the connectedness of events around in the world...And hence, getting to understand that human soul and consciousness is all inter-connected and guided by one Absolute Consciousness. Eventually, experiencing Synchronicity, when rightly followed and explored, leads to the belief in existence of God within and outside us.

Well, in hindsight it has been easy to explain Synchronicity, but it took almost a year (2012-2013) for me to understand that I was indeed experiencing this wonderful phenomemon. Though, it is not without its share of tremendous pain in all forms and at all levels. This should not be mistaken with complete ability to predict future. One of the posts in the following pages explains the pros and cons of the process of prediction in better detail.

Also my Awakening process was different from the way it apparently happens with many people. It did not start from the lower Chakras, so technically it's not Kundalini Awakening; it started from my highest Chakra, so I term it as Consciousness Awakening.

. . . . .

12. So what is a failure streak? Just some thoughts...

The batsman is not in form, the pitch is not friendly, it's scorching hot, the Sun is sapping him of all the energy and the bowler is in complete form bowling googlies and bouncers, no wides, no nobs☹...

What to do? The batsman should just give up himself and get lost for an lbw or go retired hurt before the bowler dismisses him for a run out...

What else to do? The batsman should just bang his head against the pitch, throw the bat on the bowler, yell at the crowd and run (just run as though king-kong is haunting him) into the dressing room and have some peace!

. . . . .

A man approaches a theologist to seek some thoughts on religion and help him realize God. The theologist gives the man a book to read and understand 'some (very enlightened) thoughts'. The man goes home, opens the book in all excitement and to his astonishment sees that the book is in Latin and he knows no Latin. He comes back again, the theologist gives him a DVD with some religious content. The man goes home, tries playing the DVD but his DVD player doesn't play this content, his laptop won't help even. The unrelenting man goes back to the theologist now with more curiosity and anxiety dying to realize God, the theologist gives him a slip with note "G O D I S N O W H E R E"... You know what the theologist meant and what the man understood. The man who really wanted to seek God is now pissed off with theologist's reply, so now he is set to realize God all by himself without the theologist's help...

What to do? The man should go to a deep wild forest as wild as Amazon, spot a nice clean rock and set on a penance on one leg (hope he balances himself, ohh just hope he gets used to

59

it...) hoping God will dawn upon him some day...if not God Himself, atleast His mercy...

What else to do? The man can *"Just renunciate and go to Himalayas"*!

What more to do? The man might just stop breathing, if God has mercy He will come and rescue, else he will directly reach God...eitherways he shall realize God!

. . . . .

A couple fights and each clarification leads to yet another misinterpretation. So this is how it starts...

Wife: "Honey! What does 'awesome' mean?"

Husband: "Apple (you know you look so round)! It's some awe exaggerated!"

Wife: "Stud! What does 'exaggerate' mean?"

Husband: "Chicken (you know all you do is coo coo in your closet!) You know, all you women practise this 'nefariously' when you fight with us!"

Wife: "Ahh I see! What is 'nefarious' you hackster! (You hacked my ID the other day, didn't you? So you are my hackster! Ahh, now I got a good word, I'm catching up!)"

Husband: "Awesome! You are just right on track...keep going (away, just get lost) you (dumb) DumbLe-belledDolly..."

Wife: "Did you just say I'm dumb?"

Husband: "Read between the lines!"

Wife: "There is no space between your lines, did you even gasp for a breath?"

What to do? Just shut up, don't clarify, don't even try! Don't tread the other person's path, just be yourself, the otherway round just doesn't help, in fact there's no choice...

What else to do? Refer to the above, there's no choice (it is said!)

.....

.....

.....

And the saga of 'failure streak' thus continues!

- Jan 10, 2012, 03:03 PM.

13. Surya S/O Krishnan!

This movie has had an indelible impression on me when I watched it the second time some one and a half years ago. What starts as a mere time sequence of events in the life of the protagonist Suriya, unfolds to be much more than that - a whole spectrum of emotions and ambitions a guy can possibly go through. It's very difficult to understand love and life from a guy's perspective, me being a girl, but this movie quite effectively mirrors those feelings.

The most touching part of the movie is that sequence where Suriya having lost his love, wanders aimlessly, uses drugs to handle pain, does whatever he gets to do, whatever he comes across, with no sole purpose. But that was just a phase! Such a phase never can, or rather never should remain forever. So thankfully it passes much to the relief of the viewers.

This phase (for whatsoever reasons one reaches, not necessarily due to a love failure) seems crazy and insane to many people, but no, it is not. This is when a person is not at peace with himself, unable to come to terms with himself. But people, who have not been through this, dismiss it shabbily. In fact those people are the unlucky lot, I'd personally believe. Not that everybody must go through this, but it's not as bad as people think. This is the phase which when gone through, will make one appreciate the real worth of life and appreciate oneself for what one is. You are just what you are, you just can't change that. It's always easy and good to accept rather than deny oneself. Tiding against oneself leaves one in lurch, creating a vacuum that can never be filled. One is one's own best friend then and self-help is the first resort if not the only resort. In this movie, Suriya's parents are such wonderful, non-interfering parents that they understand his emotional needs aptly and cater to them just rightly.

In fact people who go through this phase are the fulfilled lot, according to me. People end up either trusting God completely or stop believing in Him during this phase. No matter what, it is bound to thrust you to tread a different path (from the normal flow) where you start exploring some deepest truths of life. If you are lucky, you are bound to emerge successful and in fact establish those truths only to share it to the world. The other day I read an article in 'The Hindu' that people who undergo mental turbulence tend to delve into deeper levels of existence, something on a spiritual plane, it's put more appropriately in that article. All I intend to put across is, it is a scientifically established fact.

Love, I had always felt, is an extreme emotion. Perhaps it would be better to say - Love is "the" extreme emotion. It can beautifully permeate into various other emotions. When this emotion is used constructively, it works wonders, when dealt destructively it only leaves more pain. This is why I was always a staunch advocate of the idea of "get married at the right time". When one has a partner who understands and supports one rightly, one's emotional needs are met and one can focus on other things of life too. When the emotional needs themselves are not met, the struggle percolates and disturbs other parts of life too. The couple can struggle and grow together and I'm sure such hard work will be cherished when looked back at. But then, this is the *ideal* thing and there are many other factors which lead to the reality being quite different from what was expected.

Hence as I progress in life, now my convictions stand debunked, well not all, let me say 'some'! I'm not sure how many more stand to be repudiated ;-) Well, I still believe life is always a pursuit of happiness and not endurance of pain. I'm sure everybody else in this world also thinks the same. Ok to conclude it easier, there is "no absolute right or absolute wrong" in this world, as one of my friends, Pradeep, says. This opinion of his, makes things so simple right? It's easy to deal with people this way - you don't have to disagree with anybody - "this is your perspective and that is my perspective, this is just the way you feel and that is the way I feel"...well again this seems to be yet another "ideal" thing, not sure. Atleast it helps me get away with my critical nature as I'm always on my toes analyzing what others say and pass on a comment... (whether or not it's taken ;-))

Ok, getting back to the movie, it's a huge sigh of relief to see the guy falling in love again to marry his childhood friend. Look at the immense power of love, it can heal all the wounds, fill all the void and bring colors back. My favorite song in this movie is "Nidaree kala ayinadhi[1]" for I always love happiness more than pain :-) Oh yeah, everybody does!

- *Jan 11, 2012, 05:12 PM*

14. Oh God! Why should I still pray you?

I term this post - "Weeping soul - an open letter to God from an abandoned soul!" This basically expresses the grief of people waiting for God to act on their life, when His apathy has been wreaking havoc in their lives…

"I was never unresponsive, was always sensitive towards my fellow beings, their suffering and feelings, never kept anybody waiting, never left any topic dangling, I attended to every issue that I can, that I had to attend to, as immediately as I can, I took

---

[1] Nidaree Kala Ayinadi: *(Telugu)* These are the lyrics of the song from the Tamil-dubbed Telugu movie "Surya S/O Krishnan", it goes – "*Nidaree Kala Ayinadi Kalaye Nijamayinadi*" meaning "Sleep has become a dream and the dream has become true".

up whatever responsibilities came my way, tried fulfilling them. When all the girls were playing you know what I did, when the rest of them were busy gossiping you know what I did, when some of my friends were being girly you know what I did, yes all I did was being something I was not expected to do or something you didn't expect me to do. But that is something I chose to do, not that I didn't enjoy my life, most certainly, yes I did.

And after having come this far, you still test me and ask me to dream big despite your tests??? What a parody! Dreaming? Did you leave a single brain cell vacant for that? And you ask me to be patient... Patience, what patience? Can you please spell that out for me, it's already wearing thin...

What do you want me to learn from all this? You want me to get tougher... Oh I'm already tough...as tough as Silicon Carbide... I don't need anymore toughness, else even you can't break me further...

You want me to go through the suffering you 'intend' me to? Let me tell you there are many forms of suffering out there in the world, the worst of all being "loneliness and being unwanted". I have been through that for a long time and I bet you have not even sensed it. You are the God, wanted and chanted by everybody. Come live my life for a single day and then you will never ever create another destitute. I don't need a new form of suffering. I'm fine, Thank You!

You want me to feel something? So you always want me to feel something only when you want me to? I have no freedom as to when to feel what? This is so ungodly! And you want to tell me this is a living tribute of love and life? Love for what and life in which sense? This whole creation, your very own, pays a tribute to you daily, by sustaining and evolving everyday, don't you know, can't you just realize?

Or are you avenging me, just because I didn't pray you all the while...because I didn't chant your name? Do you want me to make it that explicit? To reiterate, I'm part of your creation, I'm part of you, don't you know? Why do I even have to pray you? You remember the day you gave me my first hurdle saying "Honey! Come take your first challenge!" I asked you "God, why me?" You should have made me realize that I was not like any other girl who could go on with her life as per her wish and that I was destined to suffer for a greater reason, that I had greater responsibilities to fulfill. Atleast I'd have known, but you never answered me, you never seemed to exist for me. You have been a touch-me-not ever since then, but you still expect me to pray? I tried calling out your name then, but you were not available back then when I wanted you the most...was forced to think God never answers or even exists for unlucky souls like me...were you a naive back then? Atleast I was...so I stopped praying you...yes I stopped praying you...but don't you know I'm always a part of you? Couldn't you help me just right then?

I'm a human, yet I can't bear a creature suffering before me, you being a God how can you be a silent spectator to somebody's suffering? You know I'm suffering, don't you? There's a whole lot of difference between letting somebody suffer when you don't know they are suffering and allowing somebody to suffer when you know they are suffering. God how can you be so indifferent?

Don't you know, I left a part of life by leaving and shutting out some people because I had no self-respect there... I was not given my due there.. I left them, so you know it right? You are omniscient, I don't have to say. Even those foolish and ignorant souls were better in one aspect for atleast they made me realize that it was not the right place for me, but what are you doing now, staying so indifferent. Oh you are God! You have a time for everything! You are God! So what? Be right there, be just that...

I want to cry out, not exactly for your current hurdle, but what life offered me so far...my tears dried over the years...the south pole Sun didn't spare me either, it dried up my tear glands just as much as the Sunshine evaded in the north pole. Do you know how it feels like, when one can't cry when there's a huge whirlpool churning within? I'm sure you don't know - you must have either cried out or you would have never had to cry. I ask you this one sole gift... God atleast make me cry! I want to let go my pain, I can't let my nerve centres disintegrate.

Just because I smile you think I'm happy? Oh that smile, is your very own gift, when you created me. If you ask me, if I had been living all this while, I have no answer, I don't exactly know, I was too busy crossing the hurdles you lay for me, so I just don't realize. I wan't to live life, not just pass the hurdles. I don't want to pass yet another hurdle, even if it means I'll miss out the orchard just a few miles away. I'm no Thomas Alva Edison, I'm a mere human.

There's something called 'patience' and something called 'mercy'. If you have the latter, I'll have the former. Now that you ran out of the latter, I ran out of the former... Now that I crossed my threshold, I want to get rid of clutches, be they of love, hatred or indifference. I have no second thoughts to pursue a path of peace, whatever the destination is, for life had been a bumpy ride enough, I don't know when the bumps exactly started, but I know I don't need anymore bumps...just to reiterate, there's something called patience, maybe I have a little of it compared to others, but that's me.

All I have learnt from my life is - the more patient you are, the more you are tested to lose your patience. Is that fun to you, just to watch people give up in life? To me means are as important as the end, I can't keep dreaming of heaven when I'm undergoing hell, atleast I'm not so ambitious, all I aspire for is a pretty "normal" life, no extremes. But you kept me swinging on the extremes for quite a long time, four years is a pretty long time! That's when you gave me my first hurdle.

I had always answered all the questions I was expected to answer. But my life left me many unanswered questions and unclosed chapters. I never cared, but still you are so merciless to pose yet another question. I can't guess what I'm expected to do or what I'm not...all I now know is I'm not bothered about it anymore. So, I call it quits, I'm not gonna tread your path. I can live life on my own terms and at my own pace. Do whatever you want, but touch me not!"

- Jan 30, 2012, 01:24 PM.

15. To listen or not to listen to the many voices around...

There are many stages you come across in life, when you just can't take a decision, take that call or plunge and you start approaching people for more inputs. And that is where you start inviting trouble!!! Such paradoxical situations are very funny - you can't take a decision, you are restless, so you want to talk to people just to make it clearer and easier for you, so you start seeking others' views and try accommodating them. But for the many voices around you, the situation only gets complicated, leaving you more confused than where you started first. But again, you can't refrain from asking others and go ahead handling things based on your sole exposure and knowledge.

Ofcourse, it is very well known that what others say is only to broaden your thinking, broaden the options, so you have a wider choice to choose from - so you are not missing out on things you otherwise might have not known. At the end of the day, it is always *you* who has to make the decision and yes face the consequences too.

Awesome! So why does it trouble me so much then? Actually, it troubles me when the whole world is saying something and my inner conscience prods me to do just the opposite. Sometimes, I just don't know if it's only me thinking so weirdly or am I so bad at explaining the situation out to others that everybody, virtually EVERYBODY offers me a solution I can't buy. But then, I always respect my conscience and conviction more than anybody else's experience, how much ever learnt that anybody is... So it turns out that it's very important for me to frame the right conscience and convictions. What I actually mean is that when you can't buy what others offer you, you have to be very selective of what you take from life and world on which you base your convictions and from which you nurture your conscience.

So what I really mean is - it is easy if others *share* an experience from which to draw some inferences that can relate to your own problem. It gets tougher when people start *offering (read it rub)* free piece of advice just because you approached them and start divulging your problems. So, the ball again rolls back to your own court - Approach the right set of people.

Ok, most of the decisions in my life were based on my own convictions, so I never regretted the consequences that came along. But yes, my convictions are definitely an end-product of the societal interaction that happens with people around. So the paradox remains - Others contribute to your convictions and not to your decisions just as they can only empathize with your consequences (good or bad) but can't take a share in them. I leave this post here, it certainly seems incomplete for reasons I can't figure out...it's because this is such a delicate topic that keeps recurring time and again how many ever milestones one has crossed in life. I will surely get back and complete it when I achieve a certain amount of mastery over it ;-) I might be 60 or more by then, but never mind, it is better late than never :)

- Mar 26, 2012, 10:28 PM.

16. Happiness is Infinite

What is wrong when all things work just right? People in general believe in this premise - *If the going is tough now, then there is something better in store for you in the future. If everything is sailing smoothly now, then there is some trouble awaiting you.* But I'd say, this outlook of things takes the fun out of the present - If everything is working just right, why not be happy with that, delve in that, why think about the future and spoil the fun? If something is not working right, why not accept that it is not working right, give it the due attention and undergo the pain that is needed. If you are sad now, it means you are sad, no point deceiving yourself and waiting for something you do not know whether it will happen or not. At least if you take the pain now and know that you are in pain, there is a possibility that it might end soon. This definitely does not mean there is no place for 'hope'. It only means that there is no point waiting forever for anything. Eitherways, it reminds me of only one thing which was beautifully put across by one of my softskills facilitator back in Trivandrum during TCS ILP[1] - *"Be there! Live in the present to enjoy the present called present"*.

Ok! Coming back to the actual theme of the post - Happiness is Infinite. Yes it is, atleast that's what I believe! I guess it's a premise to think that it is finite, that something - some unknown event - might knock it, hit it and snatch it off from you. Maybe it can, but that is only temporary. Happiness is a huge bounty that is always there, ever flowing from God. It's for us to realize and receive it. I strongly believe in the adage "You can achieve only that your mind can conceive and perceive". By thinking happiness is finite, i.e., by drawing boundaries and setting standards, you are confining yourselves to smaller things. When you believe that it is possible to push boundaries, you can actually push them to an extent that they become elastic, which goes to say boundaries are not rigid, they can be redrawn on a need basis. That is when you start achieving bigger things. *But is it so easy to reach that state*

---

[1] TCS ILP: TCS is the well known Indian Software Consultancy Company, Tata Consultancy Services. It's my first Organization where I started my career as a Software Engineer. ILP is the Initial Learning Programme conducted by TCS which used to span for about 3-6 months when TCS started off back in 1980s and which was for about 45 days when I underwent the training in Trivandrum.

where you actually believe that you are NOT confined by any boundaries? Definitely not! It's a constant journey in which you put some efforts on a need basis, which are in turn constantly piggybacked or acknowledged by the destiny through some results. Now that means, one has to be lucky to reach that state - the state where you are ready to set yourselves into that journey. Ok, now I definitely don't mean one should always keep achieving bigger things, keep pushing the boundaries constantly - the phrase here is, "on a need basis". Life is more about those small little things than the big achievements that keep popping up once in a while.

Ok so far so good! It's good as long as the conditions are applied. The condition here is that one has to be lucky to reach that stage. It's difficult to define "luck" here. It has different connotations. Some people are persistent, organized, methodical and achieve the results they want. Can we call them lucky? I don't know. But may be, the fact that they are being persistent, makes them lucky. Luck in another sense is that you have bagged enough good karma from your previous births to be able to do things you want to do. There might be various such connotations for luck, but to me 'luck' boils downs to the capability of doing what you want to do, irrespective of the factors contributing towards that capability and favorable consequences.

But what if one is unlucky? Well, the answer is simple. One is NOT yet ready to take on that journey.

In all cases, the Absolute Truth of life is the realization of that happiness which is infinite and never a destination but a journey in itself. Ok that is my inference from my life thus far. Who am I, by the way to conclude anything? So nothing can be written in stone and concluded. Things keep changing from time to time and so will our convictions. But again, there are some universal truths which are timeless and have stood the test of time. So I guess this inference coincides with what our ancestors have preached us through their works (literary), which are a result of experiences of many over a period of time. So, to me, it seems like the truth is always simple and most of the struggles culminate in such simple yet similar truths. I mean, all of us take different paths to reach the same destination or atleast milestones. And yes, when one reaches such milestones, one got to pause and celebrate. And that leads to another favourite adage of mine, quoted in my Xth class English Text Book - *Life is the celebration of being alive!*

I might sound like some philosopher when I talk all this. But people around me say I'm good at it, so may be I am :-) People take to blogging for various reasons - blogs can be used as personal journals, diaries, to vent out pent up thoughts, to socialize so on and so forth. Oh yeah, they can even be used to enlighten others and even yourselves, but that's the most boring way of using the potential of blogging for the current ways of the world. For now, I'm blogging since I want to maintain a repertoire of events happening currently in my life and the experiences I have been gaining from them. *Now, seems to be the important phase of my life - perhaps it's like my much-needed "renaissance". I'm just penning down my thoughts so my future self knows what I was up to now.*

- Apr 28, 2012, 04:37 PM.

17. The melody this summer - A slice here and a slice there is 'Pure Mango Pleasure'!

The heat of the summer has been on in Delhi for over a month already and add to it my test series, the heat was more than what I could take. So today, my ALS Test Series[1] came to an end. And it was such a reliever! I was initially serious with my test series, but later life took the better of me, went ahead of me, dumped me with some serious problems, so my ALS test series took a back seat to bombard me with some other tests on the personal front. So UPSC Prelims completely slipped off my hands... I guess! I think I'm almost sure about that because I know the amount of preparation that went into it so far. Given that there are just 20 days more for prelims, I don't think I can do anything to change the consequences - even if I'm going to do some penance and set on for an "on-the-mission" mode of preparation. I think I know it. I can see it coming. It's almost there, over there, away from me...cheers to me, congrats to me, a back pat to me... Wow, I've done it so well!

So! It was such a reliever? Damn it! I don't even understand why I even consider it to be a reliever, because I never prepared for them and gave the exams every week as though they were some kind of rejuvenating advertisments that keep flashing in the breaks amidst the boring daily TV serial that is the so-called-life :-) And I call it a reliever? Shame on me!

Fine. IT'S OKAY. Well, seems like everything is ok to me these days. So, the test series is over. I'm happy that it is finally over.

---

[1]   ALS Test Series: It is a Test Program conducted by ALS Coaching Institude in New Delhi through a series of Test Papers before the actual exam happens.

Though it's neither an achievement nor a success by any means, I felt damn good today after I gave the exam. I don't know why. I just don't know why. Maybe it's because I'm no more interested to give the exams which I know I will flunk anyways. So why give them at all? After the exam, on the way back home, on the road, I saw two strangers having a Slice cool drink. I really thought I should say cheers to myself and cheer myself, raising a toast to this exam episode. So I immediately brought myselves a Slice cool drink. The shopkeeper didn't have enough change, so he compensated the lacking change with a Melody chocolate toffee. I was so thirsty I drank the Slice on the way itself leaving some. And had the rest of it, after I reached home. And yeah, Slice's tagline is "Pure Mango Pleasure". That is exactly what you want to cool yourselves in this hot summer. Finally, I'm able to cope up with the hot summer of Delhi, I'm in equilibrium of sorts with it. So I declare - The melody this summer is *"A slice here and a slice there is Pure Mango Pleasure"!* Sounds crap isn't it? Yes, it is! I really wish Slice owners stumble upon this blog and enhance their tagline with this beautiful crap ;-)

So that was some ranting and yes it feels awesome!

- Apr 29, 2012, 10:43 PM.

18. *What time is it now?*

An American customer calls up a Customer Service Center in India. The call is picked up by an Indian Customer Care executive. The conversation goes like this...

American: "Hi! I'm expecting a shipment from India. Can you help me with that?"

Indian: "Sure! My pleasure! Shipment ID please?"

American: "0123456789."

Indian: "Ok! Your shipment was sent to you on 27th April afternoon. That's what my system says here..."

American: "Ok! Which 27th April? Indian or American 27th April?"

Indian: "Oh this is interesting! Are you telling me we have two different 27th Aprils? That's news for me. I'm no April fool. You will always have only one 27th day in April, not two 27[th]s! 28 comes after 27... That's what I studied in my school, that's what appears in our Calendar here in India. No kidding me, no fooling me please."

American: "Hey! Listen, let me explain. I'm not saying there are two 27th Aprils in April month, I must have put it to you differently. My system here shows it's 26th April. I'm travelling out of America and I need to know the delivery time to hours precision and not date precision. What I'm trying to tell is, there is something called time zone due to which..."

Indian: (He interrupts the American...) "*Mujhe kuch kahani vahani naheen sun na hain*[1]! **'Precision'???** Now what is that? I'm not used to any hi-fi English. But then forget about it. I'm not too curious to know what it means. Keep your English with you. Do you find two 27th Aprils in your calendar out there? If so I'm not responsible. I'm not part of

---

[1]   *Mujhe kuch kahani vahani naheen sun na hain: (Hindi)* "I'm not in, to listen to any kind of stories".

76

any calendar preparation business, so I'm not responsible for any errors out there in your calendar. All I know is, I need to answer your query regarding the shipment. And I think I did that..."

American: (This time around American interrupts...)"Look! You are not giving my shipment for free ok! I ordered it, I paid for it, lot of efforts went into it and you just don't seem to understand that (Anger was building up in the American and he was almost about to burst out on the Indian, but restrains himself the diplomatic way) See! Listen to me coolly. I'm telling you about the time zone..."

Indian: (Interrupts again...)"I told you already what kind of work I'm expected to do. I did that and please don't bother me anymore. I've already gone out of my way, my job protocols, by keeping the conversation up with you this long. I'm already overloaded, so please don't bother me anymore. But I can tell you one thing for sure. Even if you are calling me after a year or even 10 years, there will always be only one 27th April in a year. Is there anything else I can help you with?"

American: "Ok! Nothing at the moment. Thanks for your help! It was such a great help... I'm glad I called up the Customer Service and you, exactly you, picked up the call..." (American cuts the call intending not to overload the Indian anymore ;-))

- Apr 30, 2012, 03:26 PM.

19. The whole is greater than the sum of its parts...

God saves at all times, He is a saviour! No matter you praise him or pray him, he saves his devotees all the time. All you need to do is to chant His name, presence and existence consciously or even sub-consciously. That is what the all-pervading nature in our ancient literature preaches us. It's there, it's just for you to see. This is depicted in a larger sense by one of the forms of the feminine side of God - *Goddess Nimishamba* blesses her devotees every minute, it is said.

Now coming to the theme - "How is the whole greater than the sum of its parts"? The very concept of God exemplifies and explains this concept. Guru or the preceptor is often considered next to God and is accorded the highest stature. To understand God, one must understand Guru and his significance first. This sloka "*Gurur Brahma, Gurur Vishnu, Gurur Devo Maheshwarah, Gurur saakshaat Para Brahma Tasmai Shri Guruve namah[1]*" embodies the concept of one-ness of various forms of God. At the end, God as a whole is larger than each of His parts and all his individual functions put together is for the ultimate purpose of *Loka Kalyanam[2]* for the betterment, well being and sustenance of this world.

---

[1]   *Gurur Brahma, Gurur Vishnu, Gurur Devo Maheshwarah, Gurur saakshaat Para Brahma Tasmai Shri Guruve namah: (A Sanskrit hymn)* "Guru is equivalent to *Brahma* (the Hindu deity regarded responsible for Creation), Guru is equivalent to *Vishnu* (the Hindu deity regarded responsible for Progress and Sustenance), Guru is equivalent to *Maheshwara* (the Hindu deity Shiva regarded responsible for Regulation, Destruction and Re-creation), Guru is the God Incarnate himself, I offer my obeisance to the Guru".

[2]   Loka Kalyanam: *(Telugu)* Well-being and prosperity of the world.

Guru as Brahma creates knowledge in an understandable way, Guru as Vishnu preaches the knowledge in a receptive way and Guru as Maheshwara regulates the student to assimilate the knowledge and that is the sequence in which the knowledge is imparted to a student. This imparting of knowledge seen in larger sense is the creation of worthy individuals capable to take on the world. And that is exactly what God as a saviour does to save this world.

- May 02, 2012, 11:58 PM.

20. The sublime plot unleashes itself as Tapestry and Serendepity intertwine in Destiny Divine...

Yesterday I had an interesting chat with my friend who is good at philosophy. We were discussing about the significance attached to the year 2012 and the many controversies it raised. Both of us felt that 2012 was more viewed in the sinistric sense. So we thought of looking at it through an "optimistic, looking forward-to" sense to paint a rosier picture of 2012. The chat culminated into a faith that "2012 is the Dawn of a Civilized Era capable to take on itself". As I recapitulate the conversation and jot down its jest, it's a realization unto itself...

Yeah, the word 'sinistric' might sound too creepy and pessimistic at the outset, but the fact is that people in general naturally tend to respond to fear more than faith. Once we believe in either of them, both can manifest into larger forms, but there's no denying the fact that faith has greater power. Once you believe in a faith, it equips you to do things you never knew of or never knew you were capable of doing. On the other hand, when fear raises its ugly head, it manifests itself into an even uglier form where you cease doing things you were already capable of doing i.e., where you start doubting your own capabilities. That is probably the reason why once the seed of doubt is sown about the uncertainty of where 2012 is heading towards, the fear manifested itself into various controversies which shielded the achievements mankind has gifted itself, which shielded the very journey of mankind so far. Is all the wisdom, knowledge, technology that churned out of the human struggle expected to go waste?

Ok that question leads itself to another question whose answer answers both the questions together. When is such wisdom, knowledge and technology worth being thrown away? When they three together impede the sustenance of mankind! Which means that when they three together make us forget the very roots of mankind, make us ignore our human side and the social perspective and last but not the least, make us forget the presence of *"God"*. These three aspects form the essence of balance of mankind. "God" to me is the supernatural power that transcends beyond the human power to supervise it.

Another important aspect amidst all this is, the Divine Play of things. The Cardinal Divine rule is the cycle of "Creation-Maintenance-Destruction". The Trinity, if you call it so. And for the agnostics, let's call it "Supervision". Can you imagine a team of people (say even 5) working together without a supervisor? Supervision is an implicit expectation when the team is diverse. And can you imagine, let alone fathom, the fact that this world with roughly 7.1 billion of population as of now, let alone the whole cosmos, is functioning so orderly without supervision? This re-engineering, backtracing or reconstructing from the present way of things leads to the reinforcement of existence of supervision. And if we treat that "supervision" or the "Super Vision" as "God", it makes me believe that "YES! God exists!" Which makes me say with confidence that we hold the answers to our own questions. So, I'm geared up to say it's very much possible to dispel the fear, the fear of the known and the unknown.

Gods spoke sex when the *'Pranava Mantra' (the primordial sound in Sanskrit)*, the eternal source of energy took birth, it is said. And from that *Pranava Mantra* - the *Omkara*, as we call it - took birth, the Mother Nature, who eventually bears us, mankind. As we know, the basic principles of Physical Geography say that Nature has a tolerance capacity and when it reaches its threshold it wields destruction so as to rejuvenate itself and balance life. This when translated to the Divine Play translates to the execution of the cardinal divine rule that is Trinity.

The pull word here is "balance". There is balance in everything, it ought to be! Otherwise nothing exists. Let's try to realize this through an illustration through numbers:

0: Nothingness to realize infinity (or the absence of it).

1: The unison, the harmony, the One Smart World (Vasudaika Kutumbam).

2: The eternal feminine and masculine power.

3: The Trinity.

4: The four directions.

5: *The five elements of nature.*

6: *The six tastes.*

7: *The seven colors*

8: *The eight forms of wealth.*

9: *The nine planets, whose working depicts the concept of Universe or the Cosmos (Let's keep aside for now, this Cosmos, which is an extrapolation of the One Smart World).*

The absence of any of the constituents in the whole leads to imbalance and the history says every entity tries to restore balance to itself. Now, that goes to say when the balance in this world is out of place, the Trinity executes itself to balance the world.

Now that boils down to *the Million Dollar Question*, is the *"balance"* in the world out of place? Well, definitely there's lot of change ever since the dawn of mankind as "we" know it, so far, which period we might fit into the word 'era', 'eon', 'epoch' or whatever, depending on the jargon used to represent the longevity of time. The era as it started has changed a lot by now, people have changed a lot, the social instinct and responsiveness varied a lot over different periods of the era, some people have forgotten the roots but again there have been enough number of people who kept trying to reinstate and reinforce the roots. So there is change, well large change, but there is still enough scope, enough space, wherein the balance can be sustained further. I mean the wisdom, knowledge and technology are still intact to balance the good and the bad. Don't you think we are equipped enough, with how much ever little scope we have, to make that little large enough to sustain the world further? My answer is a definite YES!

Human kind has seen a lot of events - lot of battles, revolutions, civilizations and many more. They all can be viewed as mere serendepity - a fortunate series of events that still kept the World intact or even can be viewed as tapestry - a series of events associated with a sublime plan - the Divine plan to keep the World intact. It is up to us which lens we use to look at it, but the fact is that the Destiny has had in it that the World is intact so far. As we progress in time, the sublime plot, if any, unleashes itself as tapestry and serendipity intertwine in destiny divine...

- May 05, 2012, 11:37 AM.

<u>*Self-Notes:*</u>

The "2012 Controversy" definitely got both my friend and me curious. So we transitioned from philosophy to some real study.

Of the many perspectives offered on this issue, the one projected from the "Mayan Calendar" perspective stands out. The most pessimistic and dreaded perspective of those is that of the *"Apocalypse"*. Yeah, because of some unfounded theories and inadequate or incomplete reasoning and analysis, 2012 has been dreaded to be the *"Year of Apocalypse"* and our brief study and consequent inferences show that this presumption/ apprehension is completely false. From the Hindu Mythology perspective, the Apocalypse culminates in Kalki Avatar - the tenth incarnation of Lord Vishnu, who is expected to do Dharma Samsthapana[1] by eliminating evil on earth and reinforcing the good, thus ushering in the *"The Golden Era"* or *"Satya Yuga"*. But just question yourselves - is there "so much" evil on earth that a complete chaos is required to establish the good? Definitely not! Has the co-existence become so difficult? On the contrary, the last century has seen the brighter side of peaceful co-existence of men.

Coming back to the "Mayan Calendar" prophecy, 2012 is going to witness a celestial event, a galactic alignment. While "time" is a measurement, a scale, most importantly it is relative. It is measured relative to the galactic phenomena. The human power and comprehendibility is too small to gauge the changes happening in the cosmos. It only points to some *divine intervention* happening in this most phenomenal period which is most probably going to play witness to some rare phenomena in the universe. Let's hope this change is going to blend well with the current way of things and is only for the better, for mankind. The Divine Intervention might reveal the changes mankind on this earth got to accommodate, as a result.

- Jun 15, 2012, 12:01 AM.

21. Oh God! How do we make people realize?

Knowledge is within and without. Everyone has two sides - the inward and the outward. When we look within through our inward side, we tap and unleash the knowledge within. When we look outward through our outward side, we wake up to

---

[1]   Dharma Samsthapana: *(Telugu/Sanskrit)* Reinstatement of *Dharma*, order, through the triumph of good over bad.

our responsibilities and our position relative to the society as a whole. Now which side is more important? There is no one right or wrong answer. But a definite answer from me is, only when you realize the person within, you can wake up to the person you are without or ought to be in the society. That is where the equations merge. And there emerges a balance, the much needed balance at both personal and societal levels.

- May 07, 2012, 01:12 AM.

22. Is truth such a bad bargain?

People might get bored, but one of my, actually not one of my, but my most favorite musing is *"How to keep a check on change that often tries to surpass and swallow its roots?"* I can go on and on about this, but I think I need to consolidate all my vague musings on this topic, channelize them to a right place and fine-tune them and hence this blog post.

To start with, we human beings have changed a lot ever since our existence started or may be the right word is we *'evolved'* a lot further. Though the evolution is leading itself further at a fast pace, it needs that human guidance - *a conscious guidance*, so that the evolution is for the betterment of humans itself. So, we need to help ourselves to *elevate* or enhance our own well-being. What I mean is we just can't let time take its own course while we keep on doing things in our own personal interests, for in that case time will reveal that the collective result is chaos. Hence it needs a collective effort on the part of everybody to look beyond personal interests, if we need to avoid that chaos and prosper into a social well being.

How do we avoid the chaos then? The chaos can be avoided when we understand and appreciate the power of virtues and well-found principles and values that have been ascribed highest importance. Let's not delve much in the ancient forms of those virtues, principles and values whatsoever, for we have long lost touch with our ancient scriptures. Let's try to re-assess those concepts from the modern perspective - Equality, Fraternity, Liberty and Justice - the very founding principles of Indian Constitution. I consider Indian Constitution as the best bet to explain this because Indian Constitution is hailed to be the largest, most descriptive Constitution of all and above all it caters to serve as the touchstone for the administration of the well being of a population as diverse as that of India. But let's apply these concepts not on India as such but on the world as of today, in general.

Equality - What is equality? Let's view this from the 'Battle of Sexes' perspective - I mean the equality between man and woman. I'd say, the word equality is largely misinterpreted and grossly misunderstood especially in this context. Equality is not being equal in just about everything. It's giving equal respect to each other, appreciating each other's strengths and weaknesses to bring about the *equality of the worth* of both the sexes. *But we have forgotten this underlying meaning and both the sexes set on a competition to establish a false equality wielding confusion blurring the role definitions.* I don't mean that we stick to our age old role definition of woman being a house wife taking care of children and man being the bread-winner going out for work. Though we have grown beyond the age-old role definitions, there are still a set of things a woman is best at and a man is best at. If I go on describing what those set of things are, it will be a blog unto itself, so I stop here because everybody knows what they are - for eg: how much ever the world has advanced to bring laws to increase the span of paternal leave, there's no denying the fact that the span of maternal leave is "usually" longer than that of paternal leave in most parts of the world. In some places, paternal leave is even unheard of! It sounds as though a Father is not expected to take care of his baby after his wife delivered the baby! How much ever women have taken to drinking, the fact is that men drunkards outnumber their woman counter-parts (ok atleast in India since I don't have any statistics of other countries). We might have one Shanthi Tigga who has become the first and only Indian Woman Jawan in the army, but she is more an exception than the norm because women don't tend to choose such professions. One can't ignore the biological differences. While it's not impossible to grow beyond the role definitions, we do so only to tend to get back to where we started, for otherwise we create *imbalance* in the society. We just experiment the change, but we can't move on with that change forever. By this, I'm only saying that the inherent essence of and differences between the sexes ought not to be ignored, nothing beyond that. I'm also saying that *ideally* Equality must be possible despite the role differences.

<u>Fraternity</u> - May be India is better at preaching some fundamental values to the world keeping aside the enquiry of whether it follows them itself or not. Yeah I'm talking about that concept of *'Universal Brotherhood'* eloquently worded as Vasudaika Kutumbam[1] that originated in and propogated by India (I personally thank my polity Sir Avinash Gowtham, who stressed this concept when he taught us the Indian Constitution). I just love this concept because these two words

---

[1]   Vasudaika Kutumbam: A *Sanskrit phrase* that propels the concept of the World being ONE family.

possess in them a world of knowledge that can explain the concept of "God". God distributed Himself into Man and Man unguided evolved himself into Devil. God intervenes to kill the Devil to bring back the Man, it is said. *'God => Man => Devil'* is again synoymous with the cardinal divine rule of Trinity - *'Construction => Maintenance => Destruction'*. All the human beings are nothing but forms of God. It's a well known belief as per many religious faiths that since God can't exist everywhere physically, He created man in an intention and expectation that man be his replica or replacement. Which goes to say that when one puts the needed efforts, one can always realize the God within oneself - the concept of *'Aham Brahmasmi'* (Sanskrit phrase which means - 'I am Brahma, the Creator'). Again, there is this *Karma Theory* which goes to say that only realized souls can do this and that it happens only by the Divine Will, i.e., God Himself should will to invoke Him within such people. I'm not adept at all those things, so I'm not the right person to say what is right or wrong. But all I feel and hence know is God lies within every human being. All the human beings put together is the Universal Soul that is God. The Divine Energy is just distributed across all the living beings rather, hence we all make *'One Family'*. Isn't this concept a powerful tool that can diminish the power differences between various countries and encourage them to collaborate with each other to grow together rather than compete with each other to create more confusion and hence more chaos in some parts of the world? I'm specifically referring to the concept and need of *'Decreasing the Gap between Haves and Have-nots'*.

Liberty - again we have seen lot of revolutions in the recent past especially in the Arab world seeking liberty from the clutches of tyranny and dominance. While liberty is liberation from the autocratic rule, it is certainly not the absence of genuine guidance and regulation. *Liberty is what we are not allowed to do as much as what we are allowed to do.* I guess we are clear on this definition and hence it doesn't require any further elaboration. Atleast I can't think much about what else to detail on liberty. Oh yeah, the liberty of mankind as a whole can be realized when we can get ourselves rid of the ill-founded principles or vices, the devil within us and start believing in the power of virtues, the God within us.

<u>Justice</u> - Justice to me is the discretion of Right and Wrong. While there is no absolute Right or Wrong i.e., the Right and Wrong keeps changing with times, at any given point of time, whatever does Good to the society as a whole is Right and whatever harms the society is Wrong. So what I mean is, *whether we accept it or not, whether it complies with our own definitions or not, nature has its own discretion of Right and Wrong.*

Now, let's put all the above four concepts together to realize the well-being of the society as a whole. Let's not divide the world based on continents or countries, based on races, sects or religions but based on the two genders - man and woman. When these four concepts are truly realized between a man and woman, it leads to a happy family. *And happy families make a Happy World.* On the outset, we might say 'It's easier said than done'. But I'd say it's actually easy, as easy as it sounds. We think it's difficult, because we submit to vices rather than to virtues i.e., the world is progressing so fast that it has placed everything else but the balance between man and woman as its priority. *The world is viewing the balance between man and woman in the context of its progress and evolution.* The balance between man and woman is pushed to background, while the riches, comforts, luxuries, technology are being given the front seat. *Infidelty, lack of trust, lack of role understanding have manifested into a web of other things giving birth to the devil within us.* But the God within us can be realized when we try to axe this problem from the roots and build it from the atomic level. *May be it's time we look at the whole thing, the other way round, we might have to view the human progress and evolution in the context of balance between man and woman instead.* We got to understand the power of virtues - Love, Trust, Sharing etc and surrender to that power. What else but Truth and Truth alone can be the highest of all virtues.

The tunnel of human problems is just a mirage that seems endless because it's viewed from the lens of the vices. When we surrender to the virtues and consequently to the truth and let the truth lead us to the light, there's always light at the end of the tunnel. God is in the details and God dwells in the Truth and Truth is His abode. So why can't we all just surrender to Truth?

- May 15, 2012, 04:57 PM.

23. Fanaa! Why I liked it...

Fanaa *(means destruction in Hindi)* is a love story with many facets, not one. Or may be it's the story of two persons' life. Or is it both? *The story of love and life.* I somehow end up liking love stories with depth and to top it, those with a sad ending, I once thought. So that once upon a time, I was really scared of this fact, especially when I applied the principle of 'Secret' - 'You receive what you like and want'- on it. *Which means, the more one likes pain, the more one receives it.* So I looked back and pondered deep and was relieved to see that I was wrong in my initial statement. I like many movies where love had happy ending and many romantic comedies too. So to correct that statement, I like love stories with some depth and have 'life' element in them, well who doesn't?

Some say that when true love happens, one can never see anybody else in that light, never ascribe that position to anybody else, never love anybody else as a significant other again, how much ever one's life demands it, how much ever one's situations compel it, for that is the commitment true love inspires. True love happens only once, it is said.

My definition of love evolved over time along with my life story. To many, the boundaries between affection, infatuation, liking, love, seem a blur. Yet we all know that love stands out from the rest. When I first attempted to define love, I felt it's some feeling which evokes a smile at the very thought of beloved. And then I thought, it's something which lets you be yourself without any qualms and enhance you as a person. Then later I thought, when you love a person, you are more than happy to spend a lifetime with that person. At the moment, my definition for it is, when you love a person, you can surrender your ego to that person and he/she can protect it just as much as theirs'. Rather, it's a derivation than a mere definition. *Which means love has to be mutual, only then can it take some meaningful shape.* One sided love ends up as hatred at worst, admiration or adoration at best, I guess.

Coming to the movie, I seriously loved the portrayal of the character of *Aamir* as *Rehan - 'The Man on a Mission'*. That mission might have been for an entirely wrong cause at the societal level or a much larger level, but that's what he believed in. He dedicates himself completely to it and pursues it relentlessly and persistently. On the other hand, I liked the discretion or the judgement call demonstrated by *Kajol* as *Zooni*. The stand the character is shown to take to choose the less worser of two bad things is amazing. Coming to think of it, how many women in our current society can take such a stand? Well, I think the number is definitely not zero and I believe, at the current juncture, we do have considerable women of such strength.

That's *Fanaa* for me - a man on a mission and a woman with discretion and the story of love and life between the two. The lines *"Tere dil mein meri saanson ko panah mil jaaye, Tere Ishq mein meri jaan fanaa ho jaaye*[1]!" and *"Sahi aur galat ki beech faisla karna bahut aasaan hain, lekin dho sahin raastho mein se behtar chunna aur dho galat raastho mein se munasif yaheen hamare jindagi ke faisle karte hain*[2]!!" are two golden lines from the movie *Fanaa*. *Fanaa* might not be my most favourite movie, but it has a special place for me. At the end, the fact that emerges out is actually amazing - *life is larger than love*. I mean love must complement one's life, enhance one as a person and make one's life more beautiful, but must not eat into one's own life. What if one were *Zooni?* Instead of answering that, one might want to just swiftly switch the frame to another epic of Aamir - Ghajini and get *fanaa'ed* in the sheer intensity of passion the character exudes.

- *May 18, 2012, 07:27 PM.*

---

[1]   *Tere dil mein meri saanson ko panah mil jaaye, Tere Ishq mein meri jaan fanaa ho jaaye*: (*Hindi*) "Let my breath find a solace in your heart, may the life inside me, be consumed and destroyed by your love".

[2]   *Sahi aur galat ki beech faisla karna bahut aasaan hain, lekin dho sahin raastho mein se behtar chunna aur dho galat raastho mein se munasir yaheen hamare jindagi ke faisla karte hain*: (*Hindi*) "It's easy to choose between right and wrong, but to choose the greater of two goods or the lesser of two evils, these in essence, make the choices of our lives."

24. The mystery of myselves...

Ever since my childhood, ever since I started speaking English fluently or atleast ever since the time I can recollect, I have been using the word *'myselves'*. In fact that word 'myselves', I assume, doesn't exist if one has to be grammatically right, there's only 'myself'. But I, don't know why, get hooked up with using this term. I just can't say, let's say, 'It was me myself who did that', never! I'd instead say 'It was me myselves who did that'. My friends tried to correct me at various times, but I'd never give up. I thought when 'you' can refer to both singular and plural you, why not just assume and live in the comfort that I was respecting myselves by using the term 'myselves' (the plural form of myself). Moreover, in languages like Hindi, 'hum' (meaning 'we') is a common usage while referring to one's own self. I believe it happens in many languages, in a slightly different way though, when aristocratic people address themselves. Grammatically for me, 'myselves' was right. But then, I'm not that bad at English grammar after all. Perhaps my brain was just wired that way...

- May 19, 2012, 12:59 PM.

25. Parrot in a cage!

Ever wondered how the life of a parrot in a cage feels like? Ok, let's just assume for a while. Say, you are a parrot, but caged. You look so beautiful with those colorful feathers and all. And then you can even utter squeaky sounds that entertain the human folk. You are such a wonderful creation by God. Yet, yet! You are not living your life the way you would, had you not been caged. It's like dreaming a dream in which you wake up to the light of the day while you are still sleeping in the darkness of the night. It's a state where you can only entertain but not get entertained yourself... Parrots! Poor parrots! Now I can understand the merit of the act of freeing a parrot...

- May 21, 2012, 02:22 AM.

26. When do we know it's over?

Sometimes we are stuck in a vicious circle. We have both long term and short term goals. And to work towards one of them we compromise on the other. How best we optimize them both, is in our discretion.

Sometimes it's quite difficult to know when it's over - be it love, job, it could be anything. When do we know that the game is over, when do we know it's time to move on for the next phase? Sometimes, by the time we understand the rules of the game, the game is almost over. It's really hard to know when it's over, when to call it off a day. I personally feel that when we are after worthy things we struggle to attain success. Even if the failure does happen, we persistently try again to attain success. How long we try, how many times we try depends on how important it is in our life. We know that we have to try again, when there is that feeling of hope or doubt lingering. We know when it's done, that it's done, that we have attained. But how do we know when to give up? When it's over, we just know it. We don't need any voice outside us to tell that. And when we know it's worthy enough, we would never give up. It is said, most of the unrealized victories have lost their place in the history because the people who struggle so hard for it do not take the plunge to grow beyond their self-defined capabilities. But if we are lucky enough, I'm sure we will certainly know when to take that much-needed plunge to thrust us towards the success. I'm sure I have taken the much-needed plunge when the time was right for it and I would always go for it because I believe I would just know it.

- *May 26, 2012, 12:36 AM.*

27. *The story of Valmiki*

The story of Valmiki[1] - the man who grew from a thief to a saint - has always fascinated me. Especially the penance which he starts by saying *"MaraaMaraaMaraa"* only to come out of it chanting *"RaamaRaamaRaama"*. I wonder if things like that can actually happen. Is it the human will or the divine will? Atleast I believe it's due to the Divine Will. Valmiki before and after the penance is just a man, the only difference is his transformation from thief to saint. Ofcourse, he could have evolved to become an incarnation of God too, but that would have required divine will. The divine motive must have been different, for His plan for Valmiki was to write the epic of Ramayana which would be read for generations to come. For that matter, even Lord Rama and Krishna were believed to be men, sheer men, not actually Gods (because Gods don't dwell on Earth in physical form), despite they being the reincarnations of the Divine. They had their own purposes of life and they humbly carried on the duties assigned to them. I guess, same is the case with all of us too - we have

---

[1] Valmiki: *Valmiki* is the author of the great Indian epic *Ramayana*. According to Uttara Kanda of Ramayana, Valmiki was born Ratnakara to sage Prachetasa, but turned into a robber as he grew. His contact with sage Narada is said to have led to his penance which transformed his life. Valmiki in Sanskrit means the one born out of ant-hills.

our purposes assigned. The only difference being - the realized people know their purpose and others don't. But with or without our knowledge, we end up fulfilling our purpose of our lives.

God must have exercised both silence and tolerance when Valmiki was a thief, He might have come into action to make Valmiki realize the purpose of his life, when the time was right for it, atleast that's what I believe. In this sense, *God is both a spectator and perpetrator.*

- May 26, 2012, 01:55 AM.

28. *Traversing the paths you would never tread!*

Have you ever traversed the paths you would never actually tread? Dreams, I guess, offer such wonderful opportunities. The more creative you are, the wierder the dream gets, it can be more fun depending on how much creepiness you can tolerate. I had one such dream recently. It says that the people I left behind still love me and practise the truth (read it free advice) I shared. I actually mean that the dream showed my after-life. It was quite freaky at the outset, but probing deep I was happy.

On a different note, I read two different updates on facebook posted by different people. One was a joke which goes like this - "A man gets a call from police saying that his wife is supposedly dead as she met with an accident. The police want the man to confirm this and hence offer to send him the pictures of the woman who was dead. The man asks the police to post the pictures on facebook and says he would like the update if the pictures were those of his wife". So those are the heights of facebook'ing these days. The other update is a melancholic story about a man whose wife is dead. It goes to say - "I feel like a part of me is dead. Where are you when I need you the most, when I want you to heal my dying part?" Which one is better? If I were the wife, I'd choose the joke, feeling happy that atleast my death has given solace to my husband. Just kidding, you see!

- May 26, 2012, 02:21 AM.

29. What does it mean to excel from the house of the Dollar?

As I was walking down the road of Satya Niketan, the place I had been residing in Delhi since August last year, which I will be leaving tomorrow, since I'm done with the purpose of coming here - taking coaching for UPSC, I read this on one of the pamphlets lying on the road - *'Excel from the house of the Dollar'*. I didn't bother to read it deep enough, so I didn't venture to pick up the pamphlet and I already reached the end of the road. The pamphlet was gone, but the thought of what exactly the advertisement was all about kept bothering me. I'm in no moods now to get creative to probe what the advertisement exactly was, but I'm certainly up to create new meanings for the sentence.

Hmm, "Excel from the house of Dollar" - it could mean 'n' number of things. It could be a persuasive effort of an entrepreneur persuading another entrepreneur to leave India and enter the land of opportunities - the house of the Dollar which offers more promise in entrepreneurship as such. It could mean x, could mean y, could mean z...but I will settle with this now, now that I'm superbly bored with my creativity.

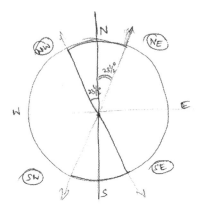

Fig 1 – Dollar and Earth

- May 26, 2012, 02:36 AM.

<u>Note left by Betsy:</u>

Your creativity goes into amazing directions when you are bored. This was very helpful, it answers a question I've had for some time.

- Nov 15, 2013, 07:08 PM.

30. *What is winning all about!*

Winning or losing is relational. Sometimes we lose by winning. Sometimes we win by losing. I like win-win battles though, of course if only the other side wants to win (otherwise I'm all geared up to win, you doubt?)

- May 28, 2012, 10:56 Pm.

31. I too had a break - A story :-)

No! This is not a sarcastic take at the book - "I too had a love story" by Ravinder Singh - at best, it's a tribute to that title, I like the title. It expresses the pride people take to say, they were not left out of the much talked-about experience and emotion, people say one must go through one's life. I have not bothered myself to read the book though, because I thoroughly believe in the practice of *'cerebral hygiene'* coined by the Sociologist Auguste Comte. I practice this on and off almost continuosly so as to keep my brain clean and unaffected, for my own writing ;-) I'm very lazy and don't read books casually to kill my time, because it feels like bothering my brain with stuff I don't need to be bothered of. Jokes apart, I'm a very sparse reader of books for other reasons in fact. I would rather prefer staring into space and think, just think some absolute non-sense, it's funny, but that's me. That said, having been accustomed to either full time study or full time job, I've been very bad at developing good pastimes. I must perhaps learn now so that I spend my next break better.

So, I too had a break - my first break ever, for about over a month since the end of May. There was one point in my life when I was really yearning, in fact almost dying for a break. A point where my personal life reached its trough leaving no motivation and enthusiasm to work, let alone making it big in my career. But paraodoxically, that was also a point when I couldn't have afforded a break because given the emotional turbulence I was going through then, idleness would only have fuelled more negativity. That is when I set on to prepare for UPSC (which was my childhood dream anyway) and I don't regret my decision. I am still not sure if I would be sticking to my preparation, now that I've come back from Delhi, but I must say the period I spent in Delhi during UPSC preparation was worthwhile and rejuvenating. It actually landed me up in that situation where I could be ready to take a break.

I had always understood the importance of a break at an apt point of time in one's life. I used to strongly feel that people should take meaningful breaks once in a while. Ofcourse, they must be lucky too, to be able to do that. I compare it to the journey of the particle treading simple harmonic motion. A particle starts upon an external thrust and moves on to attain maximum amplitude, but then the energy dies out gradually to reach the equilibrium point. If you are in the *retrograde* phase of energy and still expect yourselves to do as much work as what was possible at your maximum amplitude, then it means tiding against one's capabilities. We all have a tolerance limit and it's foolish to push ourselves too much when we know that it's just not working. Ofcourse there will be times when we need to push our boundaries too. But that works only when we are in that *prograde* phase of energy. One just needs to know where one is located at, before pushing it too hard, otherwise it only means harming oneself. The point of zero energy could either mean dying out or a point of equilibrium where one can set on to reach even higher amplitudes hitherto unattained, depending on whether one gets that external force or help.

Previously, when I yearned for a break, I knew that my energy would be dying out, had I called it off a day then. I knew that I would be in that zero energy state for a long time to come. The software profession which I was already working in, would be like the breeze that might set the particle again in some motion, but not strong enough even to thrust it to the previously possible energy states. I would be treading the same path, which I previously did with an equal or even lesser momentum and that was not what I wanted. The UPSC preparation was like that external force which gave me enough momentum. Now, even if I opt to go back to my old profession, it's only with a renewed zeal. All in all, I'm currently feeling optimistic and more confident to take up one of these two paths I'm already acquainted with. Wish me more luck :-)

Reading my own post, it seems like I find solace in physics, when I can't find it in time, the moment I live in. I look forward to learn more physics, apart from that learnt in college, to use it in such needful times ;-)

- Jul 09, 2012, 10:19 PM.

32. The Social Debt - its burden and our reluctance...

We both inherit from the past and also pass on a modified inheritance to the future. Among many things, we inherit resources, privileges, rights, responsibilities - the tangible and the intangible. When we talk about inheritance, things that first come to my mind are the knowledge and the social debt we acquire - the intangible and often overlooked parts. While we *use* and *abuse* our rights and resources, we are often oblivious to the fact that we need to pass on an added knowledge to the future generations and pay off the social debt while we live and delve in the present to sustain the present generation. It implies we are expected to live in such a way that our existence and sustenance does not impede the sustenance of our future generations, the essence of which is all summed up in the word "Sustainable". 'Sustainable Development' forms the fulcrum of a lot of technologies being adapted currently to meet the needs of future generations and I'm sure any International Meet/Convention these days is incomplete without this word being heard.

While the concept of 'Sustainable Development' can be viewed from many perspectives, its common usage is in the context of 'conservation of natural resources' - the tangible things, tangible here most importantly meaning 'measurable'. I would like to generalize this concept to the two intangible things I was referring to earlier - the knowledge and the social debt. The social debt is nothing but the Karmic Debt, if one is to properly understand the concept of Karma. While we might well boast of the current technologies doing a wonderful job in easy creation and dissemination of information, I would argue that a lot of information we create today is time-sensitive, it perhaps makes sense only to us and not much to the future generations not even to a generation, two centuries ahead of us. I really doubt if mankind has created any new information in the last century which is timeless and relevant for all times. Yes, we have journals of scientific discoveries, repertoires of what's happening in our day-to-day life, but think of those times when Science is too advanced that this knowledge is not of huge importance or such times when science does not even exist and this information cannot be rightly used. This highlights a simple fact that it is not 'technology' which is essential for the creation of such information, but that a conscious awareness of the necessity and *the Will* to create such information are in itself important for such creation. While information itself is one thing, the media through which it is passed on, is another thing. Let's call this information and media - 'Sustainable information' and 'Sustainable media'- that information which can withstand the passage of generations and still be useful and the media that can successfully do this job by sustaining the passage of time and withstanding the power of nature.

Let's just, for the sake of discussion, bring the Hollywood movie - '2012' and let's assume that a major destruction struck earth in 2012. Also assume only a bunch of people are left on earth to carry on the heredity. Oh yes, the unsaid things that all our internet servers crashed and the books written on recyclable paper have just disappeared responding to the power of destruction nature can wield especially since they were housed in libraries which comply with neither earthquake, tsunami nor fire disaster standards but only meet the growing population's needs. It's scary, yes, but well I'm really optimistic that this apocalypse doesn't happen in 2012. So this is all just an assumption, but then abiding by the Kalachakra Dharma[1] it is bound to happen some time or the other. To make things sound better, let's say this happened some years or centuries down the line. Do we really expect that bunch of people to start everything from scratch and what if those people are not even knowledgeable and capable enough to dismiss such an important responsibility? Or are we expecting that a century or two down the line somebody will do the needful to create such sustainable information over a sustainable media so that the bunch of people are relieved of such responsibilities? If we ourselves haven't felt the need for such things, the probability of some of our successors doing it is lesser, if not zero.

Ok, to simplify things, let's just see what could be the sustainable information with a flavour of the current technology that would really be needed by our future generations. To start with - the

---

[1]   Kalachakra Dharma: (*Telugu*) The laws and nature of the wheel of time.

kind of edible foods we ate, our agricultural techniques, the tools and equipments we used for agriculture, our knowledge of astronomy, our housing patterns, the architectural finesse we had, how we protected ourselves from natural calamities, the clothes we wore, the transportation mechanisms we employed, how we arrived at our primitive inventions or discoveries such as that of fire, wheel, power of steam etc etc, our religious faiths etc might form few first things that might need to be passed on. Perhaps even the art of sex, despite we not imbibing it appropriately from the knowledge passed on about the ancestral ways through books like Kamasutra. But then this thing, I thoroughly believe comes along naturally, it's rather a natural instinct than something that ought to be studied from elsewhere. Like many other things, it's like the truth we have always known but only lost the awareness of it for a while. The next set of things might be the major events that happened - the battles, revolutions, civilizations and the renaissances, how we as mankind have fought the change and brought the change. While we all now know how all this happened and is happening and take for granted that our future generations too will know it naturally, the reality is that the future generations would not automatically know it in exceptional situations. *In fact when the technology wasn't too developed, people felt this need to convey their present tense to the future.* The knowledge was embedded in buildings, monuments, inscriptions, books whose paper stood the test of time and were housed in places that could survive the calamities (for instance the wealth that came out of Padmanabhaswamy Devalayam of Travancore speaks loads). Who took the responsibility of doing this then? The rulers themselves! But I guess, the current day rulers or leaders are busy safeguarding their interests and power. In fact that is one of the side-effects of Democracy. Doesn't it seem that the technology without farsightedness is so vulnerable?

It also seems to me that we started interpreting technological development and innovation as real development, while an ideal sense of development could be a different thing altogether. Are we really developed, given that we live in times when we are not even aware of how much uncertainty we never addressed? Did we all become less inquisitive? Where is all our collective consciousness hiding?

Coming to the social debt part of it - not everybody is indebted equally to the society when they have not taken equally from the society. The *energy consumption* by different countries is different which is not even in line with their *energy needs*. When the resource consumption is not even, so will the consequences they face be. Let's take the Kyoto protocol abidance for instance. It's been quite a struggle for the developing countries to come to a consensus with the developed countries. When the rules are framed by those who are more powerful, no doubt they are framed as per their convenience. Who is there to tell them what is right and what is not? None?

I know, I've just ranted down the problems and just went on and on with them. But then what's the solution? I personally feel this unresponsive attitude of a given segment of people towards the collective well-being of the society, *really calls for some good-spirited individuals as leaders*. I know a good change in leadership has a whole web of latent issues that seek to be addressed.

But then, it is really that simple too. It just needs good leaders. One can't expect the whole society to change, every individual to change, to elect a good leadership...that never happens! Our history is replete with examples of able administrators building great empires while selfish administrators bringing down the same. ***A top-down change is often easier than a bottom-up change.***

- Jul 17, 2012, 11:24 PM.

33. Alchemist - An Arabian Knight's way!

An Arabian knight set on a voyage to explore truth - he wanted to crack the mystery of life and existence. With a cat as his only companion he started on a voyage from India, sailed across many oceans, walked his way out of deserts, climbed voluptuous mountains and finally reached a very old Indian temple in America.

In America, he started to lead a very sparse and nomadic lifestyle. The cat too started troubling him, but that did not make him give up his ambition in anyway. One fine day a ghost entered the cat and the cat started talking. The knight for once thought that his penance is on its way to yield results. He assumed that the cat was enamored of God and thought that God Himself descended upon him in the form of cat to show the light at the end of the tunnel. "Which better form than that of my beloved companion can God take", he thought. He now started asking cat the directions that lead to his treasure.

The cat, on the other hand, was struggling its way out to get rid of the daemon that possessed him. So both of them were struggling but neither knew the other's struggle. Days passed, time just flew by. The cat out of its satanic instinct said that it was possible that the treasure might be hidden in the pyramids of Africa. So, now both of them started on a voyage to Africa from America via Atlantic. Yes chill, ultra chill Atlantic! They halted on islands on the way, they swam when the water was shallow and allowed them to...wondering whether the water can be shallow mid-Atlantic??? Well, near the islands it can get shallow or the knight was too good a swimmer that even the deepest of waters for normal humans seemed shallow to him. The cat doesn't know swimming by the way, so it was riding on the knight's back (yes, with all its satanic thoughts in its head). At times, the knight insisted the cat to swim, for it proved too heavy a sack to carry on such a long journey. He tried to teach the cat how to swim, but the cat never put an ounce of effort in learning to swim for its satanic side got the better of it.

The Arabian knight and his cat companion finally reached the Egyptian pyramids and wondered what secretive treasures have been hidden there. The knight who was well versed with the ravages of life by this time, given his long voyage, started pondering over the metaphorical meaning the gigantic pyramids before him seemed to convey. The pyramids are known for mummies conceptualizing the possibility of dead returning back to life. He extrapolated this to understand that every spirit needs a body to inhabit this earth. Going further, it meant that we as human beings are only carriers of a higher thing - called the soul - we are the travellers - ***we travel and travel until we burn our energy***. This life, as we perceive in a single birth is but a sojourn in such a long journey. The aim is not merely to appease the body with luxuries and comforts but also attain soul satisfaction. And that soul is very much within you, the secrets to appease your soul also lie very much within you. It is your inner conscience whom you should appease, it is your inner voice that you should listen to, a *'you at peace with you'* is the best gift you can gift yourselves, the pyramids seemed to tell him. Before this voyage and all through out the voyage he thought he would be at peace once he gets to trace his treasure and go home. After this long journey, he left for his home which was nearby, along with his cat companion and joined his family. He was finally at peace with himself and he knew he traced the treasure. He wasn't too sure the journey was worth it, but time will tell if it is, if he could use further in his life, the treasure of knowledge he attained through this journey. The satanic instinct of the cat too seemed to vanish on his way back home. He realized it was his own anti-voice which played the Satan all the while. He realized he was his worst enemy, he was now on his way to become his own best friend, guide and philosopher.

By the way, I missed this in the beginning - the Arabian knight came to India first based on some sage advice given India's spiritual history. Not that India is not the right place for seeking the treasure, it's just that the African culture was something he was able to connect better with. Now that he successfully accomplished his journey, India must have definitely proved a lucky start for him (not to miss the cat, because after this, the cat was well fed and its needs were completely met).

- *Jul 18, 2012, 11:30 PM.*

34. The God particle and the God sense!!!

The discovery of Higgs Boson particle famously termed as *'God particle'* definitely got me curious. My initial response to the search CERN was pursuing for this God-damned particle, when I first read about it a year ago, was skeptical. I had this 'one-in-the-flock' opinion that *these scientists just dig into nothing to create something, both of which cannot be discerned by laymen - they start with some assumptions and not any ground reality which means nothing to a layman and they claim they have found something?!?* So that's my very naïve side looking at it, with my scientific and inquisitive side shunted and silenced off. I didn't understand of what value this search for an elusive particle is going to be, for a common man or mankind as a whole. More importantly I was threatened by the layman opinion populated on the internet that the CERN LHC[1] experiment might mean a voluntary solicit of the doomsday by the arrogant mankind, that it is, revelling in the glory of a chequered history of scientific accomplishments and innovation. And that history dating back to utmost four centuries, let's say if we start with those times when Netwon discovered gravity, which is very short, in fact equivalent to an infinitesimal point when compared to the span of evolution of universe – 13.8 billion years (an estimate arrived through that very science)! And when I started applying my own sense of science, the threat appeared even dangerous and all the more fatal. Here's my logic for that: They (the scientists) are trying to find God particle through high energy collisions in the LHC and this discovery is aimed at unravelling the mystery of creation and fabric of universe. If that was really the aim, they are trying to simulate (or emulate) almost a scenario which happened during the creation of the universe. And if we intrapolate negatively, such experiments result in the God particle being traced, immediately followed by the state of nothingness from which the universe emerged and that state of nothingness implies destruction of earth, atleast, if not this universe.

---

[1] **CERN LHC:** The name CERN is derived from the acronym for the French "Conseil Européen pour la Recherche Nucléaire" or it's simply "European Council for Nuclear Research" in English. The Large Hadron Collider (LHC) is the world's largest and most powerful particle accelerator. It first started up on September 10, 2008 and remains (as of July 2014) the latest addition to CERN's accelerator complex.

But wait, that was only my presumption! A presumption to start with…to get curious and explore further, not that I thoroughly believe in what I just said now! This presumption stemmed primarily from my inquisitiveness of why the Higgs Boson particle was termed as God particle in the first place. They (read 'they' as scientists henceforth) say that Higgs Boson is responsible for the mass of every thing tangible (or should we say every material???) on earth (or is it the entire universe?) and is expected to travel faster than light. So how do those properties make it the God particle? That was my *million dollar question*. Was it because they believe that Higg Boson emerged *during* the creation of the universe and didn't exist before? Because, if it existed before the creation of the universe, it means that material and thus mass existed before the creation of the universe. But any material can't predate the creation since it invalidates the very concept of creation, so that possibility of Higgs Boson existing even before the creation of universe can be completely ruled out. So that means Higgs Boson emerged *during* the creation of the earth, grounded on the assumption that Higgs Boson is fundamentally responsible for the mass of any object/material/matter on earth (and perhaps even in universe). Again emphasize the fact that it is 'during' the creation that it emerged and *not something that evolved after* the creation for that means the material matter didn't exist for some time after the creation of the universe, which again invalidates the concept of creation and hence cannot be the case. And since Higgs Boson is something that emerged during the creation of universe, it is very apt to call it the 'God particle'.

And now to the point, how my presumption stemmed from the above reasoning behind the special naming attributed to Higgs Boson. My assumption was that the scientists were emulating/simulating those very conditions during the creation of the universe to find the God particle. *If my assumption was right*, my premise of, the tracing of God particle resulting in annihilation of earth might be right, atleast that's what I thought. But when I gave a bit of further thought, I felt my assumption itself might most possibly be false. *To trace the God particle, one need not go to the point of its creation.* Since it always existed ever since its creation, the task at hand is more to trace the particle which is elusive, given its sub-atomic dimensions and not necessarily to go back to the point of its creation and then trace it. My assumption being false can be validated by the public announcement CERN made and also some information on their site, which says that CERN LHC does not produce such high energies that existed during the creation of universe, but in fact only that set of energies which are produced constantly in the universe, hence safe. But my question still remains, is CERN really sure of what amount of energy is produced by the high energy proton-proton collisions in LHC? Is the energy produced predictable and does it always fall in a given energy-range? Those questions still remain unanswered to me, atleast I have not browsed deeper enough to get answers for those.

Just being optimistic, let's just assume that the high energy collisions of CERN LHC do not produce those set of energies capable of annihilating life on earth. Now that's an assumption, which only when made, can we proceed further towards some analysis. And that's the way of science :-) So, we proceed to a phase where CERN LHC is functioning within a safe energy band (8 TeV).

Two questions which I would like to analyse through this post are:

- Is Higgs Boson a particle or material? ⇔ Is Higgs Boson 'God particle' or 'God matter'?

- What does its discovery mean to the world of science and mankind in general?

The first question stems from the question the Director-General of CERN Dr. Heuer himself posed - "Is it **THE** Higgs Boson or **A** Higgs Boson?" While this question can be interpreted in anywhich way, my interpretation is that - can Higgs Boson particle exist independently or did the scientists trace one of the bunch of Higgs Boson particles which cannot be separated, in which case it becomes a Higgs Boson matter. The immediate question that might just pop up is, if it was one of the bunch of a similar group of particles each of which cannot exist independently, how can only one particle be traced? I answer it by saying that, no body has ever stated that a single particle has been traced. It's just the existence of a hypothetical particle, which they believe to be God particle, that scientists have validated through abnormal energy values observed in their set of graphs, in which band the so-called God particle is believed to exist (energy treated equivalent to mass here). By that I mean, the scientists have not claimed that they have *'seen'* the God particle through some high-resolution microscopes. The presence of a new particle was validated through abrupt energy bumps (125 -126 GeV with 5 sigma level) in their observations.

The second question is pretty interesting and questions the whole worth or value addition vs financial investments of the CERN experiment. They say that the long-term motive or the holistic aim of finding the God particle is to unravel the mysteries of the creation of universe and discern the fabric of the universe, i.e., what is matter and anti-matter composed of? Is there a way to harness the abundant energy constituted by the anti-matter which permeates through about 90% of the universe?...to answer questions like that! I don't exactly know if dark matter and anti-matter are perceived to be same. As a layman, it's very natural to resist this discovery and rule it out saying - *"Ok, God particle always existed, so what? How does it matter to us?"* It's very much like Newton's discovery of gravity - gravity always existed, but the discovery of its existence served as a key to further progress of Science. It wouldn't have made any sense to people when scientists like Rutherford and Bohr proposed atomic models but then those models are basis to the understanding of atomic structure. Application of that knowledge to things like nuclear fission and nuclear fusion, when rightly used, makes harnessing of abundant sustainable energy feasible. And now Scientists are even talking about harnessing the **Zero Point Energy**! (which I personally consider as an intrusion of space, mankind is not aware of). Now, come to think of the progress Science has made!

I'm not a scientist by any means to understand how the discovery of God particle can help discern the fabric of the universe or unravel the secrets of the creation of universe. I know that fire is produced when two rocks rub against each other. In fact I can see the fire, but that by itself is not enough information to understand the chain of events that happen when two rocks rub against each other. I would in fact go a little further and say, you don't even need fire to understand that chain of events. Yes, it's only after fire is produced that we know that the friction between rocks was capable enough to produce fire. But once the fire is produced, there are n number of ways to understand friction in detail, we don't need fire per se, atleast that's not the only way.

To me, this is what tracing of the God particle means. The God particle is elusive because it decays in the order of millionth of a billionth of a billionth of a second (10^{-24} of a sec). By tracing the god particle, the technolgy has evolved to a stage where there are high precision instruments to trace what's happening in 10^{-24} sec. It implies that is the fundamental unit of time in these experiments - which means the scientists can anlayze 10^{24} events happening in a second. To me the LHC then becomes a time microscope. Add to it the claim that God particle travels faster than light, we have its field of application to be *'time travel'*.

But then any observation is in accordance with science if it is repeatable. Can scientists repeat this situation as and when they want under prescribed experiment conditions? Only then, can this discovery be deemed to be a beginning point enough towards a long journey. The mere discovery of God particle being the key to explore the mysteries of universe seems only an exaggeration when scientists can't make public how they plan to unravel those mysteries. This is not a confidential piece of information and mankind deserves to be apprised of this, because it is our earth which we inhabit, that they are experimenting with.

There is non-sense and there is common-sense and then there is science to reason both. Surely, there will be some God sense too which will interrupt if and when this experimentation is fatalistic to mankind. Will time tell or will science tell?

- Jul 19, 2012, 09:43 PM.

<u>*Note left by Mr. Ron Krumpos:*</u>

The term "God Particle" came from the book "The God Particle / If the Universe is the Answer, What is the Question?," by Leon Lederman & Dick Teresi (first published in 1993 and reissued in 2006), which is in the bibliography of my free ebook on comparative mysticism.

In his 2006 Preface Dr. Lederman, a Nobel laureate in physics, wrote:

"Now as for the title, The God Particle, my coauthor, Dick Teresi, has agreed to accept the blame. I mentioned the phrase as a joke once in a speech, and he remembered it and used it as the working title of the book. The title ended up offending two groups: 1) those who believe in God and 2) those who do not. We were warmly received by those in the middle."

- Jul 20, 2012, 12:16 AM.

35. The magic that is time...

What is it with time that can transform zeal into despair, accomplishment into past glory, determination into procrastination, virtually everything that mattered into nothing that matters. Guess it lies in its power to change present into past and then dump it into a secondary memory that is not readily accessible in a flash of a second, that which cannot elicit the same emotion and intensity when it 'was the present'. There were times when I used to view life in only two shades - you make it work or you don't make it work. You work hard to achieve what you want or give up on it and work on something else that interests you. Though people might see that attitude as 'invincibility' I personally always had an honest assessment of what I was capable of doing and what I was not. It actually worked out because I did not view life in terms of capabilities, weaknesses and strengths. *I only viewed it in terms of interests.* My way of life was to do things those are of interest to me and give my complete resources to materialize them, make them happen. If they were not interesting, but yet cannot be avoided, I found one or the other way to see interest in the task/phase I was involved in. I did this by analyzing the purpose those things served. At the end of the day, it was more to believe in what I was doing and when I firmly believed, they more or less happened. And when I believed, it was always possible to change the boundaries of capabilities, risks and comfort zones.

I believed in destiny, I knew there are always many factors at work which lead to unexpected results. But I felt this is the case with everybody and everything on earth. By which I mean though the factors are variable for different people, the power of those factors is constant on all of us. Hence, when I pursued something I always chose to ignore or rather not consider that constant field, the divine field as also the human collective field (good and bad) that is supervising, overlooking, controlling, manipulating, protecting and shielding us. I was, no doubt aware of that field, but at the same time I was also aware of the fact that "I" don't have a say in that field. I'm an actor in a different plane altogether. The constant consciousness of a different plane was a hindrance to the current plane of action, in my opinon. But being aware of the existence of a different plane (in fact not one, but an infinite number of different planes from the one in which we are acting) was very fundamental to my own existence. This is how I used to deal with 'relativism', how I chose to capture certainty in uncertainty, how I seeked to establish stability in an ever-dynamic play of factors. It worked and I still believe it would work, but now I add a conscious disclaimer to it. It works if only you have the zeal to make it work. With that, I'm again back to my very first hypothesis - one can make it work, if one wants to make it work.

There were times when I was confident of the path I have taken, the path I'm currently treading. I'm reminded of a conversation with a friend who was confident that I will be going to US in a near foreseeable time given my career, background and life's circumstances at that time. My equally confident response to that friend was that on the contrary I wouldn't be going to US because my dream lied in staying in India during that period because I was pursuing UPSC. Yes, at one point I was quite determined about UPSC. My confidence lied not in the uncertainty of going to US but more in the certainty of my own goals because I believed I would pursue my goals with dedication. But now all my zeal, determination, enthusiasm seem to have died down, atleast they seem to have been taken away for a while...by whom? Is it by one of those fields, I don't have a say in? It's tough to accept that argument. It reminds me of my *human vulnerabilities*. But, very strangely I have ALL the resources at my disposal - I have all the time in the world (which I whined was not sufficient when I was working), I have the books, the right information, the right approach, everything a beginner might possibly be expected to have. I did try hard to equip myselves with everything I wanted, but in that process I did not realize that I was losing out my soul. I remeber my own words to many people when I said "Before setting on to do something, ensure that your emotional needs are completely met". I was always proud I said that. But the pathetic part is, I didn't care enough to apply my own sage advice when I set on my own pursuit of goals. It's often easier said than done. I guess being a great master is a lot easier than being an ardent disciple.

I guess I have ended up being in that phase of life I've always dreaded to be- 'the phase of being a silent spectator', which I referred to in my own blog way back in 2007, some call it a limbo state. As I lurk in the uncertainty of wait, the wait for my soul to return back and possess me and take charge, the time is evaporating in its own cyclic pattern, robbing me of the zeal to travel in accordance with it. Yes, I don't have the zeal to make anything work and a shameless thing to admit is - it has also robbed me of the beauty of my soul - the truth, I'm not even true to myself. I call this a 'vegetable state of existence'. So, I'm not even looking for a solution. Is this all the magic that time is wielding on me? Guess I'm not even bothered to know the answer...

If I'm doing anything at all, apart from the day-to-day 'living', realizing on a day-to-day basis that I still exist, it's only that I'm in search of my soul that was one with me through out my life (to the extent I can recollect) in its journey through all the highs, lows, accomplishments, failures, endeavours, endurances and the pursuit that transcends them all - my pursuit of happiness and the quest to accord my life with a meaning of its own in my terms. I've taken my soul so much for granted and now I realize it isn't. Ok, doesn't that go to say I'm still hopeful? Perhaps I am. A paradox, yes! As I sail in the uncertainty, I usually search for rocks to hit upon and in the continuation of that habit, I'm trying to pick up something useful from these lyrics of a Telugu song - "*Ninnallone nindipokala nijam loki raa*[1]!"

- Aug 14, 2012, 05:31 PM.

36. The churn that creates purity...a rainbow in the making!

I'm usually not fond of writing about the gloomier side of life, but life is not devoid of this phase. When life blooms, blogging is not what people really do because they are all immersed in living it out. Yeah we do write out such phases, in hindsight though, but I can hardly recollect an occasion when I was all happy and immediately felt like elucidating that on paper. Anyway, leaving this bragging aside (because that is not what I really want to do now) let me just start with the topic of the post - Purity!!!

White! Is it absence of all colours (definitely no, I know, because that's black, so why do I ask? It's just for the posterity, just to paint a gloomy picture of ummm...what...well yeah... me pondering and brooding and all that ;)) or the presence of all the colors? Ofcourse, the latter. What then is 'purity'? What is 'pristine'? I once mistook 'pristine waters' for 'water devoid of contamination'. Probing further, 'purified water' also comes under my connotation of 'pristine waters' (now that says a lot about my English vocabulary, doesn't it? ;-)). But actually

---

[1] *Ninnallone nindipokala nijam loki raa*: (*Telugu*) *"Don't consume my yesterdays, come into the present and become true!"*

'pristine waters' are those original waters which didn't even know what contamination meant.

If we assume 'pristine' and 'pure' mean one and the same, purity means absence of impurity, the innocence (or is it the naivete?). Well this is getting too ambiguous and boring because an English word means different things in different contexts. So, just let me put this discussion in the right context. I'm referring to this word when it is used to qualify the character of a person. Purity in this context is often synonymous with the color 'white'. Drawing parallels with the original definition of 'white' – "presence of all colours" – purity then must be the conglomeration of various possible psyches of human character. Not actually a conglomeration, but the culmination of human psyche after having been introduced to a huge spectrum of emotions...that stabilisation after being:

tapped - to see the vastness of this universe when you were born

lavished - with comforts

pampered - with love and affection

encouraged - to observe everything around you and learn

fed - with opportunities to grow

challenged - to compete and excel

surprised - with unforeseen yet pleasant experiences

embarassed - with situations that can't be dealt effectively in real time *rewarded* - with results commensurate with your efforts

punished - as a result of your vices or ill luck or for no obvious reason

transformed - as a result of passage of time from one phase of life to another - ageing

tempted - to try out irresistible paths

beaten up - with the harshness of life, that shows up itself once in a while

introduced - to the feeling of love

seduced - and lured to delve deeper into the above emotion

tormented - to realize that love can sometimes be synonymous with hurt when you end up loving a wrong person or a wrong cause

calmed down - to realize that life can just move on

enlightened - that life is indeed larger than what we know

bestowed - if we are lucky enough with another opportunity to follow some passion

trapped - to believe that life is indeed a pursuit to realize the purpose of life and fulfill it...

advised - (for free!) that life is life, no matter what - this through a plethora of challenges again thrown for free! (Now this is where it really gets irritating, daunting, boring, jarring and what not and then all the more interesting)

re-introduced - again to love, be it for a person or a profession or some concept or aspect of life that is worth pursuing. So, GO BACK TO '*introduced*' phase and try your luck if you can escape that '*tormented*' phase and directly jump to the next phase below

gifted - with a re-discovered 'new you'! Now you can either get married or work on one of your passions/purpose of life/ dream of your life

And now just live and live and live, until you break free of this chain of life-death-re-birth and finally achieve salvation to dissolve into the oneness of this Universe from where you have been initially been tapped and trapped into the above chain :)

Well, there must be a lot after that 'gifted' phase, because after all you were gifted in the first place! Weren't you? Yeah, if you chose to get married after being gifted, children are the next possibility and *then facilitating this cycle of events to them!!* Ofcourse that might mean a new set of emotions altogether, but atleast I'm not introduced to those emotions as yet, so let me refrain from discussing them. Because, that is a huge deviant from the current topic, for I've already deviated quite a bit...

Well, let's go back to that *gifted* phase. By this time, as an adult we have been introduced to enough of spectre of emotions. As a child, this chain of emotions as I thought of, was perhaps more simple (not that we really think of this at that age, but I'm just trying to pen down a sub-conscious expectation by memorizing my state then, you know, really I swear, I tried

:-)) : *encouraged-fed-fulfilled-married-lived happily ever after-retired.* Now that *fulfilled* stage sounds so very bright...fulfilled what? Well, everything, you set your heart and mind on, ofcourse through enough struggle by overcoming the obstacles. Now that is innocence or let's just say naivete. Should we refer to that phase as a pure phase, the pure side of our character? Definitely not. When we don't know what bad is, being good is not all that tough - that is just a monolithic perception of life. *The naivete of our character is not purity by any means* - well ignorance is bliss, but unfortunately we are not allowed to remain in that bliss forever - atleast time doesn't allow us to.

[As a side note, today I was reading the 'Religion' section of 'The Hindu' Newspaper and came across a very convincing explanation of God - Lord Krishna in His Geethopadesham[1] tells Arjuna that He is the Time. I was totally convinced with that definition. From whatever I had experienced in life, I had come to believe that God is nothing but the collective consciousness encompassing the spatial and temporal existence of Universe - that all-pervading energy. Not that I'm a great fan of God, but yes I believe in Him and in His plan for all of us]

The purity of our character lies in picking the right attitude despite the harshness life has wielded on us. When badly hit, some people get disenchanted sometimes, disillusioned, disheartened, dis-oriented and keep wandering endlessly around illusions and vices - they lose the zeal they initially had, in short they lose hold of themselves. Nothing wrong with

---

[1]   Geethopadesham: A *Sanskrit phrase* used to indicate the narration of Gita (more popularly regarded as *Bhagavadgita*) by Lord Krishna himself to Arjuna, when the former rode the chariot of the latter during the famous war of *Kurukshetra*. *(Geethopadesham = Gita + Upadesham (which means narration)).*

them, that's indeed a natural response to hurt, they just didn't have the right set of people and events that can channelize the grief into useful lessons. They just didn't have the right anchor. On the other hand, there are these other set of people who come out even stronger.

I guess as long as we have that hold on ourselves we are good. As long as we are hopeful that we can overcome the despair in life, because after all life has gifted us with a variety of experiences from which to learn, we are good. I consider that quality of being hopeful, and being rightly hopeful as we rightly discharge our duties, despite the plethora of evils one has encountered, as the purity and the strength of our character.

Vedanta[1], the culmination of Vedas, indeed seems a paradox of all that is preached by Vedas. Vedas give a whole lot of rigid set of data and concepts, Vedas do not really question anything, it is said (I've never read any of them). *Vedanta apparently sets on that process of enquiry, putting the preachings of Vedas to application.* In that sense Vedanta, though sounds an end, is actually the beginning of the process of enquiry one is expected to do, not just to achieve salvation but also to lead a meaningful life. I guess, one can even hack this underlying implication and tend to do that enquiry on and off, even if one has studied neither Vedas nor Vedanta.

---

[1] Vedanta: '*anta*' as suffix in *Sanskrit* means '*end*', so literally the term translates to 'end of Veda'. There are four Vedas in Hinduism – *Rigveda, Yajurveda, Samaveda* and *Atharvaveda*. *Vedanta* is one of the six schools of Hindu Philosophy and the term has different connotations as per context. *Vedanta* as religious scriptures composed of Vedic literature is simply referred to Upanishads and some see it as the school of philosophy that interprets Upanishads. In a more general sense, the term is sometimes broadly used to refer to Ancient Indian Philosophy itself.

A transcendental journey of a spectrum of human emotions culminates into an altruistic purity of thought and character just as the colours merge to give a pure white light. There is no pure white light as such, it's just the embodiment of all colours within itself. The co-existence is beautifully depicted when that very pure white light refracts into a rainbow. *We just need a prism for that beauty to manifest* :) In fact, all that our character needs, to get to know its various shades, IS a prism!

But frankly the knowledge of all this and the right/wrong interpretation thereoff is no solace. Altruism is not easy to embrace especially when there is no outlet. People around you don't need it! Given a choice, I would prefer naivete to altruism, the bliss of ignorance to wisdom, how much ever small, of altruism and a finite set of colors to the purity of whiteness. I'd really like to believe that purity is elusive atleast for a human, *at this current juncture of the world*, for the bitterness of altruism just shows in the fact that altruistic God Himself is accepted by people through the filters of their faith and beliefs instead of the fact that He is God. I really wonder if this earth has become such an ungodly place that God is unwilling to establish His true identity. *The bitter fact is that purity has no audience until it refracts.*

- Aug 24, 2012, 10:24 PM.

37. The patterns around...the life and the spiral...

I have always been fascinated by the patterns nature creates and nurtures. Sometimes, it feels that the nature really beckons us to take notice of them. The occurrence of patterns around us in the nature only indicates the existence of an architect above us, according to me. Anyway, what triggered this post is the Spirometry test I happened to come across yesterday. Back to Spirometry later, I'll first talk about the most fundamental pattern we all know, fundamental in a sense that it is fundamental to our lives in many ways...

Scientists have known it much earlier and postulated it for the larger mankind to know. According to Rutherford's atomic model, the electrons in an atom revolve round the nucleus in elliptic orbits and the nucleus consists of protons and neutrons. The closest analogy to it is our system of planets in the Milky Way, where the planets revolve around the Sun in elliptic orbits with variable orbital spans in all the three terms of distance, time and velocity. Obviously it was called the Planetary Model. The Solar System revolves around the Galactic Centre in elliptic orbit. Extrapolating it to the Universe beyond the Milky Way, the galaxies themselves revolve around a centre of mass probably in elliptical orbits. Anyway, our science textbooks back in school have confined our knowledge to the Milky Way and only hinted that multiple galaxies do exist. Reasearch indicates that the Universe expands constantly. That is exactly where the spirometry test comes into picture.

In the spirometry test, when the subject (the person under test) inhales, the spirometry equipment indicates the breath graphically as an upper arm of a curve (similar to ellipse) starting from origin and then when the subject exhales, the graph completes with the lower arm of the ellipse not going back to origin ofcourse, but meeting the x-axis with some shift. The deeper the inhalation or exhalation, the bigger is the semi-elliptical curve. If the subject goes through an ascending cycle of almost equal inhalation and exhalation spans every time, then the combined graph looks like a spiral. It is notable that when the subject pauses for breath for a fraction of a second (or even a second) in between, the graph does not go to its origin, it just stays there. Anyway, I might not have been exact, but I guess I'm close to describing it appropriately. Breath is usually regarded synonymous with life, so the spirometry test seems to indicate that, just as the breath gets larger it traces a spiral path, so does life in this universe. As the life expands, it seems like the galaxies inherently trace a spiral path to accommodate more and more life. I have not collected any scientific facts to substantiate it, but just a presumption through analogy...

Coming to think of more patterns, it is said that the composition of water in human body is equivalent to that of water on earth ~ 70%. Seems like that's how life is balanced, this equivalence strikes to me as the concept of similar triangles an instance of which is the concept of Sierpinski triangle. (Now don't ask me what is the composition of water in any other living organism - animals and plants... I don't know!)

And then the famous Golden Ratio towards which nature exhibits an inherent affinity in creation... the phi and the fibonacci series (for the mathematically inclined people!) That's perhaps why wise people have mimicked nature to create bigger and better things - internet perhaps inspired (atleast conceptually) by neural networking of the human body, nuclear fusion to create sustainable energy from an understanding of the fusion process in Sun and so on, the list could be very long if attempted.

I'm intrigued by the wobbling effect of the earth being compared to that of a wobbling top. We know that the top wobbles because it spins on its axis, one end of the axis being held by the ground. How then does the earth wobble? What holds the other end of the earth's axis?

Whatever it is, I'm fascinated by these patterns that can scale from microcosm to the macrocosm...

- Sep 07, 2012, 05:33 PM.

38. What if the earth was to set on a time travel?

Now don't say I'm wierd to have thought that. Then all those Hollywood directors would be labelled being 'wierd' instead of 'creative'. So what if earth in an endeavour to catch up with time (or shed off excess time), was to set on a time travel? I mean, catching up with some Cosmic Time which is on a different referential frame, say time frame of that of Milky Way itself or may be some other galaxy which we ought to be synced up with! Who knows if Earth and Man are really on the same time frame as that of Milky Way?

I watch English movies sparsely, so to give you a better understanding I'll take you to the Telugu movie "Aditya 369" :) The hero, heroine and a third character (a police constable) in that movie set on a time travel through a time machine without appropriate exposure of how to operate that machine. In the movie, the machine just spins off in a spatial plane at a very high velocity and just vanishes from there to travel into the temporal plane. To me that seems absurd, because a travel is always two dimensional - both space and time dependant, so it must traverse through both the planes simultaneously. Well, the time travel of a human mind might just involve the singular dimension of time alone. Many people are said to have done it over the years and that is how they came to predict the future. But that's not the kind of time travel man these days is aiming at, right? If it was the time travel of consciousness alone, one would be able to do it (through Divine Will, I believe), roam across multiple worlds sitting under a tree itself. Anyway, now let's get back to the concept of *physical time travel* (yes, I have innovated this term for a two-dimensional time travel ;-)). Now, what if the earth as a whole was to do that, *the time travel?* The endeavour here has two possibilities:

- Case 1: To catch up with time i.e., travel into future and transform it into present - compress the present, traverse through it at a faster pace. (faster relative to the usual pace)

- Case 2: To shed off excess time i.e., travel into a different variant of future which would have been past for that future and transform it into present - magnify the present, traverse through it at a slower pace. (slower relative to the usual pace)

Here my assumption is that you are not allowed to go back in time. Practically speaking there is no going back to past, we might want to travel into past, the earth as a rotating body might be required to travel into past, but all the entities in the universe might not go back in time homogeneously to recreate the past as it was. So to shed off excess time, we must just travel slower than our usual pace, starting from now into the future, so that in the due course of time, we (I mean the earth) shed off the excess time.

In case 1, we must traverse through the present tense at a faster pace. So let's say we have to catch up one year in a day (the year and the day here are those time periods as experienced on earth 'usually'). So we need to experience 365.25 days + 1 day (along with the day currently being traversed) by the end of that day. So we get to see 366.25 (367) sunrises and 366.25 (366) sunsets in a single day!!! Wow!!! That must be such a wonderful thing to experience!

I say 367 because the remaining 0.75 can be assumed to be the continuum leading to next day. Don't go into the exact details anyway, this is all just a fun-talk and we don't even know how nature responds to it. Nature might reveal its own way of accomplishing this task when posed with such a challenge.

And in case 2, let's say we must shed off a year in a day. This can be done when we have only one sunrise and a sunset in a whole year.

The beauty here perhaps is that when we have to catch up, we live the real time of one day (experiencing a year virtually) and when we have to shed off, we live the virtual time of one year (experiencing a day virtually) in reality.

Now the big question here is, this can be accomplished only if the rotational and revolutional velocities of the earth increase or decrease proportionately. What must be the impact of life on earth in such conditions??? I don't know and I'm just wondering...

(As you might have understood, I considered distance traversed in space constant with varying time and velocity. And ofcourse the whole Milky way, the system in which the Earth is just a part, must go on a time travel if this were to happen when the syncing up is with a different galaxy altogether! Above all, the biggest disclaimer is that this is my personal hypothesis, a mere hypothesis.)

- Sep 07, 2012, 06:34 PM.

39. *Satyam Shivam Sundaram!!!*

I have a deep reverence and admiration for this beautiful phrase 'Satyam Shivam Sundaram'. And we also have another phrase 'Satyame Shivam'. A couple of months ago I bumped into a documentary on a Telugu Music Director Satyam. It's named 'Satyame Sangeetham'. The documentary narrates the mark, the music director has left on Telugu music. Anyway, all this talk is to get to the root of significance of Satyam[1] and Sangeetham[2] when it comes to understanding the **Shiva Tatvam**[3]. In Hinduism, the *Shiva Tatvam* is too intricate and deep and really requires a lot of soul search and self-exploration to understand its essence. While I have not yet made any deliberate efforts to understand and realize the essence of this philosophy, I have been fortunate enough to get a few glimpses which actually initiated and stimulated my interest towards this. My understanding of it so far is based on the beauty (Sundaram/Saundaryam[4]) of duality it symbolizes, the synergy of complementary energies it signifies and the possibility of co-existence of paradoxical worlds it exemplifies. All in all, to

---

[1]   Satyam: *(Sanskri/Telugu)* Truth.
[2]   Sangeetham: *(Sanskrit/Telugu)* Music.
[3]   Shiva Tatvam: *(Sanskrit/Telugu)* The aspect, nature, way or Philosophy of Shiva.
[4]   *(Sanskrit/Telugu)* Sundaram: Beautiful; Saundaryam: Beauty.

me, it's about staying attached, yet detached, selectively and conditionally based on one's discretion and circumstances. One of my fellow bloggers has once referred to 'Sivoham, Sivoham[1]'. This post is to try my hand at understanding these phrases based on the little understanding I have. Perhaps someday I shall gain more insight into this philosophy enabling me a better grasp of these ideas.

<u>Sivoham, Sivoham</u>: The literary translation of it says that ***Lord Shiva is the Truth, the Pure Consciousness and the Bliss.*** My understanding was that it depicts the concept of God at a holistic level - that He is beyond form, emotions, attachments and the physical senses. That means, when you transcend through and beyond the plurality of the existence, the purity can be realized. Lord Shiva Himself, as said in Hindu scriptures, ardently practises detachment. But He is always tagged along with His consort Shakti and pondering deep, God never prescribes detachment *per se* as the path to salvation. In fact salvation is not the sole purpose of human birth, rather it is the fulfillment of the purpose of the birth first and then attainment of a stage where one can let go of that attachment the human journey spawns.

Now, to the phrase - <u>Satyame Shivam</u>. It literally means that ***The Truth is Shiva, Shiva is the Truth.*** It is said that Lord Shiva is Layakaara[2]. *Laya* is an inherent aspect of the concept of "Srishti – Sthithi – Laya[3]", all the three elements being integrally related. In that sense, Lord Shiva establishes the basic truth that *All the matter that was created from the eternal energy needs*

---

[1]   Sivoham, Sivoham: (Sanskrit) I am Shiva, I am Shiva.
[2]   Layakaara: *(Sanskrit/Telugu)* The one who establishes Periodicity.
[3]   Srishti – Sthithi - Laya: *(Sanskrit/Hindi/Telugu)*
       Creation – State – Periodicity.

to dissolve back into that energy someway or the other, some day or the other'. THIS is the truth which was always there - whose beginning and end we never know. In the world of music, *sruthi* and *laya*[1] are regarded as mother and father of music respectively, which means that there is no music until they both fall in place. My Music Teacher Sri Vasudevan (for Indian Carnatic Vocals) says that there is no object in this universe without a *sruthi* and *laya* of its own. In this sense, **Lord Shiva, the father of this universe is the one that establishes 'laya', the much needed periodicity, which is fundamental for sustenance**. And sometimes when the *sruthi* is out of sync, the *laya* becomes pralaya[2].

Now, to the first one! - <u>*Satyam Shivam Sundaram*</u>. It's the same as the second one, almost. **The truth gets beautiful when Lord Shiva establishes it...**

- Oct 05, 2012, 03:22 PM.

<u>*Self-Notes:*</u>

Shiva and Shakti unite with their roles swapped and recreate each other when a *Pralaya* needs to be avoided. This is *Shiva Tatvam*, the beauty of *'Satyam, Shivam, Sundaram'* and a very subtle variant of *'Sivoham, Sivoham'*. This is how the Absolute Truth that Shiva and Shakti being two bodies but one soul, the paradoxical concept of duality is established and this is how Shiva who is usually perceived to be a destroyer becomes a creator!!!

- Dec 16, 2012, 09:50 AM.

---

[1]   Sruthi and Laya: *(Sanskrit/Hindi/Telugu)* Base and Periodicity of music.
[2]   Pralaya: *(Sanskrit/Hindi/Telugu)* Chaos or Disaster.

40. The hierarchy of need!

It's really boring and at the same time daunting to say same things over and over again in different forms, from different perspectives, but this time I really need a vent out and hence this blog post! As far as this concept is concerned, perhaps I never gave a meaningful and comprehensive shape to my feelings, in fact maybe never addressed them under an appropriate heading even and hence they crave to be expressed over and over again...this time I would like to make a successful attempt at this, so I stop floundering along!

This is about the hierarchy of need. I'm sure there are many theories out there. The hierarchy of basic, economic, political needs and then comforts as sought by human beings, the hierarchy of freedoms, the hierarchy of problems a government is expected to address to establish good governance, so on and so forth. But this attempt of mine is to word out this issue as I see it, uninfluenced by the knowledge of those theories. The hierarchy of needs for an 'average' human being of the current century perhaps would be:

1. to stay alive

2. to satiate one's hunger (food)

3. to have somebody whom you can relate to (family)

4. to stay healthy

5. to have a comfortable place to reside

6. to satiate one's sexual drive (tagged with nature's requirement for copulation)

7. to earn money to meet other needs

8. to earn other means to place oneself at a better position in society (education, earning more money, earning more power)

9. To earn more knowledge to have a better world view and satiate oneself spiritually

Anyway, these are vague headings - 'needs', 'knowledge', 'comfortable' are all relative terms and depend on one's own desire and ambition. But that is not the argument of this discussion. It's rather about how the *8th* need is assuming higher priority these days than any other need perhaps to an extent that if it is not met even the 1st need does not make sense.

Let's consider this scenario. Say you are touring with a backpack equipped with fundamental and costly accessories, with a jerkin on. And you come across shivering children on roads without basic clothing. Would you venture to give your jerkin to them? No, definitely not. It's not necessarily the brand, the cost, but because of the basic feeling that 'How many people would I be able to help after all, so this one charity wouldn't count anyway'. And thinking that way, you move on. And then let's say you come across some children languishing for food. You would perhaps offer them a penny or two, but wouldn't go to the extent of parting with good amount of money to an extent that you satiate the hunger of the whole bunch of children. And then finally let's say, you are on some nature touring and suddenly a tiger starts running to catch you, I mean to actually eat you. What would you then do? All you would think is to lessen the burden on you as much as possible and run, just run for your life. In that process, you wouldn't mind throwing your bag, jerkin and what not. I mean this is such a predictable scenario and there is nothing too fancy about it. But the point I'm trying to make is, in the moment of disaster, we all stop being rational and get back to our very basic instincts. During natural disasters, it is said that even the set of animals (snake and frog has been the most cited pair) those are deadly enemies (or the predator and the predated) are said to pair up and help each other to save their lives. I mean that's the point where one sheds even one's natural vices one has acquired out of one's birth and upbringing.

Now let's consider another scenario. This one is about how we all get pampered gradually but get regulated all of a sudden, owing to the sudden mix of situations. Let's consider a family in which the Mom is a housewife and doesn't earn on her own and saves money in the kitchen-tins from what her husband gives. Also let's say Dad is usually not concerned about how much money he earns and gives to his wife and how much money is spent, so money management is more or less in the domain of Mom. So Mom spoils her children by feeding them with pocket money day-in and day-out. Dad is completely unaware of it while Mom indulges in spoiling her kids. I mean that's such a sweet thing to indulge in, but consider this situation, let's say when Dad runs out of work for some reasons and stops giving money to Mom and then the chain of events that get triggered - Mom doesn't give pocket money to kids, kids' needs are not met and then they resort to some acts of venting out their pent up frustration which shows up in very different and unrelated situations in front of their parents and then

Mom and/or Dad suddenly resort to straightening up their kids' behavior. An ideal situation would be gradual pampering and regulation of kids, but that's not what usually happens.

There are other situations too. Parents and teachers give the sense of free play to kids to give them a sense of judgement call to inculcate in them effective decision making skills, to make them feel that they are growing and that they can handle their progress on their own. Some elders do keep a keen watch on their kids in the background and come to the foreground only when needed and do the needed regulation. And again that's an ideal scenario and I think the current day activities of both the elders and the kids (with lot many avenues opened up for both entertainment and distraction), it's not really possible to effectively monitor children. Regulation then happens all of a sudden and it is not easily accepted by children too. It's usually seen as taking away their freedom. At the end of the day, monitoring and regulation are not easy responsibilities.

Now another situation! Say, there is a family whose members have heavily disintegrated from the setup of family and are on their individual pursuits without giving space and concern to other members. Such a condition actually steals each member of their energy and creates an additional stress and lack of fallback mechanism of de-stressing. In fact family, according to me, must serve as the vital fallback mechanism in conditions of distress, but the modern society has so shaped itself that sometimes family itself is the cause of major stress. Let's say in such a condition, a family member is affected by some major illness and needs sudden attention. If the family has initially started off with healthy bonding, I'm sure the members unite and wake up to the situation and strike on initial family ties and bonding and might even go through a cycle where they retrospect about their deviance and how much of a quality 'together-time' they have lost. They might even realize that their own individual pursuits are not an end in itself and that it does not make any sense at the cost of losing the setup of family and that it is definitely possible to strike a healthy balance between 'individual passion' and 'family integrity'.

Anyway, I have cited various kinds of situations and it might not make any sense to connect them all. But all I'm actually trying to put forward is, ***the hierarchy of your need is shaped by the resourcefulness of the framework you are part of.***

Let me cite another very different situation that does not fall under the category of above situations. I've read recently about the huge number of people in India who are being arrested on baseless charges of indulging in terrorist activities - this without any formative evidence! And then they are interrogated (read it harrassed) for a number of years and when the interrogation does not go any further, they are released on the grounds of lack of evidence. And it seems, the police have been clinging to a set procedure in following their interrogation. And it seems, all these fraud cases that have been booked on the innocent populace have a very common pattern. It just reflects the lack of basic procedures. And even if there are set procedures, they reflect the lack of implementation and the lack of will to actually nab on the real culprits. Forget about that, but the pathetic part is that there is no fallback or coping mechanism for such people after a long languish, to join back the regular walk of life. And they take a couple of years to overcome such trauma and gain confidence and required skills to even lead a basic existence. Such people really do not have energy to indulge in the normal 'conflict' or 'selfish' patterns of thinking like - 'Hey, why the hell the government runs like this?', 'That class of people is responsible for the downfall of society', 'Oh! There is corruption all around and there is no place for truth or merit', 'Ah! This population, this pollution, these roads, these policies, man this system in India!', 'This fetches me more money and I don't care who is being affected in this process'... All they would really ask of the society is - *"Could you give us some scope to live?"* But this situation of theirs arises with no fault of theirs! That is how society, situations and above all, the destiny of a person shapes his attitude and ambition and that is how his needs get shaped accordingly.

It is in this context, I would like to bring out the role of a disaster on a macro scale. People say that conflict is very much part of society and consensus is usually elusive. Agreed! People say that *'Man is a selfish animal'* and some even go further and say that it is that selfishness which has accomplished big things in the world. Agreed! Some say that, we all have a tendency to group and divide ourselves out and that world fraternity is not just ambitious but impossible. Very much agreed! This is all true, BUT this is true only because it has been THAT way. The world, as we know it, has based itself on selfishness and man has evolved to be selfish. ***In fact history has shaped itself that way.*** There is nothing wrong in being selfish, but there is that thin line which must not be evaded so as not to overreach the society. It is this discretion that man today is lacking - that decision to strike a balance between the individual good and social good. Fine, when nature has enough resources and people didn't have enough technology to abuse it, it was all good. And then man started getting cleverer and more selfish and once having started that journey in a given accelerated gear, man was never able to pause or change the gear to see what damage he is doing to the society and how he has been abusing nature's resources. Inspite of being aware of the damage, he was not able to change the gears, his selfishness has defined for him. I'd say, *wind back the clock and implant that discretion in human brain to strike that right balance*, then this huge population would have been a boon and not a bane while the nature would have still been at its best. Growing population is just a reason we cite to compensate for the selfishness which we do not want to stand accountable for! **We are just tied down by our past when we state that we have such and such behavioural traits.**

It is actually a change in the attitude of the people that's essential and that's the need of hour, we do have all the resources at our disposal. To say that we do not have enough resources is such a blatant lie. We must rather say we do not know how to use them or say we have a bunch of friends or a set group of people whom we want to share them with, just because we have some personal interests served that way while not wanting to give that privilege to others. Come to think of it, while we have a good bunch of countries with no proper governance, millions of people starving for food and shelter, millions with no education and atleast a billion of them undergoing some or the other kind of abuse everyday and while we do not have enough resources or enough skills to use the resources, itseems scientists want to research in time travel and warp drives that consume energy equivalent to the energy-mass equivalence of Voyager 1. Ok talk about time travel (of consciousness) of some enlightened souls, fine. Talk about the spiritual upliftment and Trikala Gnanam[1], fine. But come on give us some food and then

---

[1]   Trikala Gnanam: (*Sanskrit/Hindi/Telugu*) The knowledge of three states of time – past, present and future. (*Tri* – Three, *Kala* – Time, *Gnanam* – Wisdom).

embark on your creative flight that is SOME food for your thought!!! I know, the governments invest based on a trade-off between current needs for development and long-term goals and visions for development and progress as a human race, but this is too costly a trade-off to be tilted towards investing huge money in *Time Travel* (I personally believe).

Coming back from time travel to the conflict vs consensus theories, I agree with all of what people say and also add that though conflict is the tendency of human beings per se, it must be the vision of leaders to unite people. ***People may be cynical, but leaders must be a fine blend of being idealistic and pragmatic*** - Idealism to dream big and pragmatism to pin down the underlying problems and implement their idealistic policies. The end result would be atleast double as good as it would be when people think that 'class concept' is inevitable. But then, good leaders are hard to find these days and that's a different story altogether.

If one goes out and preaches "Brahma Satyam Jagat Mitya" (Sanskrit phrase which means – "Brahman alone is real, this world is just an illusion") or "This is good and this is bad and this is what you ought to do", one really runs the risk of being beaten up thoroughly, yeah complete black and blue at that! "Yeah seriously, who are you to teach me anything, how dare you!!!" Sadly, people learn the hard way! They need to realize their mistakes on their own. ***It is only in the face of disaster that people (atleast today's people, given their discretion) unite and then do some retrospection*** – a disaster through which the humanity is expected to pay its Karmic Debt as a race. Perhaps that's the only scenario in which all the class conflicts, racial differences, economic gaps and all other divisions and boundaries cease to make sense and living, just being alive, makes sense.

Ok, I know that I have started with something and ended up writing something. A more appropriate title would have been "The essence of disaster in change management", but still *I'm looking at how a disaster shapes the hierarchy of need*, so I will leave it just that way...

- Oct 09, 2012, 11:48 PM.

41. Mitigating the cascading effect...

This one is about one of my experiences during my role as an onsite co-ordinator, back in 2008. Keeping the technical details aside, I'll try to explain this more in laymen terms. The product under discussion is used by client locations distributed world-wide. There was one feature which was needed by few locations (including mine) and not needed at the rest of the locations. While there was a simple and detailed 'HowTo Manual' on how to use that feature (how to use and how not to use - activate/deactivate), some client locations felt that knowing that procedure in itself was an extra burden since they didn't need that feature in the first place. This triggered long chains of mail communication between heads at various levels, in fact involving such higher-ups who were not technically well versed with the feature. Hence they (leads@Development Centre) in fact genuinely backed up the feature and started arguing that the feature was indeed robustly developed and all locations might possibly sense a use case in the future and hence urged them to 'learn' how to deal with it and deactivate it. While the leads were right from their own perspective, I as an onsite co-ordinator understood what the clients were actually intending to convey - this due to the close interaction I had with clients there and hence the awareness of the knowledge of the product, the way they use it and the amount of exposure/isolation of certain features they expect. It is plain simple, clients view the product through the filters of their usage, hence they just don't want to deal with things they are not required to use. Well, to certain extent they would deal, but that procedure needs to be as simple as possible, that is the basic requirement.

The client lead at my location had some technical knowledge of the product, so he sort of played an intermediary and explained to our leads the actual problem before which our leads sticked to the defensive mode. It is only after that, they understood the problem and ordered for an immediate service pack that might address this problem. The solution meant that the feature has to be deactivated by default and only the interested parties activate it as per their need. Again different solutions were proposed by us, the Development Centre and some solutions came up from the client quarters too. But again consensus eluded and a lot of halla-gulla[1] ensued. It's because the activating procedures either affected the environment of those client locations where there was a use case and which change they didn't afford to take or the procedure was a bit cumbersome. This mode of trying to address the problems of non-use case client locations posed problems to those locations which had a use case in the first place. This proved more counter-productive. This is where naturally onsite coordinators ought to come into picture, so I did. The solution offered then was to introduce a simple environment variable which has a default effect of numbing the feature and which when set explicitly activates the feature. This solution of mine, such a simple one, was greatly applauded by my immediate leads. But, that's a different story anyway because many other areas

---

[1]   Halla-gulla: (*Hindi*) Hullabaloo.

of my work in which I kept my heart and soul into never got as much attention, owing to fewer business scenarios in which the work was used. But pragmatically speaking, this is the way of things because, the more the impact of one's work, the more the recognition or attention. Such direct proportionality does not exist between quality of work (dedication, skill, efficiency) and recognition. It's as simple as that - the more your work affects others, the more importance it assumes.

Anyway, this example was more to use as a base for a bigger problem. How in general can *Cascading Effects* be mitigated? I know it's not simple and there does not exist one solution and more importantly it is subjective to the problem and system at hand. But then, this is to try my hand at figuring out a generic approach possibly. And I'll attempt this from the software solutions perspective. Let's say we have a core system => Level 1 systems => Level 2 systems => Level 3 systems ...... and so on. The core system is the core of the system as the name says, the set of fundamentals, assumptions, hypotheses, etc. that the whole system is based on. And let's assume each level evolves from the immediate lower level and is dependent on that level only and does not speak directly to the levels below the immediate level. And also assume that the sub-systems within a level speak to each other. So every level can only speak to its immediate lower level - that is the basic assumption.

Now let's say there arised a scenario where there is a change in the core system. The core system, ofcourse being the core, has an impact on Level 1 system, which has an impact on Level 2, which in turn has an impact on Level 3 and so on. So that's a cascading impact. Ideally it means all the systems will have to be changed in order to deal with this core change. But then, that's big work and is time sensitive and cannot be done immediately, it takes time and nevertheless the whole system has to move on and keep functioning and cannot afford any downtime. In such a case, how do we deal with this change and how do we address the resultant impact? The solution can perhaps be two fold:

- If there are enough resources (time, money, flexibility and robustness of the existing systems, knowledge, skill, personnel) - change all the systems so as to address the change.

- If not all resources are available, let's say most importantly if there is no time, an immediate approach by any software engineer would be to build a *'wrapper'* which takes the immediate impact from the core system, translates it in an understandable way to level 1 giving it an illusion that nothing has indeed changed so that the rest of the system functions in a similar way. In the mean time, a possibility of employing the first mode of solution can be looked into, depending on such a use case.

It all depends on how best a wrapper can be created so as to mitigate the cascading effect with zero or minimum downtime. The idea is to keep the interfaces same as much as possible by creating an additional intermediate layer.

- Oct 14, 2012, 12:29 AM.

42. Saralee Swaraalu :)

Ok, I just started off with my music classes and I already broke my voice, that's because I already gave some naive performances before some kids who are not adept at music and hence were comfortably all praises for my voice. I twisted my voice to the level of braying, so no wonder I broke it. I'm now in the process of getting it back on track. But the fact is that I just started off with *Saralee Swaraalu*! (means the simplest of musical compositions) If this is my condition for the first steps in music, I should see how it goes in the future. Jokes apart, as my music teacher says, music is a journey of lifetime and I'm getting to realize how true that is. I can't deny that I've started enjoying it, nevertheless like any other artform, it requires time, dedication and commitment.

Anyway, Saralee Swaraalu gives one, the scope of learning music and at the same time be creative about it. My favourite Swaram as of now is this:

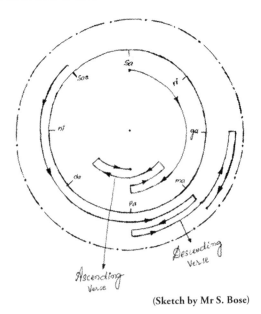

(Sketch by Mr S. Bose)

Fig 2 – Music Verse

In aarohanam[1], while ascending (in frequency ofcourse), the note (frequency) *'pa'* is used as a proxy to descend, alternating between *'ma'* and *'da'*. In avarohanam, while descending, the note *'ma'* is used as a proxy to ascend, alternating between *'pa'* and *'ga'*.

The details are boring as I explain, but it gets beautiful as one sings and I'm tending to sing all the swaraas[2] in this fashion, so my teacher says I'm more tuned to these frequencies :)

- Oct 27, 2012, 12:30 AM.

43. Freedom Struggle - as an evolutionary process

History was always interesting, even to study and recapitulate. Yes, you heard it right! I was not one of those students to whom history meant one of these - boring, jarring, monotonous, scary or threatening. And this, despite the fact that I'm not very good at memorising facts, especially names and dates. It's because I don't see history as a factual compilation of data (events, happenings, processes etc). To me, history meant the missing link and handle of the past providing a platform of continuity to sustain in the present. Back then, I used to really enjoy studying history part of my social text books and preparing answers of my own with long list of bullet points. I also felt proud when my Social teacher said after my schooling

---

[1]   Aarohanam & Avarohanam: *(Sanskrit/Telugu) Aarohanam* and *Avarohanam* represent the ascending and descending sequence of a musical composition respectively.

[2]   Swaraas: *(Sanskrit/Telugu)* Plural of *Swaram*, which means musical composition.

that my Social Science answers were always looked upon and raised the bar for other students. Yeah, to this day I pride on the fact that Social Science was my highest scoring subject in Xth (whose place is usually taken by Mathematics and other Sciences). I wish I was atleast half as enthusiastic, methodical, organised, diligent, committed and clear in thought now. Ok, I was to write about the history of freedom struggle, but here I started writing about my personal history, well this nostalgia never goes. But, now into the actual point of discussion, let's get into the past, into the 19th Century India (I always had a problem with 1800-1900 being regarded as 19th Century, my mind would say oh you mean the 18th Century)...

Ok I might have boasted a lot about my flair for history and Social Sciences in general, but reading about Freedom Struggle of India lately, took me by total surprise. Yeah, as a student this was the impression I had - different revolutions: French, Russian etc had their place in history. They had a cause to contribute in the evolution of mankind in a very important way. But, I feel Indian Struggle for freedom did not find its right place in the history, not even in Indian History. I say this because, after being through text books, Indian Struggle for freedom in general meant - British conquered India, exploited economically and while they evolved into a developed nation we moved to an underdeveloped nation, our wealth has been drained, we did not even know for a while that we are being exploited and when we knew it we set on to a long struggle to unify India for a common cause of 'Swaraj'. Well, there could be many great history books which I might not have come across, which had deep and personal accounts of various people who participated in the struggle and they might have offered beautiful, real, not-so-general perspectives, which we didn't have the luck to be aware of. Another point is, Indian history to a majority extent was narrated by British writers more than the Indian writers, so obviously a lot of Indian perspective was missing in the history books. Atleast in World History, the Indian struggle for Independence finds a place more from the British perspective than from Indian perspective.

But, my basic problem is that the Indian school textbooks themselves which are expected to inculcate basic values and knowledge in the young citizens and give the much needed impetus for self-exploration have been successful only to the extent of invoking a patriotic fervour in us when we think of the freedom struggle. When we read deep accounts of freedom struggle, they actually stand out as witnesses to India's greatest transformation of all times (atleast dating back to those times from which history-keeping is accounted for). And the transformation has been for good. Yes, there have been turbulences, but how Indians have involuntarily welcomed Europeans, how the foreign evil and selfishness joined hands with the local evil and ignorance, how the combined evil grew together and forced the subdued strengths of Indians to surface, how British exploitation has set a platform for the renaissance of India and how the Indians have crossed that threshold and barrier to overcome years of languishing, perhaps needs a different take at history viewing it as an evolutionary process - as the evolution of a struggle.

I will just cite three excerpts of the freedom fighters' views on how they see themselves in the history (from the book "FREEDOM STRUGGLE" by Bipan Chandra, Amales Tripathi, Barun De - National Book Trust of India). Those excerpts will speak for themselves and need no further explanation as to why I'm citing them here in my post.

(*Context*: The freedom struggle here is seen as having evolved into two eras of Moderate nationalism and Militant/Extremist nationalism, the former being ahead in time. The Moderates were moderate in their approach to fight for freedom. In fact they didn't even have a platform to fight, they had to set a stage, they had to weave a thread that can unify the distinct classes who suffered for distinct reasons (including those who didn't even know they were suffering). And that stage was to arouse nationalism in Indian minds and the weapons were primarily Newspapers, Journals, Mass Meeetings and Political Associations which were mostly self-financed by the leaders initially. (Imagine, can we now even think about devoting our earnings and accrued property for a cause which we are not sure would fructify in our own lifetime, let alone sacrificing our life??? The moderates were apparently more considerate of British rule and more polite (read it diplomatic) in their ways of approaching the British. The Extremists on the other hand were more radical and demanded the freedom, their *due*.

- When in 1891, young Gokhale expressed disappointment at the two-line reply of the Government to a carefully prepared memorial* by the Poona Sarvajanik Sabha, Justice Ranade replied:

    o "You don't realise our place in the history of our country. These memorials are nominally addressed to Government, in reality they are addressed to the people, so that they may learn how to think in these matters. This work must be done for many years, without expecting any other results because politics of this kind is altogether new in this land."

- The preliminary character of the struggle can be seen from a letter by Dadabhai Naoroji to D E Walcha dated 12th January 1905:

  o "...The very discontent and impatience it (the Congress) has evoked against itself as slow and non-progressive among the rising generation are among its best results or fruits. It is its own evolution and progress... (the task is) to evolve the required revolution - whether it would be peaceful or violent. The character of the revolution will depend upon the wisdom or unwisdom of the British Government and action of the British people."

- Lastly Gopal Krishna Gokhale, the last of the great Moderates, put it this way, while evaluating the role of the founding fathers of Indian Nationalism:

  o "Let us not forget that we are at a stage of the country's progress when our achievements are bound to be small, and our disappointments frequent and trying. That is the place which it has pleased Providence to assign to us in this struggle, and our responsibility is ended when we have done the work which belongs to that place. It will, no doubt, be given to our countrymen of future generations to serve India by their successes, we of the present generation must be content to serve her mainly by our failures. For, hard though it be, out of those failures the strength will come which in the end will accomplish great tasks."

(Excerpts completed)

I guess, *it requires not only wisdom but also self-appreciation and contentment to appreciate the transitionary progress of one's own struggle.* True, results are the visible parameters based on which success is measured, but success again is relative and considering the timing of one's place in history, failures for those times are a form of postponed or translated success for future generations.

The sad part is, our text books on a high level have only glorified those leaders who were instrumental in the process "when" the freedom was obtained. It was only a matter of timing. Fine, I'm not saying that our text books should glorify all the leaders, but I would definitely and earnestly ask for the process to be glorified atleast. The accounts of the anguish, the fervour, the lives that permeated and got blended into the struggle can only be brought out by a historian who lived in the same times, interacted with them directly and was as much passionate as the fighters themselves. The exact story can never be out and it lies silently in the graves of the people who fought as much silently and selflessly.

It is like this, for me. It takes generations for a language to evolve...those times when people didn't have anything to communicate and had to come up with sign language, pictorial representations, gestures etc and then evolved into a langugage to speak, read and write. And then, it might take just a year for that great epic of evolution to be beautifully marvelled into a book. We don't know the people who framed the language, but we sure know the people who used that language to mould it into prose and poetry.

History does not highlight everybody who was part of it, but it stands on the skeletons of those who went into its making.

- *Nov 10, 2012, 09:41 PM.*

44. These are my interests - So what?

A discussion I had with one of my fellow bloggers a week ago has been a revelation of sorts for me on many levels. The blog post there, as I see it, is about how difficult it is to arrive at an optimal goal for oneself when one is part of a system that is not apparently organized. But what really caught my attention there was a problem in case that specifically talks about local-global optimization.

Seventh Daughter-In-Law scenario:

"There is a story of seven daughters-in-law with each having their share of duty during dinner time. So, the first one's duty is to lay out the table, the second to bring rice, the third one to bring water, and so on. The last one's duty is to clean up. One day, all of them begin their duties at the dinner time. It so happens that their men folk are delayed coming to the dinner. So, the last one cleans up everything before anything is eaten, because that's her duty - A hilarious case of 'local-global' conflict."

So this is a scenario which is based on an inherent assumption that the daughters-in-law are non-intelligent beings who could not assume a global goal based on "past knowledge" of roles (of daughter-in-law or even people in general serving as part of a family) and systems (family). Not only did they not assume a global goal, but also they could not rise to a situation where they could try and initate a communication with other parts of the system and arrive at the need of the hour and what is expected of them. So it is a little tricky (and might even feel wierd) to inspect this system where in human beings act like non-intelligent or non-living or non-feeling entities in a system. That way, I guess systems composed of living beings and systems composed of non-living things form entirely different threads of discussion.

Anyway, this blog post takes it a bit further on this, growing from this. I've arrived at the following definitions and concepts to understand "System Optimization" better:

- A generic system for a generic discussion can be viewed as a "Whole of parts" irrespective of the plethora of categorizations available technically. (I know, you may say, *Ok! A system is ofcourse a whole of parts, what is it that you newly understood anything?* BUT! I'm greatly delighted by this understanding :))

- "Who is optimizing the system?" is an important criteria - I mean how the person/entity as an 'actor' is related to the system. More importantly is the 'actor' inside (if so, at what level of) the system or outside the system? Both the actors have their pros and cons. An important consideration - An actor outside the system 'might' have a complete view of the system (for whatsoever reasons) but might lack an understanding of inherent features of the system, its actors, but might again well to do to easily alter the course of the whole system, like a research guy who researched an ant colony as discussed in a similar case in point. The actor inside the system (ant), on the other hand, might lack a complete view of the sytem, but knows completely well the inherent features of the actors and partly of the system. But, sadly a single ant, with its inherent disabilities might not alter the course of the whole system (in a desired way) and it takes the evolution of the ants' colony as a whole to reach a stage where the struggle between the actors is not very high.

- The system definition is different to different set of actors.

- Every system is at a point of evolution. To a *system B* at a different point of evolution, *system A* might well fall in the database of 'previous experience/knowledge' or *system B* might be superior in some ways so that it can exploit/enlighten *system A*. Hence, interactions between different systems might speed up (or alter greatly) the evolution of one/some/all of the systems. (Eg: India - British contact).

In hindsight of the discussion, this is my understanding of how systems that emerge on one's own (without an evident system administrator) might evolve. It might well seem that the parts are on their own for some time (like the countries of the world which did not have knowledge of other countries or even the characteristics of earth as a whole until some time), the parts might not know the existence of other parts or of a higher system apart from its own local system (even in a *top-down* system when the top never communicated with the constituent parts). While it is true that the parts have to balance both the local and global interests appropriately, the question that arises is - *What is **global interest** for a part that does not even know the scale of **global**?* So carve it on stone, ***a part can never know global interests on its***

own by any means or standard. And now progress a bit further into the stage of evolution and just assume that the part is now aware of some parts or even all parts in which case it is a whole (not necessarily constituted/represented by an exclusive entity/ power at the top). The awareness is ofcourse due to contact/ communication. So now the 'part' knows the 'global scale' for its purposes. But, who determines 'global interests'? Another pertinent question I'd like to ask is - *Why is a part interested in global interests?* Is it out of pure reasoning that - "There exists a global entity and for my own well being I need to serve its interests"? Well, even in that case, there is no way that a part alone can determine/assess 'global interests'. I think in most cases it is the *'cause-effect' relationship*. While it is true that you as a part might affect every part of the system in one way or the other and hence also affected in a similar or a different way, I guess the important fact is the *'awareness'* of it and *the need to act* for certain change. What I mean is, unless you are affected by other part(s) and hence the system, you don't notify the other parts that they are affecting you. Depending on the impact of the effect, you notify the impact. Your interaction results in some set of common/global (in case of all parts) interests and perhaps even a better realization of your own local interests. You are not going to accept common interests at the cost of your survival. This is where you try to optimize local interests, where you are trying to accommodate global interests into your own set up and see if they can gel well with your own interests as a whole. Sometimes they just don't clash, so you go ahead to do the needful so as NOT to negatively affect the 'part' being affected. This is then a revelation for the part that it has not been catering to the global interests properly.

You would usually reject the global interests that intimidate your own interests. And with the remaining set you see how the global interests impact your system and what modifications your own system has to undergo so as to accommodate them. You handle this set because you are part of the system and if only when you do not have the power to continue as a *'parasite'* or have enough reasoning that you don't want to continue as a parasite. Another scenario is, when another part is more powerful than a given part, the former could override the latter's interests to establish its own interests, if it believes that's in the best interests of everybody or if it lacks the generosity to let others survive. An important revelation for me is that you act for a change only when any 'foreign interest' becomes your 'own interest' at the end of the day. To summarize, I believe, you act for a change and start thinking of the global interests only when you are aware of/notified of the need to act for such interests.

Applying this to real world, to the current state of our world, a lot of countries (parts) might know that they are negatively affecting the system (this owing to our stage of human/consciousness evolution) but

i.   might not just act upon it because there is not enough pressure or

ii. even if there is, the serious clash with their own interests or

iii. the lack of will to even do such an assessment of optimization or

iv. even worse, the lack of an effective assessment strategy.

But living in the information age that is today and for the intelligible beings that we are today, I guess the last case should not arise unless there is a lack of will to initiate it. The problem is that certain parts have inherent advantages or disadvantages (eg: geographical location of certain places). And some have acquired advantages/disadvantages in the process of their evolution (economic/cultural/political status – can be summed up as *power quotient*) and hence the negotiation naturally becomes difficult. But then at the end of the day, it again boils down to how different parts can optimize each of their own interests. But the growing trend is to have organisations at the top, instead of having to deal with individual parts (countries). Eg: UNO; Country groupings such as ASEAN, BRICS, SAARC, G20, G8; European Union; IAEA, IUPAC, ICANN etc.

Viewing India as a system, it too was chaotic in a previous stage of evolution. But each of the parts of its organic whole sensed the necessity of an organized central government and representative power at the top for their sustenance and well-being for easy future negotiation and evolution. India (and hence its parts) took cue from the democratic winds that started trending the world back then. Again, it is to benefit each of its own interests. In fact, only such entities/parts can group, else they stay out of the system. This is where the "whole of parts" is tempting to discuss. The system is always a whole for the parts that want to be part of it and hence the integrity of the whole is important, as long as you deem it a "system". Ofcourse this is for intelligent systems again! In fact the whole discussion above has been for intelligent/living systems and not non-living systems.

The system as a "whole of parts" beckons two beautiful and extremely excellent examples that perfectly fit that system definition:

- *Human Body*: A human body consists of different parts and the human brain more or less commands the other parts. Ofcourse there is a consciousness that masters the brain, but we in general stop at brain/mind today and get satisfied with the answer that it is the master of the human body. Keeping that debate of brain and consciousness aside, let's delve more on the parts of human body. While all parts are necessary for effective functioning of body, it is non-debatable that certain parts are more crucial than others. Human beings have progressed to that stage today where we get certain parts repaired or replaced for longevity or better functioning of life. What if, the parts are too stubborn not to listen to us and become resistant to repair or replacement, basically any treatment? Imagine how chaotic the human body then becomes; fathom how fatalistic such trend is to our existence. Think how ridiculous it shall be, if all parts demanded autonomousness and expect to be their own master or if kidney aspires to become the master of the body! This highlights the essence of *master-slave concept* in the system of human body. We can state, without any doubt that the parts MUST listen and respond appropriately to the mind, for the best interests of the body as a whole.

- *India as a Union of States, with Federal character at state level*: India is one of those countries that truly exemplify the concept of *'Unity in Diversity'*. How difficult must it be to govern such a country varied with so many features? The Indian Constitution declares India as a Union of States, with Federal character at state level. I guess no other layout fits India as perfect as this one. The states cannot secede from it having once joined the whole that is India and become part of it. The federal character pertains to the need of some degree of autonomy at state level. It means that the states can aspire to get separated, within inside the country. But the terms of separating or joining states are more the domain of the Centre than the states, as per Article 3 (which also deals with the precedence of Centre over the states in the hierarchy when it comes to border issues too). But during emergencies, the federal character becomes temporarily void and the states are expected to rise to the expectations of the whole, even if it means that the Centre is dictating terms.

Actually, in that discussion with one of my fellow bloggers, we lacked certain information due to the sheer nature of discussion and lack of professional interest/setup. I did sense the need for system definition in hindsight, but that definitely does not mean I be given a clear-cut complete definition of what it is all about. Because there is no standard for a definition and somebody below my knowledge might need more oxford and wikipedia links and somebody above my knowledge might not need any, at all. And then blogging is done purely for different purposes and not to cater to every set of audience. This is actually the data I was missing with regard to my response to the discussion there - How did the daughters-in-law arrive at the roles, who set the roles, in short I was missing the background of the system's evolution and that without my knowledge created a great confusion!

I don't really think the parts intentionally optimize or balance anything. Each one of us is inherently in that process of balancing oneself and optimizing one's own interests. I would say, we are just evolving! Oh yeah, I did leave that part on how this whole discussion falls in the set of my own interests - how it answered one of my musings – *"How to draw that thin line between personal and social interests so as not to overreach the society".* That, I guess is a topic for blogging for some other day!

- Nov 15, 2012, 02:39 AM.

45. Personal interests vs Social interests

I know this is an oft-abused topic and is highly subjective and we also have some references and legacies set by our ancient Gurus! I have not read the original (Hindu) scriptures in any detail except reading excerpts from school text books or watching the movies based on them, so this is to be seen more as a continuation of my previous post. All said and written, no single piece of write-up/a case of research/consistent set of rules agreed for a discussion can serve as a reference for a series of discussions that ensue in the process of evolution (of a discussion as also of that of a system). And that holds good even for a top-down system with a *system administrator.* The person who created the system might have done it with a defined objective initially, but as the system evolves, the administrator too needs to evolve to be able to catch-up with it. That is where he *serving as the representative of the top of the system* becomes part of the system and experiments with his parts and understands the parts more. In some cases he might be amazed at the parts/system he created and how magnificently they have grown. Consider the set of students a Guru nurtures. Sometimes the Sishyas (students) might even challenge the knowledge/skills of Guru. The Telugu movie

Swati Kiranam[1] portrays a rare case of power-conflict in Guru-Sishya relationship.

Now that I was talking about *evolution* and highly obsessed by that term at the moment, I must bring the Universe into picture. Yeah, the Universe is evolving continuously and we are part of that evolving Universe. And if I have to apply my previous post to this evolving Universe, would it serve to any end? I think, how much ever you generalize you have to be subjective again, just as how much ever you try to make something unique, it might after all have some redundancies.

I read somewhere that it is *Love* that knits and binds this universe. I believe in believing this. It must be true because even greed, selfishness, hatred that shape the society along with love are indeed some form of love on certain scale for something else. The word 'Love' per se is perceived in a different sense though. The *local and global interests unfortunately cannot be applied to the resources purely, unaltered by these intangible factors of human psyche and that is the underlying problem.* Can you define love, greed, selfishness, hatred per se objectively or even subjectively? All of them defy logic and of all love defies all the logic that is rationally arrived at. Whatever is in general a social evil to an average person in the society can well be in the interests of a person in love. I mean, we have seen many examples, where people in love go to any extent to serve the interests of their love. It is because love per se or the person they love is their own interest. And this cannot be put to discussion and negotiation with a set of people to whom you cannot objectively define love. When in love, killing a person

---

[1]   Swati Kiranam: *(Telugu)* It is a Telugu movie whose title means White or Pure Ray.

for the sake of love, is justified too by those in love, but not by the society ofcourse!

It is said mother's love is unconditional. We have seen many people sacrificing their lives for social causes mainly as part of struggles to get political independence. *Is it really because all of them have put societal interests before personal interests?* It is perhaps true and most definitely true for any body except them. But when it comes to them, they have found their calling in serving that cause and they just don't see themselves not catering to those set of interests. Sure, they have put societal interests before their interests but those societal interests are completely in their interests. A mother indeed seeks satisfaction by fulfilling her motherhood. That satisfaction and the consequent power/burden involved in motherhood are her interests. Let's consider Gandhiji, the "Father of our Nation". He stays in Indian History books for a primary reason that he could translate societal interests to all parts of the society in a way each of them could appreciate and understand and in turn contribute their turn. Phenomena like 'Anna Hazare Phenomenon', 'Malala Phenomenon', 'Arvind Kejriwal Phenomenon' are not new these days, they just come and go, but yes when they happen they catch the attention of a majority. It's because they happen to strike at the root cause and translate to others, the societal interests to personal interests. It's again for those 'others' to decide how they act on such a translation. It is important to understand that all these people do have their own interests in serving such a cause, it could be love for the cause itself, selflessness, fame, power or even money.

Whatever it is, they enjoy both the burden and rewards of such a cause. While I and you or any particular individual in the society might have any impression on such set of people, at a societal level such people are indeed a rarity (because moving masses is not easy) and hence the recognition or attention. On a different note, the term 'selfless', I believe, exists only in the mere sense of the term, but does not make any sense in reality, because everybody has some or the other 'self' interests when they take up a task, be it fame, money, power or even internal gratification which in a religious sense can be perceived as soul satisfaction or even Moksha[1].

All I'm trying to get at is, well, one might put global interests before personal interests, but one will be able to serve such interests only when those global interests become one's own.

Now to that important question on how not to overreach that thin line between personal and social interests:

- When one *gets to know* (*become aware of*) that one's personal interests are affecting one's roles in the social domain and if one cannot control the societal role in a desired way or if one cannot give up that role, one needs to look at optimizing one's personal interests.

  Here the scenario is that you are unable to control the societal roles in a desired way, so you must try to change your personal interests. So here, you have allowed the societal interests to take the precedence (i.e., override personal interests) especially since you are trying to alter the society through that societal role.

- Now to the other possibility when you cannot let go of your personal interests. Here, you are not ready to

---

[1]   Moksha: (*Sanskrit/Hindi*) Salvation. *(Telugu)* – Moksham.

give up or change your personal interests. In such a case, you must look at either optimizing your social interests in a way that you do not affect the society negatively. Or if that's not possible, you must give up that societal role.

Because you have now reached a scenario where your personal interests are coming in the way of your societal interests and you are not ready to give up/change personal interests. You are not ready to let the societal role come in the way of your personal interests, so the only possibility is to change or give up the societal role. So here, you have allowed personal interests to take the precedence by choosing not to alter the society negatively.

- Ofcourse, luckiest are those scenarios when you can balance both personal and social interests by optimizing both.

The GOAL for all the three scenarios is: Given that one is aware there is a thin line between personal and social interests, how not to overreach it, so as not to trouble oneself and not overreach the society. In brief, **the goal is to balance one's personal and social existence**.

- Nov 16, 2012, 12:40 AM.

46. Good thief and Bad thief!

Ok, I know, my last post was highly biased towards *'good'*, good as perceived in a general notion by the society. I'm a good person by the way and hence my writing is heavily tilted towards that! :-) But let me write about the *'bad'* now.

Ever watched the Telugu movie 'Kick'? The flashback episode is more interesting. At one instance, the hero Ravi Teja happens to bump into a twin suicide (by a couple who do that to escape the apparently 'anticipated' death of their daughter suffering from some disease, which they couldn't stop due to lack of finances) and the note they left. Moved by that incident, the hero goes out of his way to collect the finances and get the girl operated and save her life. But he doesn't stop there! Once he sees the happiness in the eyes of the girl after her life is saved, he gets to realize the amount of help needed by the multitude of orphans in the state. At once, he realizes his calling to help them, but where would such large amount of monies come from? So he decides robbery as his path to realizing his goal. He starts robbing the filthy rich of the society and passing over the money to the needful orphans and fix their health. His friend stops him by asking *"Endukuraa veellandari gurinchi nuvvu risk theesukuntaavu?"* (meaning: "Dude! Why are you taking such a risk for all these people?"), the hero then says, *"Nenu evvari gurinchi emee cheyyatledu, naa gurinchi nenu cheesthunnanu, endukantee daantloo kick undi kaabatti"* (meaning: "I'm not doing this for anybody, I'm doing it for myself because there is some kick in it!"). That sums up a novel instance of the discretion of Swadharma[1] and Paradharma[2] for me.

---

[1] Swadharma: (*Sanskrit/Hindi/Telugu*) Fulfilling duties/acts as per one's conscience, as guided by one's own consciousness. *Dharma* has different connotations as per context – sense of morality/principles/discretion of good and bad/faith/religion/duty.

[2] Paradharma: (*Sanskrit/Hindi/Telugu*) Fulfilling duties/acts NOT as per one's own conscience but as per others' sense of morality. *Swa* => Self; *Para* => Others

So now tell me, is that thief a good thief or a bad thief? If you have to frame a generic rule for the society, then it has got to be - *A thief is an evil element to the society!* But, in this case, the prevailing inequalities and the gaps in the society would have made the rich richer and all those orphans would never have got an opportunity to live a decent life with good health, so at a higher scale it does good and nothing bad to the society. So, *sometimes* it indeed is all relative.

How about we apply this concept of relativity of good and bad to Natural Calamities on earth? Calamities on a large scale create wide range of destruction and shatter the lives of many people. As Science is progressing, we have turned our focus on how to circumvent the effect of disasters by predicting and forecasting natural calamities and avoid the loss of life. This is a good improvement. Even Disaster Management and Disaster Preparedness are good developments in that area. But we are not doing enough to introspect why natural calamities are occurring in the first place and what is the contribution of man in such disasters? The human race is not doing enough self-introspection there. It is confining its scientific progress to forecast disasters and try saving lives, but not to assess human contribution in the disasters and decrease the rate of disasters on earth. Basically, we are not doing enough to protect Earth, but trying in vain to protect ourselves. I've qualified that statement with *"...in vain..."* because we cannot protect ourselves when we are not protecting earth, because Earth is our home. Can we protect ourselves while our home is collapsing, while we are still residing in it?

We must understand that earth too is an entity and chaos is usually seen as earth's way of protecting itself. Earth expresses its angst and burden (that we ourselves have put on it) in the form of natural calamities. It is basically responding to the pressure we are laying on it, as we are marching our journey towards scientific and technological advancements. Basically, all it is doing when such natural calamities happen is - *it is tackling that pressure, that human pressure on Earth.* I have seen some atheists and agnostics alike, question the occurrence of such calamities saying – *Where is God? If he was there would such things even happen?* I don't understand where their rationality is sleeping during such analysis. Does the existence of God imply magic where there is abundance all the time? A true God believer understands that both Good and Bad are part of God's creation and that God is always in the work of containing that Bad as much as possible.

We usually think of the lives lost during calamities, but earth as a planet in a bigger system got to safeguard its own interests too. What might be perceived 'bad' for the humanity can be 'good' for earth at the time of disaster and might be good for humanity too in the long run. So how about we see Natural Disasters as earth's way of prioritizing things to maintain the planet safe for the long run and ensure *Sustainability* - yes, the big term we all abuse so fondly.

- Nov 17, 2012, 06:21 PM.

47. Context Switching and Relativity

In my last two posts I was talking about good and bad. But at any given point of time, there cannot be all good or all bad in this society. It shall be composed of various groups, a composite of good and bad, determined relative to the collective well-being. So it is not really the complete elimination of bad that is in the best interests of the society. Actually both good and bad have their respective contributions to the society. It is their *net effect* on the society which is more important – whether that net effect of the merging of good and bad enables the society to move forward. In that sense, I realize that without 'sustainability' there is no progress whatever be the interests of a society or a person.

Ever since I started my UPSC preparation, I had to learn context switching. Not being able to switch between contexts effectively, made issues difficult with my family. Amidst something, I see my family as a society (that I keep studying as part of UPSC preparation) and use all my problem-solving skills on them. Time and again, I would expect them to understand my expectations and even have very aggressive quarrels, read it family rift :) - though for all practical purposes a family is a 'whole'! I juggle between multiple roles these days and keep telling people to understand my expectations and act accordingly. But to have expectations itself is a losing battle sometimes. Looking back at all my successful and contented years, they were all years of self-discipline. Looking at it in terms of horoscopes, favourable time, family situation and expecting others to understand my expectations is all a background noise. Everybody has that background noise and are struggling with it.

But with some analysis of my past, it is not that I never had my background noise. But I was able to exercise that self-discipline because I was *tuned* to my pure self. I was a successful student during the age I had to prioritize academics, I was a successful software engineer when I had to prioritize career. But when I wanted to prioritize family and specifically marriage, destiny didn't let me and it still kept me hooked to prioritizing my career. So I was not tuned to my pure self and hence the background noise. If I have to objectively put anybody's purpose of life, it is *'tuning to one's pure self'*, as Satya Sarada Kandula puts in her blog that self-realization is the greatest service one can do to oneself.

And I want to discuss about relativity too. We have different systems and different frames of reference, but to be right or wrong one must stick to a single frame of reference. Else it shall be a zero sum game as one of my friends says and I fondly call it the coffee cup theory. Strike a conversation with me if you want to know more about this theory in detail :)

- Nov 18, 2012, 04:20 PM.

48. Music class - through the words of my Guru

Friday's music class was very enlightening. In the very own words of my Guru* without manipulating it through my filters of reasoning and intuition (I might not be verbally exact though, despite my sincere attempt to translate it from Telugu to English), it goes this way:

"Many years went into my learning of music and I usually encourage self exploration. And with practise everybody can attain one's own level of perfection and people can even reach the same level. You have your level and he (the other student) has his level, but with different amounts of practise you reach your best levels.

Music can be excelled at, through ardent learning and mastering of the seven notes per se. And those are the basics.

Giving more time to basics is important. You can entertain audience with just those seven notes when they are mastered properly. You don't need more; each of the notes must be pure.

When I started music, I was not able to utter the note 'aa' properly. I knew that it didn't come out right. Not knowing you are right is an eligibility to learn music. Being right, you are fortunate to learn music. If you can judge your own notes you are a musician. If you can judge others' notes you are a good musician.

Assign 20Hz to 'sa' when a man utters it (female and male voices have different frequencies as one knows), then the 8th note 'saa' is 40 Hz. This is the 8th note for first scale and becomes the first note for the second scale or second floor. Every floor has a frequency double the original. Keep doubling and reach say 20,480 Hz and then imagine how many men have come together to utter 'sa'. Imagine how it sounds when all the men in the world come together and utter that note or frequency!"

Coming to my own terms…It is said that, if you give your soul to music, the music that comes from you, from within you, becomes the dance of your soul, the pure dance of your soul.

(*Guru: Different people have different connotations with respect to the concept of "Guru", but one statement that attracts me is: "Anubhavaanniki minchina guruvu leedhu" – in Telugu means, there is no Guru superior to Experience).

- *Nov 18, 2012, 05:00 PM.*

49. The Man, The Woman and The Trinity!

I've known this story for a long time, because I watched a Telugu movie (I don't remember the name) on this when I was quite quite young at about an age of 7 or so, on the occasion of Maha Shiva Rathri[1], when my Dad used to both fast and be awake all night to observe the rituals of the festival (he has stopped observing the rituals over the last couple of years though). Perhaps, we all know this story but we just don't tend to realize. Wonderful were those days when we had very few channels and were streamed quality programmes (relative to the current times). I keep sensing this story on and off, sometimes even without my knowledge because when we observe things young, they are just etched in the sub-conscious very strongly and always there for you. People might ofcourse also reason out that I'm biased by such knowledge, that's a different story, but they are very free to believe so, because it's genuine on their part.

Ok, the story is that at the beginning of the creation, God (as a power He is) has split Himself (Herself/Itself, the way you perceive God or His absence) into Shiva and Shakti, the first beings of material existence and they in turn have created the male and female counterparts of Trinity out of either of them to handle different roles to carry forward this creation.

---

[1]   Maha Shiva Rathri: *(Telugu)* This is a Hindu festival largely celebrated in India as well as in Nepal in reverence of Lord Shiva. It is observed on the 13th night/14th day of the new moon in the Krishna Paksha (dark half) every year of the month of *Phalguna* as per Hindu Calendar. The legend has it that this indicates the day on which Shiva and Shakti converge or get married. Devotees perform *Upavasam* (fasting for the whole day) and *Jagaran* (waking up all night and chanting hymns in devotion of Lord Shiva). *(Maha – Great, Shiva, Rathri - Night)*

The other two couples as per the legend are Vishnu-Lakshmi and Brahma-Saraswati. In that sense Lord Shiva and Goddess Parvati are their own children along with the other two couples (ofcourse all these are the names according to Hindu mythology). There are different legends behind the birth of deities and this is one of them. The three couples of Trinity are said to carry on three functions fundamental to the sustenance of the Universe:

Brahma-Saraswati: *Creation;*

Vishnu-Lakshmi: *Maintenance;*

Shiva-Shakti: *Regulation, Destruction and Re-creation.*

Hinduism has different stories on how Shiva has promised to be the son of Brahma at one instance, etc etc and how the Gods of Trinity have swapped their roles (of parents to each other) on various occasions. But my understanding is that with the evolution of creation, different Yugas or cycles of time after Maha Pralaya have seen such variants of God hierarchy, but I had always "felt" that the story I cited earlier is the most original version when this creation started.

And from this awareness tagged with some reading of few but quality interpretations of Bible, I thoroughly believe that Man and Woman on this earth were indeed created as a replica of God. That goes to say that every man and woman are a combination of three roles of the Trinity emphasizing their importance in carrying out a meaningful life:

Creation-Maintenance-Regulation :
Wisdom-Wealth-Spiritual energy,

former being the functions of the male Gods of Trinity and the latter being the aspects of their female conserts, crucial to facilitate the execution of those functions and in fact the cause and necessity of those functions. In fact this is equivalent to often-discussed concept of balance between man and woman. That is why perhaps it is often said that God can be realized through the harmony between man and woman. Also check the *Yin and Yang* theory! The *Pranava Mantra* and the *Mother Nature* discussed in one of my previous posts are indeed perceived to be the Masculine and Feminine Energies of Nature. It is also believed that there is swapping (or even subversion) or balance of power between these energies to create either chaos or sustenance leading to *pralaya* or *laya* according to the cosmic need and timing. That is perhaps why we see images like this in local folk lore.

Fig 3 – Maa Kaali

We have heard enough stories on Adam and Eve, the first man and woman on earth at the beginning of cycles. Those stories which say that woman is created from man's rib, that it was man who came into existence first and the desire or the search for his other half that created the woman, that the man was always fascinated by feminine mystery (perhaps not that the vice versa isn't true, but our paternalized history keeping has always suppressed the complementary reasoning). Atleast the human evolution was so that, man is associated with brains (accomplishment) and woman with beauty! And also there are those stories where Eve served as mother, sister, friend and wife of Adam and so did Adam (by serving corresponding multiple roles). But most importantly they were man and woman to each other. The Hindu religion has very aptly described a wife to be "Karyeshu Dasi, Karaneshu Manthri, Bhojeshu Maatha, Shayaneshu Rambha, Roopeshu Lakshmi, Kshamayeshu Dharitri, Shat Dharmayukta, Kuladharma Pathni"[1] but failed to elucidate on what is expected of a husband. A husband is first seen to be a man, that's it and at the most qualified as "Bharinchevadu Bhartha"[2]! (atleast my general awareness does not speak more about the expectations on man). I guess this constant struggle on power dynamics between man and woman is eternal.

---

[1] Karyeshu Dasi, Karaneshu Manthri, Bhojeshu Maatha, Shayaneshu Rambha, Roopeshu Lakshmi, Kshamayeshu Dharitri, Shat Dharmayukta, Kuladharma Pathni: This is a *Sanskrit prose* which elucidates the attributes expected of a woman as a wife. It means that Wife must serve her Husband like a servant (Dasi), that she must offer him wise advice in need, that she must be like a mother (Maatha) when she serves him the food, that she must be like a *Rambha* when in bed, that she must look radiant and beautiful like *Goddess Lakshmi* appeases to *Lord Vishnu*, that she must be tolerant like the *Mother Earth*, that she must follow all these six *Dharma* to be regarded as a virtuous wife.

[2] Bharinchevadu Bhartha: (*Telugu*) Husband is the one who bears. The implicit attribution is he who bears his wife in all the ways.

Now to some other musings on religion to which I have not had enough answers. The marital status of Lord Vinayaka is not very clear according to Hindu scriptures. The general perception is that Lord Brahma has created his consort(s) from him itself. Some believe he has two consorts and some say he has three consorts (Buddhi, Siddhi, Riddhi). But most importantly he is associated with "beginning" of things, that he is Aadi Moolam[1], Gana Nayaka[2], which is why the Hindus start any major pooja with Ganapati Pooja[3]. Ever wondered why the stories of Shiva, Brahma were mystic and abstract, while those of Lord Vishnu and His consort are very close to our real lives. The answer is ofcourse very simple, as we all know, because He is the God of the Earth realm. Just as every major Kshetra has a Kshethra Palaka[4], it seems different realms have different Gods and any other God can exercise his power in that realm through the leader or God of that realm. So His stories are very much our stories and need not have an explicit in-depth analysis. I've heard of the Avatar[5] of Dattatreya (the incarnation

---

[1] Aadi Moolam: It is a *Sanskrit phrase* which means the *beginning or the first source*. Lord Vinayaka is regarded to be the *Aadi Moolam*.

[2] Gana Nayaka: It is a *Sanskrit phrase* written in English script. It means the leader of the *gana* (group) of Gods. It is not leader in the actual sense of the term, but he is more the representative of the gana of Gods and his prayers are invoked first during any ritual due to a boon from Shiva and Parvati.

[3] Ganapati Pooja: (*Telugu/Hindi/Sanskrit) Pooja* means the ritual of prayer or worship. *Ganapati* is another name of Vinayaka. *Ganapati Pooja* as said above is the first prayer or obeisance offered to Lord Vinayaka at the start of any *Pooja*.

[4] Kshethra Palaka: (*Telugu) Kshetra* means region, if the strict literal meaning is to be considered. It can also be considered to mean *realm*. *Palaka* means ruler. *Kshetra Palaka* hence means ruler of a realm or region.

[5] Avatar: (*Sanskrit/Hindi/Telugu/Also a legitimate English word)* The reincarnated form of one of the Divine aspects. (Meaning as per the current context here)

of all the three aspects of the male Gods of Trinity) but not of a female counterpart, seems like the grouping between female goddesses is difficult. Not to mention about the promiscusity of masculine Gods, but female goddesses were mostly depicted to be one-man women. Both the Gods and society have done well to preserve the male domination, perhaps the female goddesses needed some evolution to either decrease the male-domination or they themselves needed to start dominating. The evolution of both the society and that of Gods seems to almost go hand-in-hand, either one of them is shaping the other or both are shaping each other!

Keeping the musings aside and getting back to Trinity, whenever there is a marriage crisis, role/power crisis or identity crisis, every couple can be seen as the manifestation of Trinity waiting to create a perfect family. At the end of the day, one must know thyself first. When such an attempt is made, the answer that usually comes is *"I am a person"* first and anything next!

- Nov 22, 2012, 08:26 PM.

50. A journey into the past!

At the beginning of this week, we (my parents and I) have been to *Annavaram* and *Draaksharamam* (religious tourist places in my home state of Andhra Pradesh, India) and the journey literally seemed to take us into the past. Though the purpose was mainly to do the Naga Prathishtaapana (Resurrection of the idol of Naga Deva) in Draakshaaramam, we went to Annavaram first to perform Satyanarayana Swamy Vratham[1]. Two

---

[1]   Satyanarayana Swamy Vratham: *(Sanskrit/Telugu) Vratham* means a

stark commonalities of both these *punya kshetras*[1] is that they establish the bonding of Lord Shiva and Lord Vishnu. They say that Lord Shiva and Lord Vishnu regarded themselves as equals despite the differences set about by the corresponding devotees. That's perhaps why Lord Shiva is termed as *Vishnu Priya* (the lover of Vishnu) and we all know the great epic romance during *Mohini Avataram*[2] :-) The main set of idols we see in Annavaram are those of *Satya Deva* (one of the forms of Lord Vishnu) with *Lord Shiva* and *Goddess Lakshmi* on either side.

On the first day in Annavaram, the Satyanarayana Swamy Vratham (performed by my parents) went fine, but the *vratha katha*[3] with five episodes seemed to pass by in a jiffy. After the *vratham*, the only notable place we dropped by in the *Aalaya Pranganam*[4] was at Vana Durga[5] temple. The priest there was too

---

ritual associated with certain rules to worship Gods. *Satyanarayana Swamy Vratham* here refers to the ritual of worshipping *Satyanarayana Swamy*, one of the forms of Lord Vishnu.

[1] Punya Kshetra: *(Sanskrit/Telugu)* Religious tourist region.

[2] Mohini Avataram: *(Sanskrit/Telugu) Mohini Avataram* is one of the forms taken by Vishnu during *Ksheera Sagara Mathanam* (The churning of Cosmic Ocean of Milk). The legend says that during this time, Vishnu has taken a female form of *Mohini* in order to divert the *Asuras* (Non-Gods) to save the *Amritham* (the divine nectar known to induce immortality) for Suras (Devas or Gods). The legend also has it that Mohini united with Shiva to give birth to Ayyappa or Manikanta during this time.

[3] Vratha katha: *(Telugu) Katha* means story. The *Satyanarayana Swamy Vratham* includes listening to the stories of Satya Deva, his miracles and his devotees in five episodes.

[4] Aalaya Pranganam: *(Telugu) Aalaya* means Temple. *Pranganam* means compound. Together it means, the temple compound.

[5] Vana Durga: *(Telugu) Vana* means forest. It's used to qualify the location where Goddess Durga has come up in the form of idol (here in a forest). Goddess Durga is an aspect of Shakti (The Spiritual Energy), one of the Goddesses of the trinity, the other two, so far,

benevolent to offer us the story behind the emergence of the temple (basically in the anticipation of *dakshina*[1]). He said that it was *Vana Durga* who emerged first and that in that sense She is the elder sister (*Akka*) of Satya Deva. It seems She appeared in a dream to one devotee about the emergence of Satya Deva and that is how the main idol was discovered later. I happened to come across a similar story in the past, so I understood where the story was getting to. There was hung a portrait of *Dattatreya* on the wall at the entrance of the temple too. When we three happened to sit in the temple and peacfully savouring the fresh air of Annavaram, my Dad casually asked me *"Is she Vana Durga or Vana Lakshmi?"* I laughed out the question with another question "Meeru eppudinaa Vana Lakshmi anna peru vinnaaraa?" (in Telugu means, *"Did you ever hear the name of Vana Lakshmi?"*). Dad said, "I have never in the past heard the name Vana Durga either!" Ok, frankly even I never heard that name literally in Telugu but somehow the name Vana Durga made more sense to me than Vana Lakshmi. Don't ask me why, it's the way it is - the power/role distribution among the goddesses in Hindu mythology! But then, itseems there were instances when both of them wore the appearances of the other (swapped their appearances) when such a need arised (now this bonding does not seem to be restricted to their male counterparts alone!). I happened to know this through this serial *"Hara Hara Mahadeva"* in Maa TV (the Telugu dubbed version of the Hindi *Har Har Mahadev* serial in LifeOK channel). Oh you must really watch this serial, the settings are simply great and so is the choice of actors! The recent episodes bring out beautifully the story

---

being Goddess Lakshmi (Wealth) and Goddess Saraswati (Wisdom), as per Hindu scriptures.

[1] Dakshina: *(Telugu)* The monetory offering given to a priest.

of how Sati Devi realizes to be (or was made to realize) that she is indeed the incarnation of Parvati. Watching the serial, I used to feel self-exploration was not all that easy for Gods themselves and that they treaded even more difficult times than humans when they happen to take birth on earth. On the contrary, the general notion of public might be "Oh! They are Gods, they must be all powerful and do not go through any hardships and must necessarily be performing miracles". The purpose of Gods' incarnation on earth most of the times was not to lead happy lives but for larger reasons, to establish tasks which they wouldn't otherwise be able to do sitting in their divine abode. When on earth, perhaps they are simply humans amidst humans.

Ok, coming back to the trip, that conversation with my Dad was interrupted by a man nearby answering a phone call *"Yeah! All we six are coming...in full honours!"* He uttered it so loud and so energetic, that we completely forgot about what we were talking before. All in all, the first day of the trip ended peacefully on the heights of Annavaram, with all the three staring at the beautiful landscapes and the sun-kissed waters of River Pampa around. Ok all this description is by looking back and memorizing the events, but at that moment, my mind was completely surrounded by a vague emptiness which I couldn't figure out at all! It just stayed that way during a majority part of the trip. Perhaps the vibes of devotion were working tad too much on me!

We left for *Draakshaaraamam* on second day morning and reached there by afternoon. Trust me, the view of the interior of Draakshaaraamam temple is just breath-taking and I'm sure one will be transported back to eras and not just to a couple of centuries. The temple construction and plan reminded me of the *Jagannath Temple of Mysore*, but this temple looked way too older. It seems it dated back to pre-BC era and was constructed by Gods themselves when they arrived to earth to wage a war! (Ok, I don't know the history of this place and never bothered to check, but an important part is that the *nabhi* (navel) part of Sati Devi fell here during her *Aatmahuti*[1]) This entire story was told by the priest in-charge of our Pooja who accosted us into the premises. I must really talk about this priest - *Bulusu Ramakrishna Pandithulu garu*, he is one of the very few genuine priests I've come across, in fact if I have to be frank, he is the only genuine priest I have ever come across who did the Pooja (a big one at that, covering second day evening and third day morning!) with such lot of sincerity and detail, expecting no extra money at all and did it with all surrender to God. When I was performing the rituals all I could hear were the mantras uttered around by about 7 priests and my own internal Gaussian noise of my mind not withstanding the divine vibes flowing around. Wondering why I did this Pooja at all? I have K-a-a-l-a S-a-r-p-a D-o-s-h-a-m[2] itseems. Ok don't be scared by that (if you are my well-wisher and believe in it just like I do), I'm sure the Pooja would have cured me of all that :)

I must tell you this joke too. When we were all walking into the premises initially, the priest started narrating the history of the temple all enthusiastically. When he said that this temple was built by Gods themselves, my Mom interrupted and asked "Deevullantee? Ee Devallu? Evaru?" (in Telugu means, "Gods means? Which Gods? Who?") He started laughing and said

---

[1]   Aatmahuti: *(Telugu)* Giving up of one's life or soul.

[2]   Kaala Sarpa Dosham: *(Sanskrit/Telugu)* It is a specific dis-merit owned up by a person due to past lives' karma which is said to be salvated, compensated and cleared off by appeasing *Lord Subramanyeswara* through specific rituals.

"Beshukkaina prashnammaa! Intha varaku nannu evaruu adagaledu ee prashna! Hmm, umm, Devullantee, aa, aa Indrudu vaalluunu, Indrudu devullaku naayakudu kadaa..." (in Telugu means, *"Excellent question madam! Nobody asked me this question so far! Hmm, umm, Gods means, that Indra and others, Indra is the leader of the army of Gods isn't it..."*) Ofcourse he didn't go into much details because tell me how can anybody today know the exact answer and even if it is indeed narrated in some puranam[1] who can guage the rightness or the wrongness thereof?

Ok, the *Naaga Prathishtaapana* is all about praying and resurrecting the idol of *Subramanyeswara Swamy* (also called Karthikeya, Skanda, Muruga, Kumara Swamy), the son of Lord Shiva. The idol is that of conjoined snakes. It can be looked at as number 8, the mirror image of 3 and its mirror image (3 itself) coming together, 'S' and its mirror image conjoined back to back or for that matter even 25 written appropriately to fit this pattern. Oh, I must tell you about the pooja mandapam[2] (it was a stage elevated to a small height similar to the homa mandapam[3]) ornamented beautifully. There were lot of kalasha(s)[4], main *kalasham*, flowers so on and so forth. But what caught my attention are the four tiny mirrors (those

---

[1]   Puranam: (Telugu) Ancient Hindu scripture.

[2]   Pooja mandapam: *(Sanskrit/Telugu/Hindi) Pooja means the ritual of prayer or worship. Mandapam means* a platform for a specific purpose which is usually elevated. *Pooja Mandapam* is an elevated platform for Pooja.

[3]   Homa mandapam: is used to indicate another ritual performed as an obeisance to Fire, as part of a larger worshipping ritual. *Homa Mandapam* is the platform for performing *Homam*.

[4]   Kalasha(s): *(Telugu/Sanskrit) Kalasha* means a container filled with water, with coconut placed on top of it, the coconut draped with pure cloth. *Kalasha* is used in most of the Hindu Pooja rituals, placed in front of the deity idols or images.

round pocket mirrors) and the blades kept on the four corners of the mandapam. When asked the priest why they were placed that way, the priest said, "All the gana of Gods come tonight and sleep on the mandapam and bless the idol that you have been performing rituals on and the Gods always need weapons and food, so we placed them there symbolically!"

The nivedana pooja[1] happened on the second day evening and the actual resurrection happened the third day morning. The resurrection happened under a Banyan tree with an elevated pediment around it with hundred of other idols resurrected in a crowded manner in the past. (It seems the ASI (Archaelogical Survey of India) procures the idols every seven years to make space for new ones). The idol incidentally was resurrected at the exact south of the circular elevated pediment (there were four pathways at the bottom of the tree in all the four directions for reference perhaps) and the idol faced east as we all faced north as we performed the rituals. My parents held with their feet, an iron grid bench with three steps, to facilitate and elevate me to a comfortable height as the priests helped me do the rituals. It was a bit difficult for me to do that and especially my Mom was not completely satisfied with the way I did it. She kept prodding me that the garland was not placed right, the milk was not offered properly so on and so forth, but I silenced her with my angry but stern response, "This is all I can do located at this height and look at the orientation of the idol, it's not at a conveniently reachable distance, I cannot do any better!" I could neither tell her about the noise in my head nor the sudden emptiness that kept coming on and off, but the

---

[1]   Nivedana pooja: *(Telugu) Nivedana* means *offering. Nivedana Pooja* is usually one of the first set of prayers to offer a specific thing or request to a specific deity as part of a set of rituals.

morning air was all vibrant and very pure washing away my internal keytones my brain was emitting. The experience will perhaps be etched in my memory for a long time.

- Nov 24, 2012, 08:27 PM.

51. Memory - Mind and Soul

It seems memory is not physically stored in specific parts of brain for the brain to retrieve the memories/events from those parts. Brain is merely an organ which generates the mind by mediating with the consciousness carried by the soul. Most of the memory is indeed part of the consciousness and not the physical brain, I infer. Research indicates that it is through phylogenetic memory that people memorize their previous births. It seems the evolution of a species can be retrieved by activating this memory (a research activity in progress as I read from a book whose name goes on the lines "Amazing Stories, True Facts - II"). I've no indepth knowledge about this mind-soul interaction, but my understanding is that human soul tunes to certain distinct frequencies to communicate with the vibrations of nature to present the consciousness that identifies us. That said, a female brain operates at higher frequencies than a male brain it seems. To me, it explains the *general* notion in the society wherein it is felt that a girl of age 20 is almost as matured as guy of age 24 and that it takes more time for a guy to attain maturity. In that sense, I guess it requires FSK (Frequency Shift Keying) for a man and woman of different ages to attain compatibility ;-)

Recent times have also seen diffused consciouness. It is viewed by some as evolution of mankind and specifically evolution of human memory/consciouness on its way to suprarational consciousness. And who else, but the collective consciousness (God) can tune to all the frequencies or the consciusness of all the individual beings in a desired (yet proper non-intrusive) way! It is perhaps not easy for a specific individual to deal with diffused consciousness. Well, this suprarational consciousness sounds very good at the outset more so once the evolution happens, but reading the stories of people suffering with diffused consciousness, it really looks like a dangerous phenomenon, especially because its a very alien concept to a majority of the society and no help can be offered to the people who are suffering/experiencing this diffused consciousness to lift them into an appropriate level of evolution. Itseems people with diffused consciousness are unable to lead normal lives because of the vulnerable feelings they are experiencing due to their telepathic abilities, most of the times incomplete skills or incompletely fathomed or understood skills. This is where I seriously feel ignorance is bliss. Knowing too many things and worrying about multiple systems makes one no good for a single system. That is perhaps why there is a thin line between philosophers or Vedantis (who worry about too many things) and mad men.

The process of Frequency Ascension discussed majorly on internet also speaks of a similar process of suprarational consciousness. The discussions from most valid and popular internet sources indicate that a cosmic intercourse between Cosmic Father and the Great Mother of Galactic Center is expected to birth all of the creation into a new reality. Whether this happens in 2012 or even near foreseeable future is for everybody to watch.

That said, I have great value for intuition. There arise many situations in life to deal with, for which we don't have complete knowledge and background. Generally speaking, decisions are arrived at, through rational analysis. But during emergency, crises or for systems with half knowledge, intuition works better for me. It's much like the involuntary response of keeping our hand away from a hot object instead of rationally thinking what to do, when such a situation arises. My experience shows that intuition is much better than a rational decision arrived through half-knowledge. People tend to say, "no gut feelings, no intuition please, can we arrive at it rationally", but then seriously intuition is not irrational. To reason out intuition scientifically, it is a decision our sub-conscious has taken weighing out many factors based on the knowledge it has, without our general awareness. The same goes with music too. It seems our human brain is naturally inclined to the right notes/frequencies when we sing a song. A song is usually sung the right way either when one imitates it by listening to it thoroughly (the natural inclination at work) or when the music is thoroughly learnt and sung (general awareness - our acquired skills and knowledge at work). That is perhaps why the songs sung in films by pure imitation sound much better than those sung by people with incomplete knowledge in music. "Half knowledge is dangerous!" conveys with a bang, the necessity of intuition.

That is why I see religion or faith as science tending to infinity. I'm not saying whatever a religion preaches is true. But quite a few things preached by great religious and philosophical thinkers (which they arrived through faith) have become part of our value system and are constantly shaping our society. It might take ages for science to validate them. There were times when science striked off rebirth as religious myth, but only with advent of more research is science able to buy it now. How much ever science progresses, faith shall stay ahead and intuition plays a great role in imparting many fundamentals to the society which are unknowingly taken as inputs by science. My preference, anyday, would be a balanced analysis through science and religion. I have recently bumped into this book - *The Expansion - A Philosophy Of Consciousness, Creation and Rebirth* by *Vicky Anderson* - and it validates my observations to a good extent. This book is not to be missed, do read it if possible (I say this despite me not having completed it yet, I've just quickly browsed through those 40 few pages available on internet and it makes for a wonderful read! It's definitely on my reading list for the future).

- Nov 25, 2012, 04:37 PM.

52. The 3G Gods...

Yes, you heard it right! I'm referring to the third generation of Gods!

In one of my previous posts – *The Man, The Woman and The Trinity*, I had briefly written about my musings about religion, I mean the Hindu religion in specific. Getting back to that context, I shall start with Lord Vinayaka. The story of birth of Ganesha has not been very clear and had many versions. The story that we regularly hear during *Vinayaka Chavithi*[1] says that Ganesha is created by Goddess Parvati out of the dough used for bathing.

---

[1]   Vinayaka Chavithi: *Vinayaka Chavithi* is a Telugu festival celebrated to commemorate the re-birth of Lord Vinayaka, also called as Ganesha, Vigneshwara etc. It is celebrated as *Ganesh Chaturthi* in North India.

Now that I was talking about the children of the divine couple, I must also talk about Goddess Jyoti, the daughter of Lord Shiva and Goddess Parvathi and the sister of Lord Skanda (Goddess Valli is his wife). Jyoti is supposed to be the replica of her mother when it comes to the spiritual power and is also treated as the aroused Kundalini Shakti[1] in some contexts. One of the stories goes that the divine couple had hid Goddess Jyoti as a weapon of Skanda to protect her from something. This brother-sister duo itseems are symbolic of perseverance and strength to fight one's internal daemons. I don't know if the Makara Jyoti[2] that is said to appear in Sabarimala (Lord Ayyappa's abode) every year (on the day of Sun's change of constellation) is symbolic of Goddess Jyoti.

In this movie – Brahmalokam to Yamalokam via Bhoolokam[3], Goddess Saraswati is very unhappy with Lord Brahma that He is always busy working (writing our fates) and has no time

---

[1] Kundalini Shakti: *(Sanskrit/Hindi/Telugu)* Literary Meaning: The corporeal indwelling spiritual energy lying dormantly coiled at the base of the spine, that can be *awakened* in order to purify the subtle system and bestow upon the 'seeker of Truth' the state of Yoga, Union with the Divine, the Source. The Yogic philosophy describes it as a form of feminine Shakti or sleeping serpent. Background: We are usually aware of only body and mind, but human body harnesses and perpetuates on the *Spiritual Energy* that flows through the 7 *Energy Centres (Chakras)* connected across the spine.

[2] Makara Jyoti: *(Sanskrit/Telugu) Makara Jyoti* is the divine light apparently seen in the sky (as reported by the devotees) in Sabarimalai on the day of *Makara Sankranti*, the day on which Sun makes transition into the zodiac sign of Makara rashi (Capricorn) on its celestial path.

[3] Brahma Lokam to Yama Lokam via Bhoo Lokam: It is the title of a *Telugu* movie. *Lokam* means world. So the title means – "From the world of Brahma (who creates) to the world of Yama (who takes away life) via Earth, the world of humans."

for Her. I really wonder if He ever takes breaks apart from the time there's no life out here. Perhaps, He needs some assistant!

And then there's an interesting book - *Aryaman's Trilogy* by *Bina Saksena* - on Sun God Aryaman, the keeper of Time, according to Hindu mythology (or I must say that he is the keeper of time only according to few sources, because other sources say Stars are more reliable reference for time). It seems Aryaman started his invasion on earth to gain or refill 'light'. I don't know if this novel is pure fiction but the Preface of the Trilogy on *page 17* in particular is a delight to read.

But as it is said, the eternal divine mystery is happening all the time and it is difficult for us to catch up with it. Ok, that's too much of talk on divine realm, an unknown one at that, need to free up my mind and lighten myselves a bit... Watched Telugu movie Konchem Ishtam Konchem Kashtam[1] movie recently. The movie initially starts as a young couple trying to unite an older couple (parents of the protoganist), but finally ends up with the older couple uniting the younger couple. Good one!

- Nov 25, 2012, 08:49 PM.

53. Rewriting history...

Call it rewriting history or creating a new history, this phase or process draws a lot of attention. It might seem talking big, but leaders need to do it to move masses. To arrive at the present tense (now), I mean to relate to the present, one must start from

---

[1]   Konchem Ishtam Konchem Kashtam: It is the title of a *Telugu* movie, which means – "A little dear and a little troublesome".

the past. In that sense, past is always a connecting link between the present and distant past or even sets a background for future. Ofcourse, in a movie like *"The Time Traveller's Wife"* where the protagonist moves in time with no rigid rules, it all seems a blur. It's tough if one has to narrate the climax properly... Should we say, the wife met her husband in her present and his future (or) should we say, the husband met his wife in his present and her future (or) should we say, the husband met his wife in his past (considering he is a different self by then and relative to that different self) and her present. I give up on such a definition, I need a common reference, because all the three definitions are relative to one of the two actors and not common to both, because both of them are not travelling in the same timeline. No two people can walk the same road at two different times. It is perhaps easy to draw a common time reference, which is that of viewers in the timeline of the progress of the movie. In that sense, I guess the husband meets wife in his past's future and her present. (Don't know if I make any sense here, somebody with better brains and better versed with time-relativity can attempt this!) When the jargon is not agreed upon by two parties, it might trigger 'comedy of errors' like the one between the American and the Indian Customer Care in *What time is it now*! post.

Ok, some trivia here...this talking of past reminds me of an interesting story. Though slightly out of context, I'm tempted to talk about this, to deflect myself away from this *'relative time'* confusion. Itseems Vishnu took the avatar of *Hayagriva* to kill another *Hayagriva*, as per *Sakta mythology*.

- Nov 26, 2012, 10:08 PM.

54. Mass Media and Parenting

Today, I just wanted to write on something that affects the behavioural patterns of the society. Mass Media and Parenting occur to me at the moment as some food for thought...

I might have said 'Mass Media', but I have just the media of Television on my mind. There are a multitude of channels and then there are news channels. And anything is news for them...a robbery in the jewellery shop in the next gully[1] too. And then they don't stop at just streaming the detailed coverage of what happened, but also build up theories and sketches of how the robber might have robbed the shop and hence creating easy ways for other robbers in the making. Fine, forget the news channels, we have many telugu movies mocking them. But, seriously I hate the culture of non-stop game shows, song and dance competitions in the channels. I mean, why on earth should the current day children fill their brains with the mud of somebody else unleashing some idiotic talent of their own? Of what use is that? If playing games was considered an addiction once upon a time, watching somebody else play games has become an addiction now! Did you watch those dance competitions where the participants flaunt their bodies uncensored by any central Censor Board? Did you come across those talent shows and dance competitions where kids are being expected to shake their bodies vulgarly to the tunes of adult songs? It is not always possible for parents or care-takers to keep an eye on the kind of content, children lay their hands on, both through TV and Internet media. I don't know who regulates the licensing of all those mushrooming channels...I mean if such regulation exists at all and if it does, on what

---

[1]   Gully: *(Hindi)* A small lane or street in a colony.

basis...and after the licensing if there is any monitoring entity to keep a check on the programmes on a day-to-day basis. It might all sound like such a tedious process to regulate, but all these channels are 'freely' contaminating the brains of the current generation. The human brain thus far has evolved so very well, I'm sure Television today would do well to negate the whole progress...and even retard it.

Parenting! It's such a wide-topic and many things can be discussed about it. If I voice out all that I think about this process (the rising of working women class, late marriages blah blah blah), I'm sure this post is going to become a complete hotch-poth. I'd just like to outline the basic concern I have with it. The requirements and challenges of parenting change with every generation and it's not unknown that every generation thinks that they have brought up their children better than their parents did, despite growing change in the society. And when it comes to father-son relationship, there is this famous adage which goes this way - *"By the time a son thinks his father was right, he shall have a son who thinks his father is wrong".* With all other things kept constant, I think the attitude and approach with which a couple embraces parenthood decides how well they bring up their children. I personally feel that the current times have two generations of parents at stark conflict in the approach to parenting. Take me, a person in the later part of twenties, as a reference. My parents' generation (on an average) thinks that they always heeded to their parents' words and hence they would expect their children to listen to them and shape their life as per their perspective no matter what the age of their children. They think that children need to be disciplined irrespective of their age. Fine, its true to certain extent, but what I'm unhappy about is, they tend to do this act of disciplining keeping the society of yester-years (their times) in their mind, not updating themselves with the current ways of society. On the other hand, the approach of current-gen parents (those in my age group) usually is that they need to bring up their kids as 'able individuals'. In some instances, it turns out that the dose of individualism they nurture is tad too much. Some go even further leading their kids to assume that they are the cynosure of the world of not just their parents, but also of the whole world they know of! They become very attention-craving and take on competition in an unhealthy way. And when geographies change, perspectives change completely. There was this incident recently in the Netherlands where an Indian couple was arrested based on the complaint of their son that his parents were treating him badly in the name of disciplining. I think Indian way of parenting and European way of parenting are quite different, so the Indian parents who were brought up the Indian way might have had some problem in bringing up their son who is expecting European ways of parenting, now that they are residing in Europe. Same conflict goes with many Indian origin people residing and bringing up their kids in the US.

But then, we just don't know how the coming years are going to shape, so no comment can be made on the current-day parenting process. While a middle approach, the balance of these two stark approaches is needed, every generation of parenting is an experiment in the making and part of human evolution as a whole...

- *Dec 03, 2012, 08:33 PM.*

55. *When the time stands still!*

I'm sure all of us dream of such moments when we want the time to just stand still. This childhood favourite song – *Pade pade ventaade kala*[1] - and in fact my all-time favourite, is a perfect theme song to sum that up! As said in that song, sometimes one moment is enough for things to get true. In this context, I like the quote of *Sri Mangalampalli Balamurali Krishna* quoted by my music teacher recently - "*Graha veekshanam kanna, guru anugraha veekshanam minna*[2]". In such moments, the past and future seem to transcend and converge into the present, making it the best present :-)

Oh yeah! Whenever I think of convergence, I'm often reminded of the concept of '*Limits*' in Class XI Maths, wherein the check of 'whether limit exists or not' is done through checking if the right hand limit is equal to left hand limit. But ofcourse, such a check I guess is required for discontinuous functions and I don't remember if such a check is required at all for continuous functions. And also those limits where the function being evaluated has both numerator and denominator zero were fun to work with. Say $\lim x \to 0$ (tan x)/x is evaluated by expressing

---

[1] Padhe padhe ventaade kala: *(Telugu)* A Telugu movie song lyrics which go like this– "*Padhe padhe ventaade kala, idhe idhe kaadante ela, ivaala kalakaalamu ilaage nuvvagumaa, dayunchi oo dooramaa, ivaala itu raakumaa*" – which means – "How can I deny that this is the very dream that haunts often? Oh eternal time! Stop here now! And distance! Be kind and do not come any closer today…"

[2] Graha veekshanam kanna, guru anugraha veekshanam minna: *(Telugu)* Literal Meaning - "The sight of Guru exerted on his student to indicate acceptance is more precious than staring at Space, out of astronomical curiosity, to check if the stars are working right for oneself." Implied Meaning – "If you feel that your time is running bad, you can still fight it out with the grace of your Guru!"

it as non-zero function, thus leading to a result of 1 instead of ∞. I don't exactly remember if we worked out this particular limit using the RHL, LHL equivalence.

That's nostalgia! And Mathematics anytime rouses interest in me, that's perhaps why I initially opted Mathematics as one of my optionals for UPSC despite many people suggesting me not to. Ofcourse owing to vast syllabus and unavailability of books, I'm planning to replace it with Geography though. I did cover my Paper - I Maths and I don't regret it, because the knowledge of mathematics never goes waste, as rightly said by Whitehead - *With the calculus as a key, Mathematics can be successfully applied to the explanation of course of nature...* And those early morning classes in the cold breeze of Delhi winter will always remain pleasant memories to be cherished :-)

Mathematics and Music are considered synonymous in many aspects. While Mathematicians tend to unravel the world through the lens of Maths, I know of Musicians who tend to learn and explore the world through music. The 'UPSC aspirant' in me might have left mathematics, but the 'person' in me shall explore music.

- Dec 06, 2012, 09:38 PM.

56. Mayabazaar - The timeless comedy!

Of thousands of telugu old classics, if we have to pick up a few, the epic movie '*Mayabazaar*' would surely be on the top of the list for many telugu movie goers. Such is the grouping of the legendary actors and the sensible and matured acting they have put up. Though I like the whole movie as such, the finale Sasirekha Parinayam[1] is what I like the most, especially the performance of Savitri (as Ghatotkacha in the guise of Sasirekha)-Relangi (as Lakshmana Kumara) actors' duo is matchless and I'm pretty sure no body would ever parallel it, if there was to be a remake! While the marriage ceremony of *Lakshmana Kumara - Ghatotkacha* (Maya Sasirekha) happens on one side, the actual marraige ceremony of *Abhimanyu-Sasirekha* happens parallelly on the other side. But that said, did Lakshmana Kumara tie the knot with Ghatotkacha? ;-) I guess no! The marriage of the actual 'intended' couple happens as it should!

It might seem that Lakshmana Kumara and Ghatotkacha have come together to facilitate the marriage of Abhimanyu-Sasirekha, but it is due to the fact that the actual marriage was pre-destined, the former duo earns a place in the history of Mahabharatha in that particular context of fake and hilarious coming together for marriage - to faciliate the marriage of the actual couple at the right time and right place.

---

[1]   Sasirekha Parinayam: *(Telugu)* It means the 'Marriage of Sasirekha'. Let me also give the background of the movie for non-Telugu people. The movie *Mayabazaar* is based on one of the stories in the epic of *Mahabharatha*. *Sasirekha* is the daughter of *Balarama*, the, brother of *Krishna*. *Abhimanyu* is the son of *Arjuna*, one of the five brothers of Pandava clan as also the beloved friend of Krishna, as also relative to the family of Krishna and hence Balarama. Abhimanyu and Sasirekha love each other since childhood, but owing to certain circumstances Balarama finalizes marriage of his daughter Sasirekha with Lakshmana Kumara, the son of *Duryodhana*. Duryodhana is the oldest of the 100 Kuru clan rival brothers of Pandava clan brothers. How that marriage is spoiled by *Ghatotkacha* (step-brother of Sasirekha) who comes in the disguise of Sasirekha and how finally Sasirekha and Abhimanyu get married, is unfolded in the movie.

My favourite dialogues in that whole sequence are those by
Savitri - "*Mari Arya Putrulu maatram thokkavachunee...Amma entee
naakee allari!*[1]" :-)

- Dec 07, 2012, 05:18 PM.

57. The 'continuous' process of learning

Each of us is a student in one form or the other till we die, we are
in the constant process of learning, maybe not a conscious and
concerted effortful form of learning, but we do learn something
or the other...be it learning as a (an academic) student, learning
to be an employee, learning to be a parent and teaching the kids,
learning to be tolerant of the next generation and retire... In
that sense, even unlearning is learning and I consider it an even
tougher form of learning. We are all learning, but we just don't
know that we are. Especially, in this competitive age, people
learn every minute to expand their interests.

In this generation of late marriages (the comfortable age to get
married neatly slipping from mid-twenties to late twenties), the
conflict of learning-preaching and power dynamics between
children and parents is not uncommon in many households.
While I understand the angst of parents who refuse to learn
after certain age sets in, it is really essential that parents too
keep the learning process going. When I say learning, I don't
mean the children hold a cane and teach their parents what is
right or wrong, I just mean that the parents must be receptive to

---

[1] Mari Arya Putrulu maatram thokkavachunee... Amma entee naakee
     allari: *(Telugu)* "If the honoured prince could stamp my feet, why
     shouldn't I...Mom? What is this mischief and insult towards me?"

take things from their children, after certain level of maturity sets in the latter. Ofcourse, the onus lies on the children too to send the message home in a less offending way (which I'm very bad at, by the way and constantly try to learn).

In fact, once children reach certain age, both the parties must always be receptive to each other and the relationship must evolve into a matured phase of a two-sided give-take and not remain in one direction (of the conventional parent-to-children) alone and only then can one understand the 'intent of good' in others' words. And one can always take good aspects from others irrespective of age and one's relation with them. This, I believe, helps people in being less judgemental about others based solely on one's own experiences in life. It is usually expected that the rigidity of one's ideas and convictions increases as one ages. The idea is to emphasize the need to alter such trend by pushing for a bit of receptiveness irrespective of age.

- *Dec 07, 2012, 06:07 PM.*

58. Simplicity and Ignorance

If I have to make some statements those are timeless and have a universal appeal then *"Ignorance is bliss"* got to be on the top of my list. Ignorance *usually* has a reason to it. And ignorance is not to be confused with being unintelligent or weak-brained or less analytical or foolish. Ignorance is the plain act of not knowing and being kept in dark. We are all kept in dark by various people at various points of our lives. If a child knows the aantaryam[1] of life, that it is going to end some day at a later

---

1   Aantaryam: *(Telugu/Sanskrit)* The hidden purpose or meaning.

phase of life, the bliss of childhood would never happen. If a student thinks that all his study is not all that useful and that his job might be a different business altogether, he can never taste the sweetness of knowledge. We don't do things only because they are going to be of some use some day, we do them for the sheer of joy of doing or for the sheer pain of being destined to do, sometimes.

And when it comes to *"purpose of life"*, it might very well be true that we all are just little cogs in this machine called universe and perhaps a supreme being has already assigned a purpose, which we are adhering to, with or without our knowledge. But, we the little cogs, can perhaps get aware of that purpose if the supreme being wills to, as mused in the post – *The story of Valmiki*. But again, itseems even God is in the continuous process of learning, it seems He creates and assesses the course of further evolution through His own creation, i.e., "us", as nicely put in the book, *"The Expansion"*. I like this quote by Telihard de Chardin in that book - *"We are not human beings having a spiritual experience, we are spiritual beings having a human experience"*.

I'd like to apply this entire concept to the hype and hoopla[1] that surrounds Dec 21, 2012. There are many theories floating Internet, some people view it in terms of alien intervention and think that aliens are communicating with humans through the power of thought. Some say planet Nibiru, some say solar flares, some say galactic alignment and the scientist community rubs all this off, saying Dec 21, 2012 is just another prediction that is bound to go wrong and get dumped into the previous predictions which always went wrong. While

---

[1] Hoopla: *(Hindi)* Disturbance, confusion or mess.

I have not done any academic research about this, I stick to the Divine Intervention (as professed by Mayans), Precession of Equinoxes and Frequency Ascension theories, cited in my blog earlier. But then, as the date is nearing, amazingly, the whole world seems to be converging on to almost similar conclusions. The Precession which is expected to set in the process of Frequency Ascension is also expected to put us into the "New Age" of Aquarius. All these theories indicate that the 2012 phenomenon is happening in each and every one of us and that it has already started and IS happening currently. But wait, not only 2012 phenomenon, every phenomenon in this Universe is happening around us and through us. But wait again! I was supposed to talk about simplicity and ignorance, not 2012 phenomenon. Yes, thanks, I'm reminded! It might all seem serendipity to us, but from the God's point of view, it is tapestry. And from the point of view of tapestry, all answers are indeed simple, because the solution or problem is laid out first, ahead of the struggle. From the point of view of serendipity, the struggle comes first and the truth/solution next. But eitherways again, all answers are indeed simple. But trust me, being or talking simple is not all that easy! Of all, I understand that! It can only crop up from two things - ignorance or endurance. Ignorance of multiple systems and being good at what you are talking or endurance of those multiple systems and then be good at what you are talking. I write this, not that I'm simple or knowledgeable or anything like that. It's solely because, I earnestly appreciate the beauty of simplicity and have been its admirer for a long time and used to have theories of my own about that. I'm still ignorant of that simplicity and in the continuous process of enduring the path to arrive at its beauty :-)

- *Dec 07, 2012, 11:29 PM.*

59. The dilemma of Lord Shiva!

We all think that, to be successful, one has to be decisive. Even I attribute being decisive in critical moments as my most successful trait. But I recently watched this *Life OK's Har Har Mahadev* episode which depicts the dilemma faced by Lord Shiva. Just a quick glance at the episode might make one question why Lord Shiva - Devo ke Dev, Mahadev[1], Our Father, was so indecisive. BUT, being decisive depends on the far reaching implications and the dependents you have and the whole world is dependent on its Father, isn't it? The story encapsulated by that episode (tagged along with few after and few before) goes this way!

Sati Devi who took human birth, as the daughter of *Daksha Prajapathi* and *Prasuti*, bumps into *Lord Shiva*, who comes to save Her from the clutches of a demon *Tarakasura*. And She senses a strange kind of attraction and affection for Him. But, Our Father Lord Shiva remains unperturbed! Strange! And also some followers of Lord Shiva (damn them, I'll tell you why later) strengthen Sati Devi's affection for Him. Time and again Sati Devi tries to express Her love for Him, but one fine day She is flat blandly rejected by Him. He says that She is a human and that He is an eternal being. But all those followers who have actually shaped up the love of Sati and gave some direction don't come to Her rescue (now you know the reason for damning them!). Daksha is a staunch opposer of Lord Shiva and does not like to give his daughter's hand in marriage to Him. So, Sati Devi dies within everyday unable to give up Her love, unaccepted by Him and completely opposed by Her father and *tries* to abide by Her father's words. But the

---

[1]   Devo ke Dev, Mahadev: *(Hindi)* God of Gods; The highest form of God.

attraction towards (call it haunting from) Lord Shiva does not go away, something or the other happens that pulls Her towards Him. So one fine day, in Her angst while trying to wipe Him away from Her heart, She takes a Shapath[1] that She will give up Her life if He ever comes and faces Her. But the daemon Tarakasura does not give up on his mission of trying to kill Her. On the other hand, Daksha Prajapati fixes Her marriage with *Satabhisha*. It is in this context that the episode cited there happens. All the Gods go to Lord Shiva to appeal to Him to take a human form to approach Her. Goddess *Lakshmi Devi* specifically says *"If She can't expand her horizons, you go into Her Horizons, isn't that called Love? Take a different form, if you are warranted from taking your original form. If* Aadi Shakti[2] *Herself could take a human form and if Lord Narayana can assume* Dashavatara[3], *why cannot you consider assuming human form?"* But Our Father does not relent on his decision of not taking a human form. Meanwhile Sati Devi torments herself unable to get ready for marriage with Satabisha. This is the instance where it seems to the audience that Shiva is being indecisive and that He is inordinately delaying the decision of approaching Sati. Anyway, later somehow the story moulds into Lord Shiva taking the form of *Jateswara* and then both of them (Sati Devi and Shiva) getting married. In fact the reason for the plight was not the fault of Sati or Shiva, but it's their inseparable nature and the expectation of the world for its parents to unite.

---

[1] Shapath: *(Hindi)* Oath.

[2] Aadi Shakti: *(Sanskrit/Hindi/Telugu)* The first or primordial Energy. Sati and Parvati are regarded as the incarnates of Adi Shakti. Durga, Mahakali etc are considered to be her other forms.

[3] Dashavatara: *(Hindi)* The Ten Avatars of Vishnu.

But, the crux of the discussion and the reason for this post is different. While me and my whole family was watching the serial, my father asked if She takes a human birth, then shouldn't He too take a human birth, why should He remain in His eternal form. Yeah, I replied as though I knew the answer - *"It's not that He has never taken a human birth, He too might have did, just like Her as Sati and Parvati, but perhaps at different times and maybe we don't know, maybe Lord Shiva never wanted it to be known".* My father replied - *"I mean, why will the divine couple take human births at different times?"* Yeah I understood my father's question even before I gave that customary reply, the crux of the whole thing is why the divine couple didn't take human birth at the same time to be able to live as humans together.

If we go back to the episode, it shows how even if the truth is simple and subtle, its variants are often at loggerheads and how the Gods themselves are in conflict with themselves considering the enormous responsibilities they bear.

- Dec 10, 2012, 03:57 PM.

60. The expansion - The spiralling expansion!

"Life comes a full circle, that's the usual phrase used by people to describe the strange nature of life, where things keep changing and changing, yet they seem to remain the same, when the comparison is done on an expanded time scale. Yet, for me it seems that life comes a full circle many times in a different sense, in a sense that things don't seem to stay constant even

on an expanded time scale. In that sense, it would be better to say, life is just spiralling around me and I pause and realize that at times. I hope the spiral ends soon and I start from its centre pretty soon!" These were the lines from my personal diary a few months ago in April. Things have changed completely and I realize that I was in a very low phase back then. It takes immense strength and potential to be able to cross that point of spiral and bounce from one side to the other, because that signals a changing phase of life. Perhaps, I didn't have that strength back then and hence those lines! To go to the other side of that arc of spiral, one must be able to welcome change and that needs energy and that's exactly what I was lacking then! Now that I have, I try to cross it.

When I talk of these things, I'm reminded of the principle of "Conservation of Momentum" applied to a system in which collision occurs. I take this system as an example because the impediment to cross the spiral in the above example happens when there is collision of interests - interests to remain on one side vs interests to cross to the other side. Ofcourse there are elastic and inelastic collisions too and I don't know which category my intangible spiral falls under :-) In any case, a successful transition happens only when there is conservation of momentum and the principle says momentum is always conserved in any 'system'. So, what I mean is, a successful transition is that in which the integrity of the system is retained.

Here's an old case study that involved the spiral:

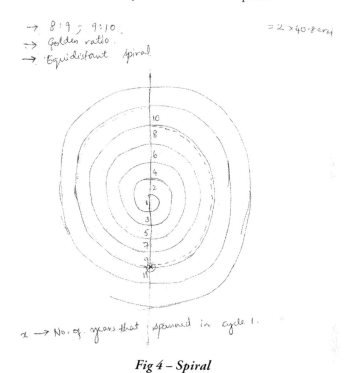

Fig 4 – Spiral

- Dec 11, 2012, 06:39 PM.

<u>Self-Notes:</u>

Let's say the law of conservation of momentum needs to be applied to this spiral at a point of transition from its 12th arc to 13th arc, we can perhaps do it this way!

Let's say in the collision that is involved in this transition, the mass of the (objects in the) system decreases from 13 mass units to 12 mass units (the objects get lighter after collision).

For the momentum to be conserved, the velocity of the objects involved in the collision must increase!

Say, 13 mass units * 12960 kmph (before) = 12 * x kmph (after)

$$=> x \text{ (after)} = 14040 \text{ kmph}$$

But for some reasons, if I'm obsessed about 12960 kmph velocity and want to retain the number (not the value ofcourse), then I must change the measurement of kmph. To retain the value of 12960 kmph as it is even after collision, I'd consider changing the next bigger scale of km-m conversion instead of the lowest unit conversion because the more atomic the modifications are, the greater the dependancies and cascading impact they have.

- Dec 13, 2012, 10:00 PM.

61. Happiness is the default state of a being...

Does that contradict the concept of happiness being infinite? I guess it doesn't! When I say that, I mean we are born with happiness... with bliss! Can anything else parallel the innocence and bliss radiated by *bosi navvulu*[1] of a baby? I personally feel that the journey of this human life spawns struggle, but the struggle of that journey very much happens on the base path of happiness. To me happiness is a path, a journey in itself and never a destination. It's like the screen saver image, well yes it's a funny analogy, but the concept remains. In mathematical terms, it's like the line parallel to y-axis, x=k whose slope is

---

[1]   *Bosi navvulu*: (Telugu) The laughs of a new born baby. Literally, the tooth-less laughs.

infinity. It's a constant line spread over the infinity of the y-axis domain. Happiness is infinite, spread over the infinitude of our life's journey, relished in finite amounts at any given point of time. And in musical terms, it's the *Shruti (base of the raaga)* that goes on and on timed by the *Laya (rhythm of the raaga)*.

- Dec 11, 2012, 07:02 PM.

62. The Sita of today!

Men are men. Times might have changed, but their thinking doesn't seem to change even after intense suffering. They think they know women, even I thought so, I believed they understand women. I've heard some men say *"Women are treacherous!"* I never reciprocated such comments because I just thought such might have been their experiences.

Goddess *Lakshmi* might have been termed Shivakari[1], but not many auspicious things happened with her when she was Sita in *Treta Yuga*. That is perhaps why Telugu people use this phrase 'Sita kashtaalu[2]' to refer to extreme turbulences in life, but maybe we are not aware of the grieving side of Rama as much. Whenever I saw that movie *LavaKusha* and that epic scene in which *Lord Rama* orders his brother *Lakshmana* to send off *Sita* to forests, I wondered how a man such as Rama could lack such little judgmental capacity. I always wondered how he could send his wife, a pregnant woman close to delivery, to forests assigning no care to her, owing to foolish words of a random citizen. How many ever times I watch

---

[1]   Shivakari: *(Telugu/Sanskrit)* One of the many sacred names of Goddess Lakshmi, which means the giver or cause of auspicious things.

[2]   Sita kashtalu: *(Telugu)* The grief, sorrow or troubles experienced by Sita.

the movie, it used create in me the same angst. And to add to that, Lord Rama is shown to be in a 'manassankshobham[1]' where he could not decide whether to choose between 'Surya Vamsha Prathishta[2]' and his wife. When Hero Rama Rao, the actor who played Lord Rama, cries in that scene, I used to think – *"Why cry? Why don't you or rather why can't you just go and get back your wife?"* I swear! I thought he must be kidding, what's with a clan's fame and buying in the feedback of an unknown citizen to abide by true kingship? I even used to ask my Dad this question, he said maybe such were the times and such were the rules. My Dad might be right in a way, so I can understand Rama's judgement call, but I never understood Sita's patience. Again maybe such were the times when women were expected to be so patient and so were they. Anyway, we don't know if the story is portrayed to be so in films or if that is the real story. And no wonder, Kali Yuga which is supposed to be less virtuous doesn't show any improvement. The *Khmer Ramakirti* account of Ramayana has a story in which *Lord Hanuman* embraces *Mandodari* (Ravana's wife) in the form of *Ravana* to evade something. But the writers portray it as a kalankam[3] on Mandodari's womanhood and not on the virtue of Lord Hanuman (Ok I have great reverence for this God, so I digress here, it's just a reference).

Lord Narayana might have did that thing with Sita when he was Rama. He might have had Padaharu Vela Gopikalu[4] when

---

[1] Manassanksobham: *(Telugu)* Dilemma of the mind (here heart).
[2] Surya Vamsa Prathishtha: *(Telugu)* Fame of the kings descending from Surya Clan.
[3] Kalankam: *(Telugu)* Blot; Ill effect; Dismerit.
[4] Padaharu Vela Gopikalu: *(Telugu)* Sixteen thousand Gopika. *Gopika* means cow-herd girl. *Gopikalu* – plural of *Gopika. Padaharu Vela Gopikalu* here refer to the group of cow herding girls famous for their unconditional devotion and overwhelming love towards *Lord Krishna* as described in the stories of *Bhagavatam.*

he was Krishna (and all of them are supposed to be sages who in some other birth were overwhelmed by devotion for Narayana - bhaktiparavasyam annamaata[1]). But, to me God was always Lord Narayana and I was an ardent devotee, not that I performed rigorous poojas or rituals. It seems like the character played by actress *Roja Ramani* in the Telugu movie Bhakta Prahlada[2] had a good impact on me when I was a child.

If Sita was born today, will she live in forests at the behest of her husband? No way! She will instead allow Rama to take his turn... I'm damn sure! ☺

PS: As is evident, written based on the Indian context specifically.

- Dec 16, 2012, 07:31 PM.

63. Dharmasamsthapana - the 'right' mix of good and bad!

Any creation or evolution is useless unless a bit of sorting out and weeding out the bad is done. While the ultimate mission of God is to save the world (not at the cost of this Universe though) and lift them to a higher possibility of life and consciousness, it is also sometimes to make people aware of His existence, the

---

[1] Bhaktiparavasyam annamaata: *(Telugu)* An actual instance of overwhelming of devotion, indeed!

[2] Bhakta Prahlada: *(Telugu)* A Telugu movie title which means *'Devotee Prahlada'*. The movie is based on the story of Prahlada, son of Hiranyakashyapa. While Prahlada is an ardent devotee of Narayana, his father hates Narayana. The father tries in vain to shake off Prahlada's devotion and even tries to get his son killed unable to accept the failure. But it is Prahlada's devotion which saves him.

reasons and implications of which are on the lines as discussed in the post – *These are my interests. So what?* I'd like to discuss the concept of *'avatar'* in this context. While human birth is supposed to be of highest and meritorious form of existence for a living being, I see Gods taking an avatar as a job to carry out certain responsibilities and they would feel themselves most comfortable in their own divine abode itself. And whatever knowledge we have about God assuming human births on earth is very little. I mean the time frame that we are aware of is pretty infinitesimal in this long continuous time cycle. While we consider Jesus as the son of God and Rama, Buddha and Krishna as avatars of Vishnu, most of the prophecies associate Jesus and Krishna as one of the sun Gods to mark important transition of their own events. Some consider Shirdi Saibaba to have imbibed Shiva's aspect. It's very difficult to reason out the logic and attribute a formula in fact. Because, most importantly time is continuous just as God is immortal and what track time takes is difficult for human beings to know.

Also, it is said that so far we are still in the descending phase of Kali Yuga and whatever knowledge we have is that of a descending arc of time and nothing more, so the knowledge of how an avatar is assumed at a point of transition from the descending arc of time to ascending arc of time is virtually nill to all of us and one can only make prophecies. If this point of time is supposed to be an event of *Pralaya (Chaos)* in Gods' calendar and yet if They do not want to let go of this evolution of life, the only way They can deal with this is to be part of this evolution. A Pralaya is usually that event in which Shiva consumes Shakti completely and hence the 'life' on earth (and not earth per se) ought to be demolished and recreated in such a case, by Shakti being born from Shiva again. It seems an avoidance of such a case is the inversion of roles wherein Shakti demolishes Shiva and recreates Him from Her (as discussed in *Self-Notes* of *Satyam Shivam Sundaram* blog post) thus keeping the Shakti intact. It seems by doing this, both Shiva and Shakti rejuvenate each other and this is the much talked-of beginning of new cycles of time, a different cycle from the one we have been experiencing so far. It is actually equivalent to *Pralaya sans complete destruction* and occurs at a point when Dharma Samsthapana (Reinstatement of Dharma) is needed on earth, because nature does exercise its discretion! And discretion is exercised only through the hate circuitry of brain and not through the love circuitry of the brain. But Shiva being an eternal being cannot be dead at any point of time, so the time He lives on the earth is supposed to be the spawned time from a different time frame.

- Dec 18, 2012, 08:55 PM.

64. *The power of Skanda!*

Yesterday was Subramanya Sashti[1] and in the early morning happened to hear on TV about *Skanda, Kumara Swamy, Subramanya, Muruga* whichever way you call him. Seems like a lot of importance is attributed to this God in a sense that he is supposed to be the Sena Nayaka[2] of all the Gana[3] of Gods. It seems, all the powers of Gods are submitted to Skanda during a

---

[1] Subramanya Sashti: A South Indian festival celebrated on the sixth day of the bright fortnight of the lunar month of *Margashirsha* (November - December). It commemorates the victory of Skanda over demon Tarakasura.

[2] Sena Nayaka: *(Sanskrit/Hindi/Telugu)* The Commander of the Army; The Head Warrior.

[3] Gana: *(Sanskrit/Hindi/Telugu)* Army or group.

war and he invokes such powers in the needful times of battles. What really caught my attention is this specific narration: Itseems after the battle of Gods, call it a war over evil in cosmos or after some task on earth, even the Good Powers *(Uttama Sakthulu)* are scattered! *Parokshamgaa unna Shivasakti ni saitam utteja parachaali antee Kumara Swamy poonukoovaalata*[1]! This is really interesting. In fact the fact that I need to know more about this God has been brewing in my mind for quite a while and this gave me impetus to do so.

I have talked about Skanda earlier in one of the blog posts *(A journey into the past)*. It's actually interesting to talk about him in the context of grouping and getting together, those conjoined snakes (two 3s coming together) symbolize it. And my interest area is the fact that his sister Goddess Jyoti is hidden with him in the form of his weapon. When it is said that Gods are residing on earth, let's say Ganesha, Jyoti, Skanda or Ayyappa, I wonder where do they actually reside.

- Dec 19, 2012, 06:07 PM.

65. Pralaya - the evitable destruction - A socio fantasy thriller!

My creative writing is evolving "by the day", hence I try my hand at writing a socio fantasy thriller story now! :-) Some of the things stated here might contradict the faiths and status quo of certain things in Hinduism, but questioning the status

---

[1]   Parokshamgaa unna Shivasakti ni saitam utteja parachaali antee Kumara Swamy poonukoovaalata: *(Telugu)* "Even if the Shivasakti (Shiva's energy) lying around passively needs to be activated, Kumara Swamy must will to invoke it itseems (only during a battle ofcourse)!"

quo is part of change and the universe is changing every minute, so I take this step and an appeal to the Hindus out there is not to be hurt if this outrages your sentiments at any point.

We all know that during Mohini Avatara ghattam[1], *Lord Shiva* and *Lord Narayana*, in the form of *Mohini*, united to give birth to *Lord Manikanta*, who was abandoned by the parents soon after the birth. Atleast that's what we were told by the religious literature. But my realization tells me that Manikanta was not the child born out of Shiva – Narayana (Mohini) unison, but the son of Narayana and Lakshmi instead. Goddess Lakshmi really wished Manikanta wins the acceptance of the Lord Shiva and Shakti couple to marry their daughter Jyoti. In a different setting, Lord Shiva was away from Goddess Parvati for a long time on his duties of watching out the world and working for its well being and progress. Time was also fast approaching for Shiva-Shakti unison. The unison between Shiva and Shakti that is the source of energy (ShivaShakti) and is the reason behind this expanding universe did not happen for a long time. This led to a lot of confusion in the cosmos and also troubled the sustenance of the earth out here. The unison between Shiva and Shakti happens periodically, the periodicity *ideally* being 12,960 current earth-years relative to the current time cycles. It is also the point of destruction and also marks the birth of a new phase of life which is usually of better quality than the previous ones. The extent of destruction whether it is minor or major depends on the amount of evil on Earth. This is Prakriti Dharma[2] and must happen for the sustenance of nature itself on

---

[1]   Mohini Avatara ghattam: *(Telugu)* The incidents that transpired during Mohini Avatar.

[2]   Prakriti Dharma: *(Sanskrit/Telugu)* The laws of nature (to retain its order).

earth. While the unison must have already happened by this time for it is time already for the expansion of Universe, it has been postponed by 2-3 Kali Yugas since that means majority of the life on earth would be annihilated. It means that more evil than what earth could bear has been fostered and surviving on earth. But human evolution reached a meaningful phase and it was difficult for Gods themselves to let go of it. So the unison has been kept on hold waiting for the humanity to ascend to an appropriate level where the evil (relative to good) decreases to an acceptable (or let's say tolerable) amount. On the other hand, man on earth was viewing nature as a resource and started exploiting it forgetting that man belongs to the earth and that the earth does NOT belong to him. The paapa karma[1] was actually increasing which the nature Herself couldn't take. In the quest for (hypothetical) development on earth, man on Earth is now at loggerheads with Shiva and with the Universe. The quest of Gods for life on Earth and their responsibility towards expansion of Universe, both the expectations too are at loggerheads with each other.

In a different setting in this modern age, we have Pranati and Manvit studying together in a higher secondary school. Eventually after the schooling, Manvit senses a strange kind of attraction towards Pranati which cannot be comprehended in this age. For a couple of years, he tries to follow what this external force was trying to convey him and is expecting him to do. The force overrided his daily priorities and made his life a hell for quite many years. Obviously, this is a unique scenario which nobody (in his knowledge) might have faced and this cannot be explained in a way others can understand and even

---

[1]   Paapa karma: *(Sanskrit/Telugu)* The sin of evil deeds; The net effect of that sin.

if it can be explained there is nothing much others could have done. He actually takes it completely on himself and follows it because virtually he had no choice. Eventually he realizes there is a soul connection between him and Pranati, but Pranati is not aware of this. Pranati meanwhile is caught in an abusive, soul-wrenching marriage with an incompatible person and tries to get rid of his clutches. It is after breaking up her virtually void marriage that she too senses the same connection with Manvit... this is 12 long years after Manvit has sensed it. She happens to tell him the same thing, but he denies it because his understanding was that they both must arrive at some stabilized conclusions through that very connection before even talking or discussing openly about it. On the other hand Pranati does not understand this and her struggle with this realization starts there. Pranati's side of understanding is that it is actually the God's soul that is guiding them in the task of uniting Shiva and Shakti to avoid a major Pralaya. On the other hand Manvit's realization ran on different lines. Whether Pranati and Manvit can solve this jigsaw puzzle is a story in the making!

- Dec 20, 2012, 07:40 PM.

66. Omkara - The Pranava Mantra!

A person performing yoga utters the syllable 'AUM' by taking in breath first, expanding lungs and stomach enough to accommodate as much breath as possible and then exhales it to utter that primordial sound. In short, *Omkara* embodies in it the whole process of life – inhaling -> creation of life (conception), holding and assimilating the breath -> living (life itself) and exhaling -> destruction of life (death). The usual perception is that destruction of life is not a part of life, but without that there can be no further life, so that's very much part of it – "it" being the life of this universe. What is death to one, is birth to somebody else. It's difficult to accept this with reference to the person dying, but with reference to the Universe, death is inevitable, so sometimes it must be understood that it's all relative to keep this eternal cycle going.

But that said, living life in the happiest possible way is the motto of any person. I personally don't believe in seeking renunciation or salvation until such an age arrives because this human life has a purpose to it - to savour the human existence and its journey. If renunciation and salvation were to be the ultimate goal of every individual right from a young age, we all rather die immediately then, because there is no need even to take this birth. Ofcourse, we have the Vedic literature talking about the four stages of life, which I'm not very well versed with. But then, the choice of all this is driven by the inner calling of a person.

Wikipedia has good description of Omkara wherein it is perceived to be an all-encompassing mystical entity whose vibration is the manifestation of God in form. As the sublime plot unleashes itself to mark both the creation and sustenance of a new phase of life, the Gods apparently would like the world to chant Omkaram and perform *Abhishekam*[1] both with milk and water to be appeased.

- Dec 23, 2012, 07:02 PM.

---

[1] *Abhishekam: (Telugu/Sanskrit)* The process of offering pure liquid substances (as per Hindu Dharma) to Gods by pouring on the idols of the deities.

67. We are just travellers - at the most we can make destiny, but we cannot break destiny!

We all are travellers and we don't really know our destination stop. Though certain things can best be appreciated only when experienced, a piece of knowledge (learnt the hard way) I would share with everybody in general is that the quest to know the unknown beyond a certain point deters the journey. Whatever we know is finite and the unknown in infinite. And a personal guideline I made to my life is to enjoy the bliss of a finite system rather than lurk in the mystery of unknown. Sure the quest must be there but not at the cost of hindering our present way of living. But then there is no single rule that can serve as panacea to everybody's life and we all choose what works better for us.

Two people may share the same road, but they cannot share the same journey unless their ideas resonate i.e., unless they are compatible. Let's say two people are treading a simple harmonic motion from two ends of the semi-circle arc and they do meet each other at various points, but only those points at which they both stabilize and resonate are the positions they actually belong to, the rest of the positions are intermediaries.

I'd also like to talk about prophecies. It is not without divine will that people like *Nostradamus* and *Potuluri Srimad Virat Veera Brahmam* made prophecies for the future. But I never understood the purpose behind it. Because God and time take their own course and the awareness of what lays ahead in the future is not a useful piece of information to anybody, at the most it deters the present course of living. And then, there is no certainty with which prophecies are made because there are always last minute changes like those decisions taken by us in very critical moments. And even if there is certainty by the person who made the prophecy, it need not be reciprocated with commensurate belief, because we all have an established system of living and we can't flee or abandon it. In fact in the time of a disaster, when thousands of people are dying, the wisest person would choose to die along with them, there is no better way. This is harsh but true and underscores the reality of mortality of human beings.

- Dec 26, 2012, 12:25 PM.

68. Sex - A soul dance!

I have been shutting my mouth on this for a really long time for the fear of hurting people's sentiments. But, I want to lay my opinion plain clear on it once because right people will always take a right opinion in the right vein. It's true that dating and sex prior to marriage is a common norm these days in some places. It's also true that healthy dating is essential to understand the compatibility and it's even more true that it's not necessary that every married couple must be compatible in all aspects and on all terms. That is why the facility of 'divorce' has been devised. Divorce is not a sin, but staying in marriage and wanting your wife to be somebody else or just keeping the marriage intact and putting your heart else where is a sin. If you thought that your mother and father's generation had seen healthier sex life, there are reasons for it. We are evolving and let's give the mothers and wives of today's generation their due places. I have seen men who ask their mother to get modern in her cooking citing today's women as examples and at the same time asking their wife to stay traditional, sober and obedient citing their Mom as examples. It's a double standard, I'm not denying that women have not changed. I have seen women playing double standards too where they can't appreciate a good man, love a dirty guy before marriage and once after marriage, expect their husband to be a true gentleman.

Coming back to the norm of *"trying"* sex before marriage (generally termed as *Pre-marital Sex*), I do not see the point of it, especially when it is practiced for the sheer purpose of trying it out. There are many side effects from this practice - Single Moms, Children born out of such relationships growing insecure, Infidelity at later stages of life, abandoned relationships as a result of sex perverts or addicts who do it for the sheer pleasure of it and not out of commitment towards the other and so many more! More than anything else, the unit of family in the societal setup gets disturbed and the society too gets shaped up accordingly. If human race considers itself more evolved than the rest of the species, then its sexual practices too must speak for that.

Sex is a soul dance when you give your soul to it. If it is seen as a sheer physical aspect, one gets just as much happiness as one gets from prostitution. A woman needs a man to do sex, not a prior experience, appreciation or taste for it. Otherwise, how could Adam and Eve copulate and create this world? Sex happens naturally between a man and a woman and that is the open Srishti Rahasyam[1]. Anything that one wants to emulate is a mere hypothesis, what one does for real is a reality. That really explains how the potency of the current generation men has decreased, treating themselves with virtual sex world on internet instead of living it out with their own wives. It's just like music - if you give your soul to music, then the music that comes from you, from within you, becomes the dance of your soul, the pure dance of your soul. When it comes to sex, it is

---

[1] Srishti Rahasyam: *(Telugu)* Sacred Secret of Nature.

said that every couple can elevate themselves to the level of Shiva and Shakti for the God lies within you and that has to be truly believed - *"You are the God of your own act...for your own act!"* If sex is not working right, then most of the times, the problem is else where, given the couple is healthy. If one has to work on anything at all, one must work on understanding the partner more and work on the equation of being soul mates, then the sex too between them would be as much divine as it is between the divine soul mates - Shiva and Shakti. All of us know this, because it is all etched in our sub-conscious, but the rat race of today's generation throws this on to back seat, unfortunately can't help it. We must try to attain that much needed balance between man and woman *(as discussed in the post – Is truth such a bad bargain?)* and make this world a happier place to live!!!

- Dec 28, 2012, 11:59 AM.

* * * * * * * * * *

"No fact is unlimitedly true."

— David Hume.

"No emotion by itself is wrong. But it should be righteous in time, space and situation."

— Aristotle.

* * * * * * * * * *

Part IV: 2013

BACKGROUND:

*B*y this time I had already gained sufficient understanding that I was experiencing Synchronicity and indeed going through a phase of self-realization in my life, guided by The Absolute. But then, this was also the period when I was quite confused. I had many questions, like - When will this heavy exertion of frequencies and energies end on me, Until when should I, specifically my body and mind be taking this burden, When will this dilemma end, Where is all this leading me to, Where is all this leading this World to and last but not the least, Why me, of all, must be going through this process – such questions and many more.

I did not get clarity on these questions ... not till the end of the year. My career in software profession was also at stake during this time. After a long break of about 1.5 years, a break that was necessitated by the process of my Realization, I made a comeback in software career by getting into Adaptive Mobile, an Irish based organization that writes software for Mobile Security.

The following blog posts in this part depict this dilemma and confusion, the split between realization and career and other day-to-day demands, looming large on me. They show how I was sailing my life, like a ship caught in directionless winds in a whirlpool very desperate to reach the shore.

. . . . .

69. The goal of the whole and the return of Gods!!!

This is the continuation of that socio-fantasy thriller story - *Pralaya* - the evitable destruction. The goal of any entity as a whole is to balance itself. And such a balance happens through *Dharma Samsthapana* - the battle of good over bad, because there would be no such thing as 'all good' or 'all bad' and if there was no imbalance in the first place, then there is no need to re-assert balance. And good and bad are re-defined over time and the usual tendency is that, whichever triumphs establishes itself to be good.

Time is fast approaching for the *'Precession of Equinoxes'* and the goal of the Gods as a whole is to save the earth as a planet during the process of Precession of Equinoxes, without being sucked into the galactic center. Precession of Equinoxes is another *cyclic event* of the nature just as the rising and setting of the sun, waxing and waning of the moon, seasons repeating etc. We all are usually only aware of the aspects of rotation and revolution of earth, but Earth is wobbling too on its axis and its locus traverses a dumb-bell path over a period of 25, 920 earth-years (current earth year relative to current time). Earth precesses 1 degree for every 72 years. Mythologically the double conical precession path resembles **Damarukam**, which is tied to the Trident (*Trishulam*) held by Lord Shiva. This event marks a change in the orientation of earth's wobbling twice in this period. At the points of Precession of Equinoxes, the laws of time are different; time doesn't obey a precession of a degree per 72 years. *It is said that, it is the interaction and inter-play of the endogenic and exogenic* *forces and the resultant features that shall decide the course of the whole process and the course of the movement of the earth there-off.*

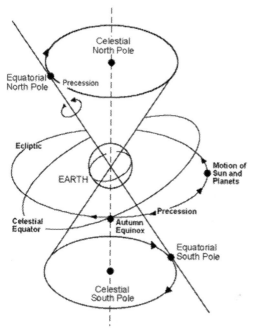

Fig 5 – Precession of Earth

(The original source of this image is <u>http://www.borobudur.tv/Image/Precess 1.gif</u>, but this reference link is dysfunctional now.)

The event is expected to birth us into new cycles of time, new arc of *time spiral* which requires higher frequencies and hence higher energies. And incidentally, this also marks the inversion of powers of Yin and Yang and passing of the cue to the divine feminine. The feminine has been tolerating for long, the nonchalant attitude of male domination and was waiting for the right time to assert its power. Apparently we are still lingering in the descending phase of *Kali Yuga*, but the fact is that we have been tiding against time and were stuck in that descending phase for quite a long time almost double its span, when we should already be in the ascending arc of time, for the time was not right and ripe to take that big leap to surge into the ascending phase. For that transition to take place, co-ordination, collaboration and synchronization between multiple worlds was needed. Prior to the actual events, the elderly Gods sent Lord Ganesha and Lord Manikanta to earth to gather some information from this realm. This information was needed to collate with the situation in the other worlds, so that an appropriate and timely action can be taken.

There's also a sub-plot wherein Goddess Jyoti, the daughter of Lord Shiva and Shakti, is hidden on earth as a weapon of Lord Skanda. And the Sun God Aryaman is on his way to wage a war on earth to gain her. So are we going to see some solar flares and some shakeup in nature and our way of living? Is the humanity geared up for Frequency Ascension? How will the Gods save their daughter and the Planet Earth? ... is a story in making!

- *Jan 04, 2013, 11:50 PM.*

<u>*Self-Notes:*</u>

The transition involves a new month in time which they named Talanuary.

The orbital velocities are expected to change drastically at select points of the transit of precession of earth. At the end of it, we supposedly reach the end of ascending Kali Yuga and make a new beginning with the ascending Dwapara Yuga.

- *Jan 05, 2013, 04:56 PM.*

70. Rewriting history - a re-look!

Seems like the evil raises its ugly head time and again. Applying this to macrocosm, over the scale of yugas, it was Ravana in Treta Yuga and Narakasura in Dwapara Yuga. So what is it going to be in Kali Yuga then? Is that fateful Dec 21, 2012 incident (perhaps the timing professed wrongly) the evil as such in Kali Yuga? Is it sun god Aryaman? I'm reminded of one of those predictions which points to Solar flares paralyzing the Earth, when I think of this prophecy. Or is it the Precession of Equinoxes as a whole, as a process, which has to be overcome or survived?

If I were given an opportunity to re-write history I would let Sita kill Ravana. The Telugu movie *Arundhati* defines such a similar sequence for me. Perhaps Goddess Lakshmi was not very happy with Lord Vishnu for not having (or not being given) the scope to do so and that is perhaps why Krishna let Satyabhama kill Narakasura in Dwapara Yuga. On a different note, the Ranganath Ramayana says that Mandodari is ayonijasambhava[1] by Lord Shiva and Goddess Parvati just like Goddess Jyoti.

- Jan 12, 2013, 12:36 PM.

71. Change is multi-fold!

Change usually is and must be a multi-fold process. Crime, according to Sociology, is part of checks and balances nature does so as to redefine laws and the discrimination of good and bad for the society. That fateful Delhi gang-rape of a 23 year

---

[1]   Ayonijasambhava: *(Sanskrit)* Not born of a woman; Not born from a woman's womb.

old (now known to the world as Nirbhaya) might have spurred a lot of talk in the social media and by the public at large, but honestly this is not new. It's been happening for a long time, it's just that this particular incident of crime happened to catch the media glare for certain distinct characteristics it possessed.

If we need to keep a check on such incidents in India (let me confine this to India, for if I need to generalize it to the whole world, many parameters might have to be considered whose background I'm not well versed with) the solution is multi-fold: Change in the judiciary (stringency of laws), education system (sensitizing children towards gender-equality, understanding of and respect for the opposite sex), our mass media (needs to atleast come up with meaningful programmes instead of plain gameshows, serials and stuff which only feed the lower side of human emotions and not really harness the good potential) are first few things I can think of. But of all, if I have to point at one thing that has largely fed this male chauvinism in Indian society, I'd clearly point my finger towards Indian way of parenting and specifically the role of mother in India. It is Indian parenting system that nurtures male chauvinism and specifically the Indian Mom who over-does (literally *petti-poshisthundi*[1]) it. I myself have come across many incidents wherein if a girl raises her voice and asserts a thing, they say - "*Enti maga raayudi laaga maatladuthunnaavu?*[2]" and if the girl happens to assert her knowledge then they see it as over-confidence, arrogance and plainly can't digest it, while if its from the other sex, they welcome it and see it as an expected thing and totally acceptable. You might be surprised to hear

---

[1]   Petti poshitundi: *(Telugu)* "She feeds and nurtures it carefully."
[2]   Enti maga raayudi laaga maatladuthunnaavu?: *(Telugu)* "What? Why are you talking and behaving like a man?"

this if you are from an upper middle class background/upper caste/liberal upbringing. Again things can't be generalized but the situation on an average in the lower strata (caste wise/economically/exposure wise) is not really bright for the Indian woman.

Anyway, my concern here mainly is about the role of Mom in breeding male-chauvinism. I'm specifically referring to the mother and not the father here because in our system mother indeed plays a powerful role in bringing up her children and father usually tends to play a relatively lesser role there. But, I must say that the mother fails time and again to contribute to a 'net' positive change in the society due to her inability to look through the faults of her son. Not only mothers, but many women in general do not recognize men's mistakes as mistakes, but are otherwise very much ready to criticize, admonish and find faults with fellow women both in family circles and societal circles. If a woman is raped, it is usually women who come first to offer their sage opinion (instead of empathizing with her) that it is her negligence or dressing or lack of alertness that has invited the rape. Inspite of women making progress in all the fields, it is the inability of women to share domestic chores with their partners or their inability to delegate it to children, especially sons, believing that as "Woman's Arena", is what puts women at enormous double stress. To cut the long story short, women are more understanding of men and less understanding of their fellow women. No wonder the Telugu adage which means – "The enemy of a woman is another woman" is so true, in general. This again plays to their own detriment since women indeed play a powerful role in shaping the society as mothers, wives, sisters and daughters.

Ofcourse, no offences here. Definitely, women today have been doing a great job as mothers, but the emphasis here is more on the negative aspects or forgotten or not-so-well fulfilled responsibilities. I'd say if the woman becomes more receptive of the expectations of the next generation and be more accommodating and compassionate of her daughter-in-law, sister and daughter and other women around her and just not make the men around her more lazy and feel that they are 'entitled' to dominate, its easier for the system to change and the 'net' change is bound to be more positive. It might seem that women are expected to fulfill a more burden-some responsibility, but every generation needs a specific group to bear the burden to usher in change and this time around it seems to be that of the 'women' group - a larger group for a larger change!

PS: As is evident, written based on the Indian context specifically.

- Jan 12, 2013, 01:12 PM.

72. My tryst with the Radio!

My Dad has been an all-time lover and fan of radio. I remember those days of childhood when despite TV, I used to sleep out to the songs of middle-era (neither too old nor too new) telugu songs on radio, all owing to my Dad's liking for it. I was never such a vivid listener, but when I went to Delhi for UPSC preparation my Dad gave (read it sacrificed) the Radio to me so that I can listen to news, All India Radio (AIR) news. My experience hasn't been so good with it while I was in Delhi. When I was coming from Delhi while I was packing my stuff in a bumper-hurry that was the first thing I wanted to drop off (read it get rid off) there, but my friend Preeti stopped me saying that it must have been very dear to my Dad, so suggested me to take it along with me. I usually am a very sentimental person when it comes to things and when it comes to others' things I'm all the more careful, but I don't know why I had such a special aversion for this particular thing - Dad's Radio! In fact, in hindsight I understand that it's not Dad's radio I had aversion with, but the inconvenience the old Radio put me to, while listening to news.

Anyway keeping my Dad's Radio aside, for the past 8 months I have been using the Radio that comes with HTC phone and spent half my time on it. That was my pastime, hobby and the daily activity. I used to turn it on when I started to get lost with other things, only to get more lost. My brain became half-numb because of that. Again some time in middle, my Dad repaired his radio and offered to me to listen to it. I didn't want to and gave it back to him, I said I'm fine with the news on internet, *newsonair.com* is very much there, I added. My Dad is really sweet, if there is one person who withstood both my pros and cons and my behaviour during different phases of my life, it's my Dad. I'm a Dad's girl anytime, anyday :)

Anyway, let me talk about my experience with Radio in Hyderabad. The only thing on all the 6 channels I heard - were the incessant broadcasting of songs, songs and songs. Don't know why, but until my ears pained, until my brain creaked with boredom, until they both started complaining together, I used to hear them non-stop vapourizing all the time! Apart from entertainment, useful information, tips, tidbits and trivia, the radio has a plethora of non-sense and free advice by many RJs too. You must listen to Prateeka on Red FM - "Red

FM la Prateeka thoo, fultoo bindaas! Bindaas, bindaas! Eeehaa[1]!" She has two paradoxical sides to her, when somebody comes and shares their experiences she used to say - "See look, don't tell people anything, they can take care of themselves" and then she used to get gibberish, preachy, offer a lot of free advice and finally round it off saying - "Nenem class peekthallee[2]!", I used to find a few glimpses of my own self too in her, but then we are different persons altogether. When I came back from Australia owing to my own condition, my brother a big-time fan of Prateeka (then, not now) used to refer to her and say "Akka[3]! You fit that role completely well, try being an RJ it will be a great experience for you!" He knows I can get very gibberish and talk non-stop non-sense. But then I know that I did not have the talent for being an RJ or rather that was perhaps not my cup of tea, so didn't look at that option. Incidentally Prateeka too is a UPSC aspirant.

Fine, radio is also a hub of lot of both important and unimportant information. One thing that's good with it is that it reminds of various things around in the world which we wouldn't even think of otherwise, thus motivating us to give a thought, instead of solely focusing on mechanical aspects of life. There was this funny piece of info on radio yesterday. Itseems according to a survey, the decisions taken at precisely 11:59 AM of the day, a minute before noon, are 96% accurate. I don't know what's with time and decision making. Some surveys and

---

[1]   Red FM la Prateeka thoo, fultoo bindaas! Bindaas, bindaas! Eeehaa: *(Telugu)* These are actually the lyrics of the theme song of the program hosted by RJ Prateeka; Literal meaning – "Just chill with Prateeka on Red FM channel!"

[2]   Nenem class peekthallee: *(Telugu)* "I'm not getting preachy and offering you a lecture…"

[3]   Akka: *(Telugu)* Elder sister.

research can be really funny! I stopped listening to Radio since yesterday and life is not that bad, in fact a lot more cool now!

- Jan 17, 2013, 04:56 PM.

73. Indifference!

I've had enough of mockery for a long time, because I'm surrounded by people with incompatible frequencies. Even if something is said out of best intentions, it sounds offensive because of that incompatibility. The safest thing is to ignore and not even be bothered. But fortunately or unfortunately we are tied and connected to others in this society and this society is a network and we all are dependent on each other. Imagine a system of twins, where the *karma* of every wrong-doing of one twin has to be borne by the other. And the other twin doesn't even listen and comes up and says he '*believes*' in what he knows. It is disgusting all the more when that person often says he has no faith in 'faith' and 'religion', then what is the so-called belief in his own knowledge? Is that called head-weight? And then to top it, reaching out to tell is seen as rubbing off opinions, without exercising even the slightest of remorse of looking back at the whole track-record of one's own deeds! But when people are connected, is there another alternative even, apart from conveying one's opinion? When two groups are a team, shouldn't people atleast listen to the other party if not accept things?

Unfortunately this society is exactly that! It's based on that *model of twin-paradigm*, the twins being the good and bad sections of the society. It's a web and at the current times unfortunately the results of the actions of the wrong-doers are more borne by the right-doers. And in our day-to-day life, we see people who tolerate more and more being given more burden and people who stay their own way in the name of *'individualism'* are let loose. It's like people get a free right to do whatever and the results are borne by others/everybody just because we are connected in this society. It is ignorance to say that this is my way and my side, boss we are living in a society and we cannot do or be *'whatever'*! ***Our acts have repercussions and most of the times are borne by people who tolerate***. We can't always talk about laws and what is legal and what is not and justify our actions basing on law as reference. Laws themselves sometimes are flawed since they are shaped by majority expectations and laws are not without their loopholes that are often exploited by the oversmart evil and there is no regulation whatsoever. An educated adult is expected to know what is good/bad and exercise common sense and cannot just bounce off saying he'll indulge in drugs just because otherwise his brain and body can't stand it anymore. That very idea of indulging in drugs to ease off pain is evil and it's ok as long as one is single, but again remember that twin-paradigm and then assess the impact of the drug on the twins put together. This example of usage of drugs is similar to people abusing nature and extracting resources from it in the name of development without the slightest of thought as to whether or not nature (Earth) is in a situation to bear this. The acts in the name of development do have repercussions and they are borne both by Mother Earth as also other people. Imagine the pain of your brain being fried incessantly over a year. And synchronize it with the pain of your whole nervous network going numb on and off. Dying 1000 times over and over is far better than such a living hell! Imagine the plight of Bhoodevi[1] bearing the paapa karma[2] of this 7.1 billion

---

[1]   Bhoodevi: *(Telugu)* Goddess Earth.

[2]   paapa karma: *(Telugu/Sanskrit)* The sin of evil deeds; The net effect of that sin.

population! By all means I would love to have that one year back and repair my dis-illusioned life.

Also trust me, a person who is on a wrong mission will seldom know that he is on a wrong cause and such a person is usally all the more stubborn to buy others' words. Such people might be very diligent, meticulous, dedicated and more passionate (about their mission) than you and me or normal people around. It's not the person that is bad, in such a case, but the person's intentions that are bad. Who can correct such incorrigible people who want to realize and judge everything on their own as per their own discretion, without caring about the impact of their deeds on others? Ravana (in Ramayana) is one person in history, who completely fits this example.

Let's talk about scaling and relativity in this context once. My favorite video commercial of all times is a Vodafone Newzealand mayfly-commercial with a simple and time-less message. The commercial shows a mayfly enjoying its life wholesomely oblivious to any errors in the world around. The audio of the commercial goes like this – *"A common may-fly has a life expectancy of just one day. But is he miserable about it? No! Not one bit! He swirls, he flies, he savours every bit of it. If we embrace life like may-fly does, ahhh, what a life that would be!"* A common may-fly has a life expectancy of just one day. But if it gets to know that a human-being "sleeps" for half of the day and takes cue to follow the same thing, it will end up sleeping for half of its life. One must understand one's own realm first and its resources and facilities before setting on to be part of it, surpass it or rule it.

- Jan 24, 2013, 05:04 PM.

74. Collective loneliness - the emptiness within - when tapestry and serendipity are at loggerheads!

In the current modern age where individuality is the ruling aspect of everybody's life, it is really difficult to even initiate a discussion of common use, let alone putting across your point rightly. Individuality is not at all wrong, but for the majority of the people, that's above everything else, so it gets very difficult for people to initiate change. It happens everywhere, it happens in my family, in the office spaces, public spaces, governing bodies, everywhere. It is a problem because people don't want to be told anything. Most of us are willing to fail, if it happens on our own, but deny the victory initiated/imparted/inspired by others. But there are many situations where people want others too to win/get involved for a common benefit. Say there's a colony where there's no under-ground drainage facility and for many years people rant about its absence. In fact it happened in my locality (no it's not a gated community or society or a group of apartments with some in-charge taking care of it, it's a random colony that sprouted long ago). Ideally it is GHMC on whom the onus lies, but for certain reasons it did not pay attention for a long time. The usual way is that people just keep complaining about the lack of such facility. A different possibility would be if atleast one person comes up and groups like-minded people and places a request to the relevant government body. It's not that, the people who must come up with such an initiative are different, unique or have a better understanding of the society. It's just that they are more pro-active in expressing their needs and getting them fulfilled. It is that pro-activeness which takes them further to gain a better understanding. I, despite my good credentials and social standing, have never been so pro-active but I'm sure many people in our society, including illiterates, are actually more pro-active in getting their needs fulfilled and hence are helping society too in the long run at a macro-scale. In fact it's not education, money, power etc that brings change (though they are easier and the most direct weapons), it's the willingness of a group of people to work for change that actually brings in change. *But then big changes happen only when such good intentions and powerful resources come together and that's why change takes time* - to get the tangible and non-tangible resources together. This is also why many societies despite great resources don't develop for one reason that they don't have such good intentions/good leaders.

Actually our age has become too cynical and complacent to question the status-quo, more so because we do not want to take the efforts of dealing with people in the society. We are reluctant to communicate with people, develop bonding and we just don't care where we are heading to. We are ok to fail, but we just don't fail as individuals, we fail as families, in the long-run we fail as societies and then we fail as a world. We have no clue where this *individuality tangent* is going to take us and make us land. We just don't know or are we already on that tangential path? But then, we the whole mankind cannot choose to be on the same path forever. We only assume that we are in the course of betterment and development, but a detailed account of my study has proved otherwise, that as per nature's discretion we are actually on a path of deterioration since the so-called development of man was at the cost of abusing nature. There is always somebody out there who is affected by our collective deeds and they are bound to take action. And that is regulation - the cosmic destroyers do it for us.

Let's talk about the evolution of this creation. Consider, for instance, the following model for cosmic cycles as laid out by *Swami Sri Yukteswar Giri.*

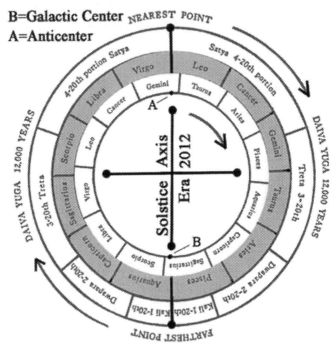

Fig 6 – Sri Yukteswar's Yuga Model, adjusted

(This image is used with permission from Mr. John Major Jenkins. This image, as the caption states, is "adjusted" from Sri Yukteswar's original diagram. Jenkins has added the Galactic Center and Anticenter points (A and B), which Yukteswar's model doesn't depict, and he had also shifted the timing of the end of descending Kali Yuga to the galactic alignment position circa 2012 AD. This follows from his analysis of Sri Yukteswar's writings in light of Jenkins' 2012 alignment thesis, and is published in his 2002 book – "Galactic Alignment". The argument is also

here: http://alignment2012.com/polar-to-solar.html. It disagrees with Yukteswar's timing for the end of descending Kali Yuga (which, Jenkins says, Sri Yukteswar has derived from Aryabhata). For more information, refer to Jenkins' 2002 book Galactic Alignment [Inner Traditions International])

As per Hinduism, virtue of mankind on earth varies in a descending order as we progress forward in time through the cycle of four Yugas - Satya Yuga, Treta Yuga, Dwapara Yuga and Kali Yuga. Through my Realization process, I have come to know another factor that supports this theory – As we traverse through the Yugas in the descending cycle, we are moving away from the Cosmic Source (The centre of our Universe... narrowing it down much further, the centre of our Galaxy, in scientific terms). At the two points of Precession of Equinoxes this alignment is inversed. So, when we are in a diametrically opposite alignment with the Galactic Centre and are in a repulsive mode, the Precession of Equinoxes sets us right by thrusting us towards the Cosmic Source... aligning us with the Cosmic Source. The vice versa happens at the other point of the double conical Precession.

So, it appears as though every age is destined to be of certain pre-defined virtue and hence that is the reason why people behave accordingly, good or bad. But the creator at best has a script and we the creation are spawning further evolution and shaping our own destiny. It's a two-way process, a mutual give and take, similar to the relationship between a Project Manager and his team members. We are a team...we are on a Project... of creating and being part of this Universe and evolving along with it! ***Both the creator and the creation play an equal and important role in shaping the destiny***. While the Creator starts with a fate - the tapestry, the Creation through serendipity unfolds its destiny and hence the fate for further course of evolution. It is when this tapestry and serendipity are at complete conflict that we perceive a lack of collective consciousness in the society - the collective loneliness.

- Jan 25, 2013, 09:44 PM.

75. God is in the details!

The majority of the humanity today mocks at the idea of God, the collective consciousness of the society and His existence. The most powerful section of the society is using and exploiting the less powerful in an unleashed fashion and there is neither respite nor remorse while they are abusing nature. In fact it is the 'freedom' given to him to enrich his life with the given resources that man is completely abusing. The God-Man-Devil concept says that Man unguided becomes Devil periodically and God exerts His power and presence time and again to steer the course of evolution in the right direction, rejuvenating the Man (the Humanity) to a better self, restoring the harmony and balance of nature.

Many spiritual gurus have indicated that time is nearing for the return of the divine feminine, re-establishing *Dharma*, giving the world a rare treasure of wisdom hidden from mankind over the ages, to enlighten them and avoid an apocalypse at the conjunction of two yugas (ascending and descending Kali Yugas) as prophesized before. Gods apparently exercise a lot of patience and complete detachment while understanding meticulously the response of Their creation to 'The Cosmic Plan' to take a call. God is truly in the details around us.

- Jan 27, 2013, 12:05 AM.

76. Cleaning!

Let's say an uncovered book shelf filled with books full of dust needs to be cleaned. The best way is to take a dusting cloth, dust each and every book, clean the shelves and then arrange the books. Another way is to use an appropriate vacuum cleaner that can suck the dust neatly. Older folks who have never seen a vacuum cleaner at work might see that process as magic. But if younger folks think that cleaning the book shelf, just means cleaning the shelves, then that's not even believing/disbelieving in magic. It actually implies that they do not understand either the process of cleaning or the harm caused by the dust lying around. Or that they just want to live with the superficial process of cleaning and breathe the dust continuously. One can get rid of dust only by dusting it off, there's no other way. One can get rid of debt only by clearing it off. Even debt wavering also means that one has to deal with the process of getting it wavered. Social debt is no different *(Remember the post – Social Debt, its burden and our reluctance?)*. Nothing happens automatically.

I'm reminded of the Telugu movie *Murari* when I talk of social debt. In that movie, the family has a curse being borne by its generations over time, at one point of which, the hero was supposed to take its effect. His grandmother takes the curse through some rituals, but that's not sans the process of the protagonist bearing the effect of that transformation of passing the curse from him to his granny.

Same is the case with social debt. We all need a saviour. We have done our acts – merits or sins. That is why we talk about end of the world, apocalypse and Gods. Humanity does it, not really in anticipation of death but it does so because it sub-consciously believes and expects that some God, a saviour, WILL save them, merely because we all have heard the story of Jesus. But then history does not always repeat and *the equation of social debt varies over time* and so will the proccess of reducing the impact of our collective deeds, the so-called *bad karma*. Even if some saviour is going to bear the weight, the humanity has to bear at least the process of that transformation.

Sometimes, looking at the greed of humanity, which is not even ready to bear that simple process of transformation, assuming that getting rid of karma is such an easy process as if it can jerk it off by whiffing it off, I wonder if the humanity has accredited for itself enough merit and worth to be saved. So we just want to do whatever we choose to do according to our own mindsets and knowledge, but at the end of the day, we want somebody else to bear the weight of our actions and we simply sit back and relax and see that process as if we are watching a movie??? No! Things just don't work that way! The humanity HAS to bear the process of transformation. The universe is expanding every minute. If the whole universe is ascending to a different frequency, can we the humanity choose to stay at an incompatible frequency and yet inhabit it? How then, can we be a part of it - *the evolving universe*? When a family grows, the children grow and so do the parents, they get older. Naturally, there's always a conflict in the thinking process of the two generations. If the children want to continue staying at home, the children either need to change their mindset so as to adjust with the parents or should go independent by moving out of home. Not changing the mindset and yet staying home is completely out of choice, because it is the parents who made and built the home over the years, not the children. It goes without saying that parents are always in the inherent process of adjusting with their children and sometimes even harsh regulation is part of that adjustment because without weeding out the bad ideas and intentions, one can never make way for better things. Only those children who can take that process of transformation stay, the rest tend to leave.

- Feb 04, 2013, 12:10 AM.

77. The daughters of Lord Shiva!

I knew that Lord Shiva has two daughters -Manasa Devi and Jyoti. Or even three daughters if we include Tara (Mandodari), different versions of Ramayana seem to have different stories about Tara's birth and parentage. But I never heard about Ashok Sundari until I bumped into *Har Har Mahadev* serial. Anyway, of the four daughters that we now know, I think Manasa is the most abandoned and tormented of all. I don't know why but ever since my childhood I was fascinated by this name Manasa, in fact at an age when I've not even heard that name. I guess when I was some 8 or 9, this was the name I architected and came up myself when our English Teacher asked us to write letters. I used to use these two imaginary names and go on and on this way- *Dear Manasa... Dear Nikhil... How are you?* and then write so many stories beginning with Kushala Prashnalu[1], as if I knew these two people for eternity. The names were indeed very dear to me and I used to obsess about this fact that I came up with these two brand new names, people have never heard of!

---

[1] Kushala prashnalu: *(Telugu)* Salutations; Checking about the well-being of the other party through questions.

Coincidentally, much to my amazement, my paternal grand father Ramaiah *garu* (a term used as a suffix for names in Telugu to indicate respect) used to call me Manasa instead of Mamata - So cool :-) - Itseems his mouth did not help him pronounce my name well, but then I thought it was easier to pronounce Mamata than to pronounce Manasa! But people used to complain that the repetitive syllables in my name actually made pronunciation not-so-easy! Anyway, getting back to Manasa, until this North Indian Trip wherein we visited three goddessess - Manasa Devi on one side and Chandi Devi, Anjana Devi on the other side of Haridwar - their temples elevated on three hills, I didn't know that Manasa Devi is the serpent goddess, daughter of Lord Shiva, worshipped more in North India oblivious to south and specifically worshipped by left hand. Apparently, that's a curse perhaps.

- *Feb 06, 2013, 04:05 PM.*

78. The mad search for a date!

Yes, there is always this mad search for THE DATE! The date when something unusual is expected to happen, name it apocalypse, the return of the Gods, the end of the world as we know it or just the beginning of an age. Why? Why is the humanity after a date? It's been happening over a long time, from the beginning of 20th century, more often as compared to previous centuries perhaps, where a bunch of prophesizers have been prophesizing some random dates and the prophecies going wrong every time and it all becoming a

'Baabooy Puli[1]' story. People now are so dis-illusioned with God that if somebody comes forward and says that God is going to appear tomorrow, most of them will come up saying – *"Ok! So what? What's in it for me? What will I be gaining? How is it of any interest to me?"* like any typical greedy selfish individual too much caught up in life would ask.

What is this mankind exactly in search of? Is it for our real identity, the Self, our inheritance, our evolution or are we in search of our future? Or is this just another business area that people want to make money upon? Equality (between the genders), more in the spirit of the word, than in letter, makes life so happy. If there is any *avatar* this time, I'd by all means believe that it will be to assert just that! That's purely my instincts at play because that is one major problem affecting the fabric of the society during the current times and avatars of Gods most of the times are supposedly taken to address the burning issues of any given time.

One thing, though slightly out of context, I'd like to touch upon is, how the information is passed across ages through evolution. I mused about it some time ago in one of my posts (*Social Debt, its burden and our reluctance*), but missed writing about the most important media used to pass information - the DNA - the perfect fit for Sustainable media for Sustainable

---

[1]   Baaboy Puli: *(Telugu)* Literally, it's a scared response on seeing a tiger. This is the title of one of the famous Telugu short stories whose story goes like this – a father puts a young boy to some work of herding sheep in the woods, in the intention of discipling him, but the son is not so interested. So in order to get rid of the work, the boy shouts that there is a tiger in the woods and calls out his father and others busy with work. He does this pretention a couple of times. This time a tiger comes for real, but when the boy shouts out for help, the father does not come for son's rescue assuming he is putting up the act for the n'th time again!

information! DNA in fact is the most sophisticated God-given means of carrying information and plays a crucial function in phylo-genetic memory, in sustaining intellect over the vast journey of time. The Tamil-dubbed Telugu movie "Seventh Sense" depicts this concept marvellously.

DNA has a mythological analogy – the *Kundalini Shakti* of Goddess Jyoti – The goddess of Aphrodite – The Venus…

- Feb 08, 2013, 12:51 AM.

79. For and against the death penalty!

Today's article in 'The Hindu' - "Sentenced to a life full of nothing" triggers this post! The article describes an incident based on an Argentinian movie in which a woman is raped and murdered by her husband's friend. The investigators fail to zero in on the culprit and hence he is not bought to book initially. But the husband gets to crack the mystery and puts his friend in his backyard subjecting him to "the vacuum of nothingness in life" for years until he is dead. The writer argues that this kind of punishment is more effective than death itself.

After that horrendous incident of Delhi-rape of 23-year-old *(now known to the world as Nirbhaya incident)*, there has been a lot of public debate in India on what kind of punishment needs to be given to the culprits and specifically if death penalty should or should not be given. After about 2 months of incident, I see that the scales more tilt towards *"No death Penalty"* and that seems to be the majority view point (from the point of intelligentsia, not from a layman's point of view). But I differ.

246

Fine, people say that death penalty is not a panacea to this problem, but the debate ends there in the public front. People really do not have any clarity on what should the punishment be, if not death sentence. A vague idea is that it must be a long-term punishment tagged with chemical castration. That indeed does sound logical, BUT I feel we the citizens (mainly the mass media and NGOs) have NOT succeeded in establishing and sending across this view-point to the right corners as much as we did in opposing the death penalty. And that's really sad! The net result seems to be that, both the law and the public at large, at the end of the day, unintentionally save the culprits rather than bringing them to book appropriately. Leaving the public view aside and visiting the bureaucracy - *Justice Verma Committee's* work is indeed laudable.

As I said, I differ from the majority view-point. I write down my case here - why I really sense the need for death penalty *at this juncture* "in India" for "horrendous" rape cases in case they do fall under the *'rarest of rare'* category at all! Not all rape cases expose the weakness of the Indian system to a similar extent - a gang rape in broad-day light in public sends a message loud and clear that there is no 'minimal' security for women in a country that boasts to be the largest democracy of the world. By that I mean, culprits of certain category rape cases do deserve death penalty and this must NOT be generalized. I strongly feel that the public debate without drawing any boundaries and just going ga-ga about "Rape cases and Death Penalty" generalizing both the problem and the solution is such a waste of time for everybody, doing more harm than good by diverting the problem and deteriorating the solution. Subjectivity NEEDS to be asserted in this specific case and that subjectivity is that - How weak is the basic security mechanism for women in India and to what extent are their basic rights ensured in

India? Kindly it's not the right to life of a culprit, right against detention, right to be defended and finally definitely not the length and breadth of the implications of death penalty.

Firstly, the crime under focus as a whole - RAPE - is very rampant in India currently and its occurrence is not sparse. When a crime is rampant, the priority is not to be bothered about how to bring about a change in the mind-sets of culprits and reform them, but actually put a check to the incidence of the crime rate. The number of rape-cases is pretty high and that must be brought down by all means, ideally to **zero**! In such a case, the justice being merely *'punitive'* is not sufficient, it's got to be *'preventive'*. Secondly, is there a way that the punishment can be made harsher immediately - do we have the means? This requires a drastic change in the judicial and police machinery of India and can that be brought about immediately? Thirdly, most of the culprits in such cases fall under that category who do not just mind whiling away their entire life in jail for the bargain of food and shelter they get. Is life imprisonment even a punishment for such people? The prisons in India these days apparently have become mere shelters feeding food three times a day to culprits who hardly toil and exert themselves to earn that.

The third factor needs to be dealt a bit more in detail. Let's consider that case where freedom fighters during freedom struggle were imprisoned by British. Then that's a real punishment for them even if they were merely locked within four walls. Because here are people with some motto in life with a burning zeal to do something and locking them up totally defies their cause not allowing them to fulfill their mission. But on the other hand, most of the rape culprits today are just a lazy lot and are we punishing them by defying some apparent cause of theirs by locking up in a prison??? I really doubt! To people who have no morale and the ability to introspect, staying in prison is hardly a punishment. They might as well group-up with fellow prisoners, boss the weak ones and happily while away their life. What is *'languishing'* to 'people with sense', is just *'whiling away time and life'* for such heart-less, sense-less and zeal-less rogues. Do you see the point? Even if chemical castration is introduced, does that impede other wanna-be culprits? In some cases, only the fear of losing life can serve as an alarm bell impeding and dissuading others from repeating that crime. In a society/group which is culturally evolved, even merely locking the culprits might become a punishment. (A disclaimer though is that I have not seen any culturally evolved societies in the world as yet. What I have on my mind when I say this is – let's say a tribe in some corner of the world which has set its own laws.) But for a group to whom doing no work, pursuing nothing in life is not a big deal, merely being locked up shall never be a punishment. Let's say the rapist is a business magnet and has raped his maid within four walls - there he is not exploiting the weakness of the society as a whole, he is exploiting another human being through his power, in such a case locking him up (life imprisonment) will actually serve the cause of punishing him.

Also, the second factor (means to make imprisonment more stringent) is something that shall not be dealt by legal bureaucracy studies and committe reports in detail because that means they got to admit that the existing punishing system is weak and flawed. It involves questioning the status-quo quite brutally and it's possible that it could be an impediment for a government servant to bring out the facts. It will be more sensible if the public debate highlights and exposes this.

The definition of punishment is very subjective and depends on many factors - the incidence of crime, the outlook of life in that region, how are we punishing the culprits by implementing that punishment, does that punishment impede enough other tentative culprits from repeating the crime. I'm sure Justice Verma Committee might have looked into this and more (I've not gone through their report) but still I have a problem with the range of the problem being stretched there. Unfortunately, some intelligentsia in India is arguing for marital rape too to be included in the scope of the problem to rope in a robust set of laws as a solution to the burning problem of rape. I'm afraid, including marital rape will hamper justice to other category (which I call the mainstream) of cases. In a country where domestic violence and dowry cases are not dealt properly to this day, I really doubt if it's possible for the police to even arrive at the basic cognizance of marital rape (that purely happens within four walls). I'd earnestly wish that this case NOT be diluted by broadening of the problem with marital rape and comparison with law and order situation of a foreign country as done in that article in the beginning.

- Feb 09, 2013, 09:31 PM.

Note left by Lakshmi Suma:

I completely agree that a punishment should be such that the fear of it should drive away any thoughts of committing the crime in the minds of the perpetrators.

- Feb 10, 2013, 08:47 PM.

80. 3G Gods continued...

I have been realizing some stories these days on the children of the divine couple - Lord Shiva and Goddess Shakti. Apparently Goddess Jyoti is the love interest of Lord Manikanta. There's another story which speaks of Goddess Manasa as the love interest of Lord Ganesha. So, while we the humanity has been aware of the 2G Gods alone and praying them, the 3G Gods have already grown old enough to get married!

- Feb 12, 2013, 12:58 PM.

81. Whole as a sum of parts!!!

"These are my interests – so what?" was the post where the definition of a generic system fell in place - *"A system is a whole of parts!"* There this definition was used to understand the process of evolution. I have always been tempted to look at the evolution of life, when I talk of evolution. And when I say *"evolution of life"* I'm not really referring here to the evolution of the humanity as a whole or its journey but more to the process of biological evolution of life as a whole on this planet. It goes without saying that it took ages for life to evolve from the *cellular level - invertebrates - vertebrates - homosapiens* apart from a lot of other evolution of that of earth itself, geographically, to a state of varied features as it is today and its huge gamut of flora and fauna. But of all this evolution, human being assumes the highest seat because he is the seat of intellect and hence naturally assumes the role of protecting/exploiting/evolving along with the nature. The human body itself is a classic example of evolution and the way its organs and constituents effectively co-ordinate with each other carrying on their respective functionality under the supervision of human

brain did not come up all of a sudden on some fine sunday morning! It took some time, in fact quite a time. And the evolution of thought and consciousness is a different stream altogether apart from the biological evolution per se. Take the brain mechanism of an octopus for instance whose nervous system is pretty complex, only part of which is localized in its brain, the neuron functionality is in fact diffused across its body. Understanding the stark difference between the diffused neuron functionality and highly centralized and networked human brain functionality as a result of gradual transition is just the tip of iceberg of unraveling the mystery and beauty of evolution. If I understand it right, humans are the rarest of rare species, apart from some other animal species, that possess the luck and dignity of having a mind, not just brain!

When children err, parents at the max, warn and regulate them, but do not kill them in the hope that they can have more children later! Because life is precious and there is that sense of belonging, for they are part of their very own blood and also for all the hard work they put in, to raise them to the stage they are today! The same goes with the much hyped concept of "*Yugantham*[1] - *Apocalypse*" too. It's not easy for Gods too to let go of this evolution so easily, which they silently created, sustained and monitored all the while and asserting their presence only once in a while. They can't keep telling the humanity every moment that they are very much there for us and cannot co-inhabit with the humanity for they too have their own work just like us and belong to a different plane of existence. They too try every possible way to protect this evolution and take it to a higher and better possibility because if they let go of this evolution they will have to bear this burden of disposing off their accomplishments, starting from scratch again, yet with no guarantee that it would evolve to as good/bad a stage

---

[1]   Yugantham: *(Telugu)* The end of a Yuga (Age; Era; Eon as per context)

it is at today! That is the very purpose of why Gods take *Avatars* with a view of saving the humanity and steering its course. That is also the reason why the *sequence of Avatars*[1] too is very much in line with the course of human evolution, happening on a need-basis, depending on the demands of the evolution of human consciousness along with the requirements of earth. I see that the concept of worshipping God is to inculcate the awareness of a higher power, ***imparting genuine accountability***, not any dogma towards the same so as to enrich one's own life. The accountability stems from the fact that we are deriving certain resources from that power. One-sided accountability merely due to power is meaningless otherwise. It is an accountability as a result of a responsibility fulfilled by that higher power. If man does not understand this, then he is inviting his own downfall.

We, the humanity are only a part of God. God is one and He has split Himself/Herself into Trinity to perform different roles in the course of His own evolution. We are just a derived class of that Trinity (if you appreciate that software OOPS jargon ;-)). When God has to assert Himself/Herself/Itself, the humanity and multiple forms of God, rise to the challenge, transcending into one, the Absolute Consciousness. ***The whole is always greater than the sum of its parts.***

- Feb 15, 2013, 06:35 PM.

---

[1] Sequence of Avatars: As per Hindu Mythology, there have been 9 avatars so far. They are (i) Matsyavatar (The Fish) (ii) Koormavatar (The Tortoise) (iii) Varahavatar (The Boar) (iv) Narasimhavatar (The Human-Lion) (v) Vamanavatar (The Dwarf) (vi) Parasuramavatar (The warrior with axe) (vii) Ramavatar (The perfect man in Treta Yuga, Rama, King of Ayodhya) (viii) Krishnavatar (Krishna of Dwapara Yuga, the Divine Statesman) (ix) Buddha (The man who sacrificed pleasures and wealth in search of enlightenment) (x) Kalki (This avatar has not happened yet but only a prediction stemmed from man's awareness).

82. The haunted!

We have seen in the post, "*The goal of the whole and the return of Gods*" that the elderly Gods have sent Lord Manikanta and Lord Ganesha to gather information for effective implementation of "Precession of Equinoxes". But Ganesha was caught up somewhere in the cosmos while the Gods wanted him on earth to carry on the task. The reality is that, due to some mishap, Ganesha was heavily possessed and haunted by Sun God Aryaman, who set on to earth to acquire Goddess Jyoti. But it was Muruga (Skanda) who was on earth in the disguise of his sister Jyoti, to save her. Because of the haunting, Ganesha was after Skanda and had to heavily take the negative impact. Apparently Jyoti was also feeling the heat of this impact. Lord Shiva Himself then comes to the rescue of His children - the brother-sister duo of Skanda-Jyoti, makes Ganesha realize that he was indeed being haunted by Aryaman. It is Lord Shiva who fights out Aryaman to save the Earth from a possible giant impact. The Chelyabinsk meteorite impact which the earth narrowly escaped on Feb 15, 2013 was exactly a result of this event.

- *Feb 17, 2013, 10:27 PM.*

83. One has to work on the relationship, if the relationship has to work

Isn't that such a simple piece of known information? Ever since I wrote the post "*For and against the death penalty*", I wanted to talk about marital rape. When I first heard this term as a teen, it felt so strange, I mean I thought why does it even happen?

Basically, it's common knowledge that a man and a woman for the opposite genders they are, have different perceptions of and expectations from sex. Apart from the love between the couple, women 'usually' require communication and foreplay to be turned on, while men 'usually' require a beautiful woman or just plain their-own-biological-urge to turn them on. Ok, I was only talking about turn-ons, but then there is something called discretion which human beings have (and animals don't) which is used to decide whether to act upon such a turn-on. That said, the biological mechanism of men is so built that it is one of their primary needs while women do not sense the same urge and this is very much part of the in-built balance mechanism of nature to keep a check on population-explosion. While both men and women, adult and healthy, can manage to stay celibate for years when needed, women 'usually' can stay so without any qualms owing to their biological characteristics. There is this Telugu movie Rudraveena in which some uneducated men who badly gave in to alcoholism approach their wives after consuming alcohol when they have not taken care of their wives or families for weeks, but just approach them for sex at the end of the day. Those men do not earn for the family putting their families in poverty and putting the burden of leading the family on their wives. I perceive especially such kind of sex to be animal sex when men expect their wives to be ready and prepared for the act when they do not spare as much as a word or a minute of attention for days together. But that, astonishingly, sounds perfectly fine for the men! Don't assume that it is fine for just those alcoholic uneducated men, it's just fine for most of the men that way itseems. Surveys and statistics indicate that many women complain that their partners would be perfectly ready for the act when they themselves are not, because for days they have never given them the attention, on how they dressed up or on how much they stressed out to keep the house intact despite their work at office or on what all things had to be taken care of towards children. And then, don't even talk about why long-distance relationships most often fail, because this equation of communication-physical intimacy never works out. It goes without saying that seeing each other periodically is the basic essence of all sorts of communication. I can't agree more on the *'Stranger effect'* often cited in the top list of problems discussed in long-distance relationships.

While women seem to understand the basic priority of men (most of the women are anxious about how they look and atleast try, if not succeed, to stay in shape more to appeal to their partners than to safeguard their own health), it is really strange why men (on an average) don't get the basic priority of women - communication - right, despite so much of human evolution across this vast span of time. Are men so insensitive to the needs of women???

Honestly, normal rape makes more sense to me than marital rape! That a married man does not take the effort of having a word with his partner and proceeds to have sex, just like a stranger, sounds completely barbaric! I wonder if their brains are all-shut when they assume that their wives will be prepared to sleep with them while on the contrary the women do not even have the basic consent, naturally for all the ill-treatment and abandonment (I have a particular distaste towards this term) meted out to them.

Most importantly, when one's partner cannot be taken for granted even after years of staying together, imagine the plight of young people who have not even materialized their relationship in the first place and do not get these gender-differences and dynamics right. This problem is more rampant in countries like India where sex-education is inadequate or even absent and people are not rightly sensitized towards the needs of opposite gender. *"Why men don't listen and women can't read maps"* and *"I married you!"* are two books I came across, that discuss these issues in simple, eloquent yet in both scientific and religious terms.

- Mar 04, 2013, 11:36 PM.

84. Exhaustion of hypocrisy!

I'm completely exhausted...of my brain power and emotional strength. But, that is not acceptable of me. It's because when things are completely fine, there are certain goals we set for ourselves. And it's very difficult to let go of them. When life's catastrophes hit us, we are completely depleted of our resources, yet to continue this journey in this competitive world, we are expected to be better than ourselves of yesterday. Even trying to lower expectations on one's own self does not help, because that by itself is a lot of work. Initially, I had some expectations from others...I realize eventually. It's not that I explicitly expect somebody to do something. I see that I'm suffering in silence and pain waiting upon something to happen and inadvertently that something lies in others' domain of action. When those others don't respond, I consciously work on finding an alternative path that does not involve action from others and also work on seeing happiness in that alternative path. But then I can't succeed every time. We human beings can't stay like lonely animals in this society, we are connected and trying to make dependence on others zero is as good as dying. Yes, how long can one stay happy and derive stability from one's own self and work?

There's no luxury of even trying to share one's problems with others in this society, especially when the problems are unique and people who are knowledgeable and can offer some advice and help on how to tackle the problem are rare. Because, most of the times, being able to narrate the problem in definable terms is equivalent to half of the problem solved. And most of the times, people I'm related to, are themselves busy with their own work and problems, so there's no expecting any solace from them, not even the comfort of striking a healthy conversation, even when I myself am ready to divulge my side of the story. It's true that they have their problems, but it's sad to note that they don't realize that there is something called *'threshold'* and pushing a person beyond that *'knowingly'* just because they exerted themselves out, because they chose to fight their daemons all on their own, is so unkind. I feel this society is starving itself with one problem of *'hypocrisy'* distancing itself of a decent progress. We are happy to keep the problem all to ourselves and showcase to the society that everything is just fine! But sadly not all problems can be tackled all alone! Forget about the society, we distance ourselves even from our family and loved ones and go about solving the problems on one's own. But we don't realize that we are not only harming ourselves, but also harming the society by passing the results of such individual actions that do not necessarily cater to the requirements of the society. We are actually shaping the society in *one-many-one fashion*, our individual actions do have far reaching implications and those far reaching implications after having traveled far enough and impacting others also hit us back someday! It's sad to see that people don't understand the joy of sharing problems with others and solving them and growing together. Do we think that family and friends are there just to acknowledge our accomplishments and not help in case of failures and down-phases? Do we go out and meet people only when we are in a *'perfect'* state and say we are doing great?

I really pity this hypocritical society composed of people full of themselves leading their lives based on their own assumptions and also pity myself for having to be part of it and sustain my life in just that hypocrite fashion.

On a different note, my curiosity on the process of 'ascension' has landed me up into a site on *star-seeds* which talks about their problems in integrating with humanity. I can't imagine their plight who get caught between multiple births and multiple realms, when we have problems having to deal with a single existence. God! Why did He make this earth such an ungodly place to live??? Isn't letting this life grow and sustain more and more when there are not enough resources, denying the people alive of a decent existence?

- Mar 09, 2013, 08:41 PM.

85. Thoughtful Art!

I have come across this article in *The Hindu* last year *(Title: "Dancing to life's Thillana", Dated: Nov 16, 2012; Friday Review, AP edition)* wherein dancer *Deepika Reddy* talks to news-writer *Vishnupriya* on the importance of being a *"Thinking Dancer"*. Thinking Dancer! That's such a nice term and beckons the inseparable nature of Art and Intellect. When I think about this, the first thing that comes to my mind is a scene in the Telugu movie Swarna Kamalam[1] which emphasizes the importance of "Bhava Prakatana[2]" in dance. Also the article cited elaborates on how an art form such as dance gets moulded when blended with

---

[1]   Swarna Kamalam: *(Telugu movie title)* Golden Lotus.
[2]   Bhava Prakatana: *(Telugu)* Expression of feeling.

thought. Though I'm writing it explicitly here, it's an inherent and implicit understanding that *Art* without *Thought* does not bring about the aesthetic and artistic sense of the art.

Thought! Such a powerful thing! Our old Telugu movies portray how people translated thought into action by the sheer strength of their will. I'm talking about such instances in movies like *Jagadeeka Veeruni Katha*[1] where Lord Indra tests the protagonist played by actor Nandamuri Taraka Ramarao (NTR) to distinguish between his wives and his mother and NTR appeals to the women convincingly so that the women in disguise shed their false appearances to assume their actual identities. It's as though the power of thought was tied to the strength of one's virtue. Otherwise, wouldn't it be such a disaster if all sort of people invoke their thoughts into action? Also recently we all have been hearing about the spate of theories talking about how all human thought is indeed connected and how certain meters measuring that strength have spiked up during events of importance and calamities suggesting an affirmative of collective thought and emotion. Just take a look at this ambition at the end of one of the related articles on internet - *"Perhaps, everyone on Earth will be needed someday to combine their thought power to divert an asteroid from crashing into Earth"*. Yeah movies like Inception throw light on how ambitious man can get!

Anyway, I'm not an artist in any sense, so I have ended up writing more on thought even when trying to talk about thoughtful art. Not that I'm so thoughtful, just that I'm not an artist.

- Mar 12, 2013, 05:08 PM.

---

[1]   Jagadeeka Veeruni Katha: *(Telugu movie title)* The story of the courageous world-winning warrior.

86. The aftermath of captivity

I've written about something of this sort before in the post – *The Hierarchy of Need*. It's specifically about how people feel when they are held hostage for a period of time and then released all of a sudden. It's about the gamut of emotions they undergo, it's about how they make a comeback and start merging into the usual walk of life, usual run of things and the usual society. Firstly imagine their state in the last days of captivity when they get to know that they are being released. And then the big day, when they are actually released! How do they actually feel? Stockholm syndrome[1] is one of the things cited to occur during the initial phases, but it's not so common. The first of the things is to fight out the feeling - "Why me? Why had I been held hostage?" Once having come to terms with it - the fact that they have been held hostage anyway, the next thing is to arrive at the first set of things to do, to merge with the reality of life and its expectations! Once these phases are over, there's a real bliss of sorts, for how much ever short span it is, the bliss that life is finally back! Life and the life in it (if that has to be worded out in pure telugu, it is – *jeevitham, daaniloo jeevam*) seeps in gradually, people then really understand the worth of life, something so unappreciated by the vast majority of people, the happiness of living it out peacefully, the peace of being able to doze off to bed and wake up happily to a new day with hope. Of all, the sigh of relief that "The Ordeal is over!" can really be unparallelled. I'm getting to understand it...now! Yayy...to my understanding!!!

- *Mar 13, 2013, 11:43 PM.*

---

[1]   Stockholm Syndrome: Wikipedia defines Stockholm Syndrome as "a psychological phenomenon in which hostages express empathy and sympathy and have positive feelings toward their captors, sometimes to the point of defending and identifying with them".

87. Energy Centres

Before delving into the real topic, here's a tidbit. Just to make you ready for a very long and possibly a boring read too. There was this valedictory function going on in JNTU (the campus in which I did my Engineering) and each stream has its own name for the occasion. There were nice names such as Sthapathya[1] (Civil Engineering), Connoissance (Mechanical Engineering), CSE's (Computer Sceince Engineering) was Quest and ECE's (Electronics and Communications Engineering) was Spoorthi[2]. While Quest has a meaningful tagline - *'Quench your tech savvy thirst'*, Spoorthi's tagline sounded tad too big-worded - *'Presenting the future as Past'*. Too bad, I don't remember if the tagline is same when I studied ECE there. Anyway now into the topic - Energy Centres!

Despite coming across counterparts of yoga such as pranic healing, art of living courses etc over the years, I've never paid much attention to the energy centres - *the Chakras*. This post is an attempt to understand them a bit more in detail. Here's a basic demonstration of the seven Chakras signifying the Kundalini Shakti[3].

---

[1]   Sthapathya: *(Telugu)* Establishment.

[2]   Spoorthi: *(Telugu)* Inspiration.

[3]   Kundalini Shakti: *(Sanskrit/Hindi/Telugu)* <u>Literary Meaning:</u> The corporeal indwelling spiritual energy lying dormantly coiled at the base of the spine, that can be *awakened* in order to purify the subtle system and bestow upon the 'seeker of Truth' the state of Yoga, Union with the Divine, the Source. The Yogic philosophy describes it as a form of feminine Shakti or sleeping serpent. <u>Background:</u> We are usually aware of only body and mind, but human body harnesses and perpetuates on the *Spiritual Energy* that flows through the 7 *Energy Centres (Chakras)* connected across the spine.

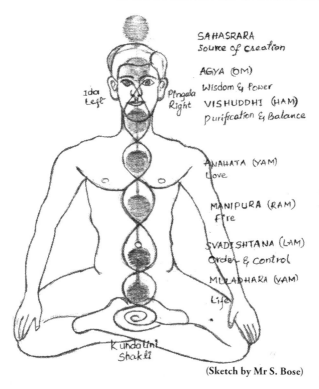

SAHASRARA
Source of creation

AGYA (OM)
Wisdom & Power

VISHUDDHI (HAM)
purification & Balance

ANAHATA (YAM)
Love

MANIPURA (RAM)
Fire

SVADISHTANA (LAM)
Order & Control

MULADHARA (VAM)
Life

Ida
Left

Pingala
Right

Kundalini
Shakti

(Sketch by Mr S. Bose)

Fig 7 – Kundalini and Energy Centres

These chakras are basically categorized into two groups - Base or lower chakras and higher chakras. It is said that, for a proper spiritual transformation to take place, all these chakras have to be appropriately activated. While, which chakras need more exertion to be activated depends on the individual calling (genetic makeup and the merit accumulated over the previous births, interestingly people of different sun-signs are prone to have certain chakras more prone itseems), it more importantly depends on what point of the odyssey, one's soul is at, in its own journey of transformation. This activation of chakras is always prescribed to be done under the guidance of a guru.

In order to understand this more, the human body is treated as a light body with a stream of energy entering and exiting it. As with any other case, the energy conservation principles hold good here. It means that there is a definite amount of energy available for all the seven chakras to be activated and it has to be distributed or rather *'channeled'* appropriately. The *'energy channeling'* is of utmost importance here to receive a proper experience. In theory, different paths are prescribed - the *Self-Realization* path (through Sahaja Yoga, Samadhi etc), the *Sexual Alchemy* path and many other methods as part of day-to-day Yogasanas and Pranayama (the *gradual* path). I'll only talk about the first path* here.

There are two issues here. *First thing* - when a person focuses on lower chakras alone or rather uses all the energy on exerting the lower chakras, he/she runs the risk of being stuck in the lower chakras for a very long time unless there is some kind of external guidance/help (the divine intervention of sorts!). It's because this is not a linear ascending/descending process where one chakra gets activated after the other and it's not the case that absolutely no work is required on the lower chakras once we move on to a higher chakra. Additional energy gets generated and even destroyed in the process. *Second thing* - the beauty or fortune of having the higher chakras activated earlier is that, the lower chakras can be taken care of easily, in fact the higher chakras bestow that capacity, they just take care of the lower chakras, they just know how the job needs to be done. Ideally, an ascending path is suggested, but that's not the only way possible.

In order to tweak from the first scenario to the second scenario, the energy channeling techniques need to be used. The energy channeling can be as simple a process as consciously focusing on NOT to use the energy at a specific time to exert a specific chakra so that the energy naturally flows to the other chakras. There can be other means, which I'm not aware of. The second scenario implies accepting a lot of pain in the initial phases. It's basically building up resilience. Another way of looking at it is, not to surrender to the call of hormones. I came across an episode (from LifeOK's Har Har Mahadev serial) which shows how Lord Indra pits the hormones of Lord Skanda against himself while he was on his way to be Sena Nayaka[1] of Gods. It's basically pitting *you* against *your* own self, *you* working out for *your* own detriment. I also came across another episode that was streamed on Maha Shiva Rathri[2]. It shows how Goddess Parvati Herself achieves her Self-Realization by going through step-wise yogic procedures by traversing through each and every chakra and finally completing it with realizing the Crown Chakra.

When it comes to group meditation or healing sessions, the presence of people around you affects the process. A guru would usually take care of how to train a group, but when there is no guru, the individuals need to co-ordinate and make a concerted effort for the optimal benefits of the group. My realization tells me that the energy sharing happens in the fashion of covalent bonding.

---

[1]   Sena Nayaka: *(Sanskrit/Hindi/Telugu)* The Commander of the Army; The Head Warrior.

[2]   Maha Shiva Rathri: *(Telugu)* This is a Hindu festival largely celebrated in India as well as in Nepal in reverence of Lord Shiva. It is observed on the 13th night/14th day of the new moon in the Krishna Paksha (dark half) every year of the month of *Phalguna* as per Hindu Calendar. The legend has it that this indicates the day on which Shiva and Shakti converge or get married. Devotees perform *Upavasam* (fasting for the whole day) and *Jagaran* (waking up all night and chanting hymns in devotion of Lord Shiva). *(Maha – Great, Shiva, Rathri - Night)*

Last but not the least, the best bet of tweaking from first-to-second scenario and get your higher chakras activated instead, is to do the energy channeling at a time when the energy impulses are extremely high!

By the way, going back to the titbit, what in this world can truly present future as past? I don't know of any, except these Energy Centres, through the arousal of *Kundalini Shakti*.

*Talking about the second path, Sex is considered a sacred act. All our religions and scriptures have taught us to initiate and explore this path 'only' when the right partner arrives in one's life. Otherwise it amounts to abusing not only sex but also oneself.

- *Mar 16, 2013, 01:04 AM.*

88. Give back whatever you take

Instances like these (Water War between Andhra Pradesh and Karnataka due to Water Pilferage in Karnataka as discussed in *The Hindu* article – *Title: "Cup of woes overflows for LLC farmers", Dated: March 17, 2013; National News, AP edition*) tell how, arriving at nice-sounding strategies (thinking) and having to implement them (doing) are two different worlds altogether. Inspite of all the resources (as deduced by a strategy), when we get stuck at initial levels itself, it tells how much difficult it is to overcome and transcend beyond the generic human tendencies of complacency and 'Chalta Hain!' attitide, more so when planning and implementation are not well co-ordinated.

266

Anyway, this post is more to take a dig at how big sounding solutions at higher levels do not see the light of the day most of the times due to a plethora of factors owing to poor implementation. No no, it's not even that, it's more on how big sounding solutions can be made to see the light of the day.

When I say high level goals I'm talking about something like *Millennium Development Goals* or those arrived at the recent *COP-11 (Conference of Parties)* that took place in Hyderabad at around Oct 2012 and the like. No, I'm not saying they don't yield results at all. Indeed it is not an easy deal at all to reach to as much as a level of *'mutual consent between all the parties'* in conferences such as these happening at the global level where *multiple interests collide.* That is an accomplishment in itself. But it does not end there. Take for instance, the history of Kyoto Protocol and then see where it started, where it is at now and where it heading towards. The net results are not very encouraging* - no **I'm not** saying this, people from suffering countries, experts and critics, environmentalists have been saying this over the years. This is my understanding of why there's a tough time materializing goals sketched at global level. The basic factors that might usually cause such a situation are:

- The goals are not realistically set - are too ambitious.

- The goals are not percolated and translated appropriately to the grass root levels.

- The consent and adherence to goals is diplomatic and not truly believed in - no real faith.

- The goals do not fit a common framework or vision.

Instead of going ga-ga and getting preachy about *'high level solutions-how to get them implemented'*, I'll sum up my ideas through a specific example/usecase - *How Environment Protection/Conservation goals can be efficiently implemented*, even when arrived at a global level.

This is my idea: *Frame the goals and implement them around a simple, practical, **workable** framework* - "Give back whatever you take!" In fact we don't have to do anything hi-fi, creative or out of the world, we'll just have to give back whatever we take from the nature. But a more important aspect is to *implement goals believing in the fact that it IS our responsibility to give back!* Then it just shows in the results. A few such global goals I can think of:

1. Invest more (in fact very generously) on research for alternative energy sources, especially solar energy.

2. Make simple rain-water harvesting system to be "mandatorily" incorporated in every house, it cannot be afforded as an option!

3. Do a constant check on what are the bodies/sectors/ industries that are resource hogging, that do not compensate proportionately for the lost resources and regulate them.

There can be many like these when the real experts come together. But let's just get started by talking about the usual bottlenecks in implementation now...

Alternative Energy Sources:

This century has seen many ground-breaking technologies. But most of them are *consumer or incentive driven*. Be it the way these tablets, iPhones, iPads, Notepads have been mushrooming one version after the other or the heavy investments that happen on things like LHC, Space Exploration Projects etc. While the former group of technologies are innovated, driven by consumerism/commercial interests and only cater to increase the comfort/entertainment factor, the latter group is innovated in the aspiration of more and more knowledge and awareness of unknown arenas or even in the aspiration of fame and power. (I don't have to explain the power wars that happen between the yester-year Power Blocs or even between the present developed nations to become No. 1 in space exploration, Nobel Prizes, Oscars so on and so forth.) While it's okay and normal for such technologies to crop up, there are hardly any, which are service-driven or responsibility-driven. Moreover what is the *'value addition'* of these technologies given the enormous amount of resources consumed by them? Even if as low as one-sixth of those efforts are spent on harnessing alternative energies, I'm sure we would have been far ahead in fighting out the **energy deficit** (power, fuel etc deficit) being faced by the world, again the burden of which is faced by us - the people inhabiting this world. Isn't all the talent and thought going so unharnessed for useful purposes? I might have used the phrase *'service-driven'*, but by investing and working on such things, we are not doing a favour to anybody, we are serving our own selves.

Investing in research on alternative energies is not really a high-budget consuming task. In India, I see that *there is a missing link between the academia and government/industry sectors.* See the lakhs of graduates who do their graduation with their talent and enthusiasm totally untapped. Some of them just wander hopelessly during their graduation because they do not see the underlying purpose of the degree viewing it merely as a route to a money-earning job. We see a lot of paper presentations happening, but I really wonder if those ideas and Theses ever take shape and not just stay on paper. Why can't the government introduce incentive-driven scholarship programs and encourage students to think and innovate? There are many burning issues in India and the mini-research projects at graduation level can go a long way in arriving at theoretical solutions for such problems. *These theories can then be imparted back to bureaucracy for implementation.* In fact, things like these will motivate the student to fulfill education for the sake of education and take up more meaningful jobs, jobs aligned to their passion, instead of run-of-the-mill jobs. This again results in increased productivity and effective utilization of resources.

Rain Water Harvesting:

In fact this might sound as a sub-heading in the above. Also there are various other things that can be discussed - effective garbage disposal, protection of endangered species etc etc etc. But conservation of water seems such a basic necessity that it deserves a mention of its own. These are the general questions that might crop up when the clause - *"needs to be mandatorily incorporated"* - comes up: Rain Water Harvesting system can be technically sophisticated, how can every home incorporate it? Isn't that too costly? The associated questions I'd ask are: Isn't a borewell too technically sophisticated? Don't we have a borewell in just every second home these days (in India)? Can't we improve the technology to make this system simpler?

A system that can channel abundant amounts of unused rain water right down to the undergrounds of earth seems not only a beautiful simple mechanism, but also a mandatory thing to support the water rejuvenating capacity of earth. When we all can spend money to buy a borewell and extract water (literally, we extract so monstrously as if Earth is serving us as a bonded labor) why can't we spend money to buy a rain water harvesting system to compensate for the extracted water. When we can take, we can as well give back. Imagine this earth as a living creature and get creative to feel the pain of water extracted from earth through high-technology borewells (for water and oil) being equivalent to cerebral fluid being pipped off from your brain and then assess that pain. Does such a pain leave you with any equilibrium at all?

Again coming to the resources that need to be allocated at the government level, it's not complicated. It requires just investing in making the system more simpler, issuing GOs (Government Orders) at the levels of local bodies of governance (it's not even a Legislature issue where passing a bill is a time-consuming process again) and assign supervisors for periodic inspection in the initial levels to ensure compliance. Atleast it can be mandatory to those homes that have a borewell fit. Doesn't that sound simple? Fortunately, it is actually that simple, atleast in this case. Surprisingly and unfortunately, there is no government intervention in enforcing this when Government Intervention is so badly needed here.

Regulation of resource hogging entities:

We have this concept in computer technologies. A UNIX Administrator runs system cron jobs to identify and act upon such resource hogging entitites. This is a very simple aspect of technology. Our technolgies have seen more evolved logic and coding, but all this caters and feeds the virtual world only. We don't harbour such sophisticated technologies when it comes to aspects of governance in the real world, yes there are genuine reasons behind it too. You can innovate and create things the way you want in a virtual world, but in real world every step needs a lot of thought, consideration of many factors and more importantly handling of people across the chain and hierarchy.

I'll give a very simple example of such entities. There are about 100 news channels in India currently. In the state of AP (Andhra Pradesh) itself there are about 12. I'll purely talk about AP now. When I listen to these channels I'm all the more confused and literally lost. It sounds like proliferation of information, unncessary information that ruins the quality of life, really! Listening to AIR (All India Radio) news once a day is such a beautiful experience on the other hand, ok that might be purely a personal choice owing to my tastes and pursuits. But now coming to the numbers, estimate the amount of resources going into these 100 channels, the power, the petrol and diesel, the paper, computers and disks, the spectrum allocated for the satellite communication and the consequent impact on nature. Now estimate the amount of value addition to the society: 'some' news and employment of some good number of people and ofcourse the huge sums of money that go into private coppers. By all means those people can be employed through other means. Do we really need to waste so many resources just to provide employment for few people? *Do these news channels give as much as they take?* Shouldn't governments incorporate some regulation here? There could be many such resource hogging entities in our world which are not really worth a penny to the society.

. . . . .

I understand arguing on these lines sounds too outdated and not being in sync with times. I understand that most of the governments have capitalistic tendencies in the guise of being socialistic too. Most of the times things are driven by market forces and private players. The governments are mere puppets in these hands and the whole world at the end of the day revolves around money, *values take backseat*. But then I don't deny the positive forces working for change, if not for them we wouldn't inhabit this world peacefully today.

Again coming back to the specific usecase discussed, this nature gives such a huge bounty of resources - forests, minerals, oceans and rivers and many more, all so pristine. But we abuse all that energy through technology, pilferage and divert it for our selfish ends and do not give back as much as we take, let alone generating more using that same technology. When the clogs in our arteries get cleansed and the mental blocks in our neural networks are removed, I mean when our perspective changes, it will be very evident that it's so easy to give that stream of energy that we take from nature, back to nature herself.

The crux of the above discussion is to emphasize and dissect how strategy making and implementation go hand-in-hand and thought process is an integral part of both, more so because learning is a continuous process and happens at every phase. Thought process cannot be in the domain of strategists alone and when the implementation suffers due to any reasons, the onus cannot be shifted to the strategists.

The net results are not very encouraging: Not very encouraging at the moment. The future might hold different results.

- Mar 20, 2013, 02:23 AM.

89. Lava Kusa!!!

Today I got to see the 50th anniversary celebrations of the Telugu movie Lava Kusa on TV. I really like this movie - its portrayal. The way *Kusa* and *Lava* are shown to protect their mother Sita and also protect each other, shows what kind of responsibilities a son used to take up in those times. The actors Nagaraju and Subramanyam talk about how the entire crew was dedicated in fulfilling their respective responsibilities, the attention to detail they had and a lot more! Itseems they were given a book describing everything, they ought to do, in a very simplified way! And my God! The music *Ghantasala garu* has given for this movie (the film has whopping 37 songs and padyamulu[1]) is such a masterpiece (they call it ajaraamaram[2], so apt!). Some highlights:

- Five years went into its making!
- This is perhaps the only movie for which when the father left the direction, the son took up the job and completed it.
- The first color movie in Telugu (very famous fact).
- Subramanyam, the actor who played Kusa, despite all the fame, leads his life as a tailor now...

- Mar 29, 2013, 06:32 PM.

---

[1] padyamulu: (Telugu) Plural of Padyam, which means Poem.
[2] ajaraamaram: (Telugu) evergreen; eternal, without death.

90. A dream come true...

Husband: I'll go away!

Wife: Where?

H: I'll go away!

W: Where? Will you stop grumbling or do you want me to get you Aanjaneya Dandakam[1]?

H: I'll go to Australia! I'm tired of this writing... I can't stay in India and do this publishing job, I'll go to Australia!

W: To do what?

H: You forgot it so soon? I like marketing, precisely marketing my ideas, in fact to tell more precisely you know that I love '*ideating*', don't you? I'll go to Australia to do just that!

W: That sounds just so wrong! When asked - what is 'Precession of Equinoxes', if somebody answers saying – it is the 'Precision of similarity of equal axes'- tell me, how weird does it sound? Whatever you are saying sounds equally weird to me! Your Ph D smartness is putting me to such a tough time man! If you wake up after a coma of one year, it shall ofcourse be like this! How else will it be, tell me! Our publishing house is in Australia, not in India! And because we ran into losses and because you couldn't bear the idea of not being able to

---

[1] Aanjaneya Dandakam: *(Telugu)* Sacred chants and hymns of Lord Hanuman to ward off fear.

immediately make our foray into ideating, you went into coma! That's what happened?

H: So what's happening now?

W: We ate ideas! I mean we are *ideating*!

H: How come we could eat our ideas? Where did you get the money to eat so many ideas of mine?

W: Honey! It's not always about money! Wherever there are values, there, people come first! There's something called *'goodwill'* and there's something called *'loan'*! It's a fact that you have dedicated sincerely many valuable years of your life to writing! Your writing not only manifested in mere books but also sustained business of many people! Those very clients, who were appreciative of your efforts, gave us some loan as a 'goodwill gesture' :) Now we have started *"Tapestry Solutions"* (I know you like the word *serendipity* more, but didn't we agree that all *serendipity* culminates in *tapestry*?) that offers ideas to deal with the most complicated techno-business dilemmas in Information Technology (IT)! It's waiting for your ideas now!

H: How come you got such a brilliant idea to shift to India?

W: That's the only idea I have got, which you did not get! I had always said that India is THE place for marketing!

H: Ok! But then you are right, that's the only idea you have got! But, whatever!

W: Yeah whatever you had been dreaming so far is our past, but all that you have dreamt of in the past has come true!

. . . . .

Not all dreams come true, but those of people who sincerely put their heart and soul into their dreams, those will definitely ideate...someday...someday!

- Apr 05, 2013, 12:16 AM.

91. Different places - different contexts

How can two people residing in two different places ever live in the same moment?

Husband in US: Your father and my mother have not stopped quarreling with their spouses and it's bothering me too much, I have really bad dreams!

Wife in India: I thought you know this. Don't you? It seems to have fallen in place yesterday, our parents have made peace finally, it's *'happening now'* in India. They are celebrating Ugadi[1] happily! You don't have to be bothered about them anymore. We just got to take care of ourselves now. In fact I'm worried about you. Maybe you should stop sleeping westwards to stop those dreams. I mean, may be west is not the place for you man at the moment, you must really come to India perhaps. Maybe a change in place would make some difference... I know you have your obligations!

---

[1]   Ugadi: *(Sanskrit/Telugu)* A festival to celebrate Telugu New Year (New Year as per Telugu Calendar).

H: No! US has become my first home, India is no more that, it's only a second home to me now!

W: I can understand, but I don't have a suitable visa that allows me to come there and work, you went to US in the first place for savings. But now maybe we have enough! Don't you think? Moreover all these days my health did not let me work, but now if we both work here together, we might have as much net savings or even more than what you might be making all alone there! And also more savings henceforth would only be at the cost of our personal life, do we need that really? You know, things are never the same and priorities keep changing, I see it as something like *Time Division Multiplexing*, not FDM or CDM! Also these days lots of money is going into long-distance calls to update each other, call it US' time lag or India's time lead, this time gap and these time zone problems can never be nullified, can they be? I wish time just stops now, so our different geographical locations don't matter!

H: (Ok! TDM itseems, FDM itseems, oh as if only this lady has done Engineering for real! ... thinking this way, the husband says...) Oh your not-so-good communication technology concepts tire me... anyway I'll give it a thought!

W: But I still don't understand if we have not reached that aspired limit of savings needed, anyway your wish!

. . . . .

Ok there goes a typical conversation of a lower urban class couple coping with long distance and life's circumstances!

On a different note I have a nice telugu song currently on my mind. The lyrics of this song are such a master-piece! I really love this line: *"Neekidi telvaarani reyamma, kaliki maa chilaka paadaku ninnati nee raagam!"* Decoupling it from its sad-context and listening to it neutrally, it means that - *"It's dark already here, don't lament in the past for otherwise you will get stuck in it!"*

And finally on a cheerful note Vijayanama Samvatsara Subhakankshalu[1] to all the readers! *Happy Ugadi*!!!

- Apr 11, 2013, 04:05 PM.

92. Freedom Struggle of India

If freedom fighters of different eras - *Moderates* and *Extremists* were to meet at a success meet of Indian Independence, this is how the conversation might run - "We (extremists) rejected the bad ideas proposed for the future to be able to arrive at a good solution for today while you (moderates) endured bad ideas of the past to be able to arrive at that very solution for today!"

I spoke about the background of these two genres of Indians once in the post – *Freedom Struggle – as an evolutionary process*. They worked at different times of the history (co-existed towards the end though), had different contexts, hence had different means, approaches and ideas, but they worked for

---

[1] Vijayanama Samvatsara Subhakankshalu: *(Telugu)* It means *"New Year Wishes for this year of Vijayanama"*. The Telugu New Year is not the same as English New Year. And as per Telugu Calendar, years repeat with a periodicity of 60, each of them assuming different names. The year 2013 assumed the name *Vijayanama*. (*Samvatsara*: year's; *Subhakankshalu*: wishes)

the same cause - *to relieve India of foreign rule.* While, whether India benefited from British imperialism or not, is widely debatable, I personally believe that India did benefit from it. *But, it would be wrong if one said that British ruled India in the best interests of India.* The British ruled India only for their own interests in reality. Indian interests were always subordinated to British interests, but in the process *a churn was triggered that made India and Indians realize what and where their best interests lie.* Hence it's Indians' response to British' moves that finally lifted India from its prejudices and ***inertia*** and synced it with the global patterns and trends.

To talk a little more about moderates and extremists... Moderates had enormous burden, responsibilities and pain, to start with. There was no agenda, neither was there any reference. *People of India then didn't even know that they were suffering*, in fact the moderates themselves didn't know. Initially, they thought that British ruled India in the best interests of the country; they gradually got to understand the reality. *They had to build a national consciousness binding the people, educate them and understand the problem at hand.* They spent a lot of time in writing mass journals and magazines to educate people. They patiently apprised the British government of their requirements and expectations. On the other hand, *extremists were more militant in nature and saw Indian Independence as a right and demanded it.* They died over and over (many leaders lost their lives in the process), unified the goals of local revolutions and arrived at a common agenda. After certain time, the approach of moderates was not working with British; in fact *the extremists were not tolerant of the submissive tendencies of moderates as much as the moderates were skeptical of rebellious tendencies of extremists.* Yet the most important fact is that, extremists had the reference set by the moderates (not officially though). They inherited from moderates in a way, though their agendas were at complete loggerheads. ***One cannot downplay either of the approaches and either of the approaches would not suit the framework and context of the other group.*** Of course post-Independence there was no demarcation as such and both the groups worked purely as "Indians" to lead India towards its destiny. To know more about this part of Indian struggle, I strongly recommend reading chapters II and III of *"Freedom Struggle" by Bipan Chandra and others.*

- Apr 11, 2013, 04:28 PM.

93. Why do people take others for granted?

Yes, why do people take others for granted? I'd elaborate this case with an example. Let's say two friends A and B set on to do a Sociological Survey as part of their research. Let's say B's forte is people interaction - identifying the right people and asking the right questions (whose answers are inputs to A) and A's forte is to observe the human behaviour and jot down notes in a way presentable in their thesis - take the relevant ideas and content and reject the unneeded ones keeping their project goals on mind which in turn is feedback to B for further people interaction. Let's say due to some time constraints, they both had to fulfill both the functions - handle people separately at different locations.

Now both A and B know their strength areas. Also assume that A has put down his requirements clearly, say he told B clearly what all he needs so that he can carry on with this additional responsibility and say B does not cater to those needs, perhaps because B has his own obligations that restrict him from doing that. And also assume that B is going about his own way of taking notes and has no complaints whatsoever. Now A also goes on doing his job in the way he pleads because B did not co-operate. In the first place, A is not aware of any common agreed rules that might have restricted B from creating an amicable environment. Now when they sit together and collate the results, A never complained about B's lengthy notes (which will consume a lot of time for A during thesis consolidation phase) because he was willing to put efforts to take care of it, but B kept complaining that A is delusional (of what is needed of the task) and not interacting with people actively. Now A admits to his incapacity in not being able to fulfill that functionality of identifying right people and asking right questions, he also cites the triggers he needs from B to be able to do that. Now B does not provide those triggers, does not want to tell why he does not want to (or why he is unable to) give those triggers. B here does not facilitate a healthy communication channel, but says that A is focusing on wrong areas and not doing the needful which is actually easy (for B). Now what might be a bed of roses to B, might be a path of thorns to A.

All I'm getting at is - *healthy communication is the root to collaboration in any project or real-life scenario.* Keeping that path closed and expecting others to work in such a confined environment only implies that one group doesn't want to get into other group's shoes. In such a scenario, both the groups lose, because it's their combined efforts and combined results that count. It amounts to consciously getting into a situation where one group does not understand the needs of the opposite group, an instance of which is discussed in the post – *One has to work on the relationship if the relationship has to work* – where the groups there constitute men and women.

If expressing ideas on paper is easy for one person, talking things out with people might be easy for others. That said, every communication path involves a bit of initial protocol-handshaking (in technical terms of Communication Networks, the control data before the actual data) and if that's not done appropriately, how many ever ideas (in technical terms, traffic, packets, data etc) flow, they go useless - they result in corrupted and futile communication.

It's easy to put efforts when on an individual pursuit, but in a combined framework, people must collaborate. If I reach my threshold of patience in such a framework, the easiest way out for me would be to give up and accept failure.

- Apr 17, 2013, 05:11 PM.

94. *The job of reporting*

Once upon a time, news reporting and journalism were two different jobs. But now with the growing business of news channels and their place in the society, there is no clear demarcation between the two. We have reporters going to the site of news and reporting the news live. And with the growing technology, sometimes those efforts too are not required, the journalism and news reporting happen simultaneously from within the comfortable cabins of the studio itself.

The collection of news involves travelling to different places, places where both good and bad happen. *The news channels report both good and bad, but that does not necessarily mean they are endorsing either of them.* Well again their personal views must not be mixed with their profession. Let's say, a Telugu TV anchor is reporting a film gossip and matter-of-fact-ly reports vibrantly that there is a growing trend in girls liking guys resembling in their ways, the top heroes of Tollywood[1] as they are portrayed in movies. That does not mean the anchor too is indulging in such dreams! Well, reporting involves the process of occasionally being judgmental about what is good and bad, but that's part of reporting, not the end aim. News channels must get into the business of reporting news as they happen, the target is to report what's happening around, but not to influence or promote what's happening around. In fact the news channels need NOT get into the business with an aim of reforming the society. In that case it either becomes redundant or even counter-productive, because when they plainly do their job of reporting, *they are facilitating the informed choice and education needed for the audience and what call has to be taken vests in the discretion of the people in the society and its agencies.* It's like the simple tip given for writing answers in exams - No need to impress explicitly, when we express eloquently, we impress eventually.

Of course that's the ideal process and the reality is far from ideal and so we have this practice of paid news being fostered. We know of the *Radia Tapes controversy* and the alleged involvement of high-profile journalists, media persons, political lobbyists, politicians and corporate houses in the decision making of appointment of a Cabinet Minister in India (*Background: Controversy unearthed by the Indian Income Tax Departement during 2008-09 for the appointment of A. Raja as the Telecom Minister in 2007*). In the day-to-day life, these days there is a growing incidence of this pattern where media people approach groups where mistakes/wrong-doing/crime

---

[1] Tollywood: *(English)* An English term used to identify Telugu Film Industry.

happen and seek money for NOT showing it on TV. We also know how the TV election poll surveys actually influence the poll results. And then going a bit further, these days there is a proposed idea of using Facebook to influence voting patterns.

On the flip side of it, sometimes the process of reporting demands the risk of getting into a hell-hole and getting killed there or return back safely. We know about the stories of journalists like Daniel Pearl, the Wall Street Journal South Asia chief, who was beheaded by his Al-Qaeda captors in Pakistan. *Actually speaking, reporters are not part of the game* (reporters or even journalists, but I'm just sticking to the term 'reporters' for now). ***But the characteristics of the game demand them to become part of it.*** The actors in the game try to pull them in, but whether or not the reporters get lured depends on their integrity, circumstances, obligations, compulsions and discretion.

Also a reporter's diary is not a bible or some kind of preachy material aimed to enlighten the audience. It's not always the case that the audience do not know what is being discussed in there. Sometimes, it's just a plain compilation of facts to record the sustenance of their own job.

My personal assessment of the job of reporting is that - the reporters have to be *'aware'* of what they are reporting (implying they must know what they are talking), sometimes they get *'affected'* by what they are reporting, but they need not necessarily be *'associated'* with (or endorse) what they are reporting. *Whether or not the societal game allows such a line of demarcation is a different story altogether, but the job of reporting essentially ends here!*

- Apr 26, 2013, 04:28 PM.

95. The balance - The Trio - The Trinity!!!

We know that the balance of a human being is marked by the balance of the spirit-mind-body trio. This trio is synonymous with the Trinity of Gods and the balance of the Universe vests in the Trinity. When posed with a question of which is important of the three: spirit-mind-body, a natural answer is that all the three are equally important. But one can't ensure the well-being of all the three all the time. *The universe too does not have all its components at its best and in abundance all the time.* Else it would be best all the time and there is no best, there is no progress, there is no deterioration and it becomes static.

Fig 8 – Balance – Trinity of Body, Mind and Soul

(This diagram is used with permission from the Faith and Health Connection ministry. The original diagram and more information

about the link between faith and health can be seen at www.
FaithandHealthConnection.org.

NOTE: The image refers to 'Soul' in the way I refer to 'Mind';
it refers to 'Spirit' in the way I refer to 'Soul', in my writing. As
for me, when I say 'Spirit', I'm referring to the 'Collective Soul'.)

When a person is born, a mother first safeguards the physical
well-being of a child by timely feeding and caring. After that,
the child feeds his/her mind by learning and observing things
around. And then the child grows and the focus is usually on
physical and mental well-being. Apparently, the soul is happy
all through out and we don't tend to take an explicit interest in
our spiritual needs until something really drastic happens (Yes
the inherent and mild fending does happen). It is because, until
then we did not even fall short of it - the spiritual strength!
We are all born with a given spiritual strength or residue,
whichever way you see it. Until our egos are badly hurt due
to rejection of our ideas, efforts, love, whatever or until some
freak accident happens or until we are inspired by a rare event
or until an automatic spiritual transformation due to the
inherent journey of the soul happens, we do not get to open
the doors of spiritual healing. *The results of spiritual healing*
are as multi-fold and benevolent as the harshness of the path to
reach there. **When all the three are balanced, the self is "at**
its own" best.

After growing into an adult, the person balances these three
based on his own needs, circumstances and resources available
to him. The actual problem arises when one of the components
grows relatively much much more than the other. Say a person,
has abundant physical energies flowing and feels very strong.
Unless the mind channelizes those energies, he will go out

and beat somebody weak. Say a person grows really really intelligent. Unless he is wise enough, he will not be able to use that aptly. The intellect there needs to be supervised by equivalent or greater spiritual strength. And say if a person is overworking his mind or spirit without paying heed to his bodily needs, the body will not even be able to assimilate the benefits from those two higher merits.

Take a pause and look at the world around you, check the history of the past couple of centuries. *This world, the earth per se, is basically the materialistic realm - part of the body of the universe.* See how we have been overly using only our 'body' and 'mind' faculties over the past years. Look at the growing intellect of people that's not channelized properly. Look at all the material resources that are actually there (if not abundantly, owing to our own virtues and vices), yet not distributed properly. Don't we see the complete absence of the third entity? Did we even allow the third element to come into play? And without that, what do we do with these resources and intellect?

What was once done using physical strength, we do that now through our intellect. We innovate and create technologies. In reality, we have either been making up for the absence of the third element and overly using the other two. Or we have been overly using the other two so as not to let the third one assert its presence. Or we have yielded to our own ignorance that we ought to overly use these two faculties, that we could not let the third one in. Whatever it is, we have been recycling the spiritual resides we have, over and over, that we have hardly any useful component left now. Man has been 'messing' up with nature, he knows this, yet he does this. Yes, in the process he has been messing up with himself too. *He has shed all his filters of discretion and started donning up all the roles possible, that came along his way,* based on his own knowledge (or ignorance whichever way you see it). He has aspired to become the master of his own destiny, become his own spiritual master, the custodian of all the natural resources and is even venturing into extra-terrestrial resources. All this is fine, but does he even pause to check if he is capable of donning all these roles and at what cost? Yes, he sees the "outcome" - he stays alive and progresses on a day-to-day basis - but his progress is at the cost of somebody else's suffering, does he check the "process" that goes into it - messing up with others - is that the process? Does he even realize this? Why do we choose to enjoy the initial free goodies of capitalism without an eye on what lies in store for the future in the long run? Who said it's ok to draw as much resources as possible without putting them back? When did we create or borrow this culture of seeking sexual favors before even owning up relationships?

Now, people talk about saviors all of a sudden! Do people want another *Bible* or *Quran* or *Bhagavadgita*, updated for the current times? Who has the patience to read through, assimilate and abide by them? Hey come on, all we people are so intelligent that we don't need any god-damn plan, template and rules for us! The intellect is just flowing and oozing out on the mega giga tera peta exa zitta... bytes of internet, we don't need some more 100 MB of data, we all are just fine, thanks!

It's not intellect that the today's generation needs, in fact today's rat race for riches and the so-called education has only come in the way of our otherwise peaceful lives and marriages, instead of complementing them. If this realm of earth needs anything at all 'at the moment' to assert its balance, it is spiritual strength. Let's hope the humanity gathers it up rightly, balances itself and sails through these tough-tiding-against-time times! *Let's not create a world where even if the Christ, the son of God, Himself is born, he would act like an anti-christ, the God of all and the know-it-all!!!*

- Apr 30, 2013, 01:16 PM.

96. Corruption - at what level? - The Indian!!!

More often than not, we get stuck with dilemmas of life and have to make a choice. To make critical decisions one is suggested to listen to one's own internal voice and take the guidance from within, one's spirit. But what if you are guided by a corrupted spirit, a spirit that's not yours? That is exactly the fight of the Indian in the Tamil movie *Indian* - the Kamal Hassan starrer. It's not about the vengeance of a father who lost his daughter for not being able to bribe a doctor, it's not about the fight taken up by a father to reform his son who is corrupted by the system (and hence in turn gets to corrupt the system more). It's *about the fight against the corruption of the spirit of a nation.* **When the spirit itself gets corrupted there is no bigger entity to save us.** Hence we see every now and then, the rise of powerful forces to safeguard it.

I don't have to explicity list down the problems due to corruption in India. But I'll discuss my views here taking a small example. Say, a person wants to extend his house by getting two more floors constructed. And he knows the rules - about all the permissions (BPS, LRS, Regularization etc etc) he needs to take, which might cost around 1.5 lakhs/-. But the problem is - he also knows that none of his neighbors has taken this and got many floors (way above the limit - an apartment of sorts) constructed by bribing all the middle players, the whole bribe amounting to some 20,000/-. One usually prefers the latter option in India because following the process takes quite some time. They prefer this option initially, get done with the construction quickly and later follow the actual process of payment in leisure. In fact, I myself am aware of people who want to follow the process - pay everything properly and then get the house constructed - but the government servants do not allow them to follow the process so easily. They in turn ask bribe (in general quite many, but mind you, not all) and keep delaying the process. We are living in a country where government fosters corruption and spoils the people and in turn people add more to corruption, it's an ever-amplifying chain, an inverter-fed feedback loop. A normal person willing to follow the rules either has to torment himself completely, much against the will of his family members and neighbours and much against the co-operation of government servants to follow the rules or must give up, get disillusioned with the system and follow and become part of the flock.

In a society where corruption is way too rampant, *it needs power to fight corruption - a power as powerful as the government itself or even more* (when I say government, I mean government and bureaucracy at all levels, not just the top layer of ministers). So who/what can be as powerful as the government? Definitely not the citizens, not even the lower layers of the government. The changing force must come from within the government itself - the higher ups who do not approve of the practices and have the power to oppose his colleagues and sub-ordinates. Somebody like a tactical PM (Prime Minister) - who would first listen to his party colleagues and nod his head to their words and once in power exercises his duties and tackles the enormous pressure of his own party which cannot approve of his ways. If there is some change in the five years, then people would know his worth and vote him back to power again, his party colleagues then will have no choice but get gradually receptive to follow his way. Anyway, *just as good can't happen forever, bad too can't be tolerated forever*. That said, corruption is best nailed down in its initial phases only, when even citizen groups with some power can control it. *Corruption when unleashed beyond control can eat those very people who are fighting it out.*

Anyway, coming back to the Indian movie, it's main theme is ofcourse - *war of a man on his own people*. When one doesn't listen even when told ardently, then he is beyond reform through mere preaching, hence the son is killed at the end. The ending seems to be done on a very ambiguous note though. One is expected to assume that the Indian just left his wife in India and went to US alone, leaving her to the care of her would-be and never-to-be daughter-in-law. I would like to assume that he took his wife along with him to the US.

Over-reaching of roles and responsibilities:

The best one can to do to one's self and society is to understand one's own roles and responsibilities, one's capacities and scope. As discussed in the post - *Indifference*, one has to understand one's own realm first before setting on to become part of it, surpass it or rule it. *Owning up roles and responsibilities that are not one's own will amount to tampering with and not adequately fulfilling both the responsibilities - one's own and owned.* Anything that is done at one's own suffering and the happiness of one's family and loved ones, in expectation of some future gains, is never going to work out, all the hard work goes in vain - because there will be nobody to share that with, not even family and your own self will never be at peace with such an accomplishment. I see a lot of advice floating on internet and elsewhere for women asking them to de-stress out, ignore the rant of other ladies, stop comparing blah blah blah, but strangely I don't find any for men! So here I go to do just that - To think that men must earn and accomplish big, owning up responsibilities that are not theirs, through inadequate resources and limited framework is going to cost them big - it costs them their family and internal peace. Even the work done in such a stressed out way, to make it big, might not necessarily be in the best interests of the society. I had always believed that a leader would allow his team members to work in such a fashion that they realize their roles and responsibilities and work to their fullest potential and satisfaction while the leader remains in the background. The leader would surface only when there is a problem to steer the direction towards a collective benefit. *In a healthy environment, one must be able to only sense and differentiate the absence, not the presence, of their leader* and seek a resolution for his timely action, because he would only do careful monitoring of his team members and not micro-manage them.

One breathes through nose, thinks through mind and is guided by the spirit. If somebody comes us and asks us, *"How about we breathe through our minds?"* Now tell me how ridiculous that sounds? Overreaching of roles is just as ridiculous, it spoils not only the parts, but also the whole!

I talk about this in the context of corruption because *corruption is fostered by people who want things big, way beyond their resources can allow them and in the process they get into roles they don't really fit in or roles not carved out or meant for them.*

Regulation - Lord Shiva's way:

It's not just India that is corrupted, the consciousness of humanity itself is corrupted. Man is carrying his own virus - greed. *In that process, we become auto-programs programmed for self-destruction.* And with other vices tagged together, we have been spawned out of some malfunction to harm and destruct ourselves. Evil begets more evil, setting a descent that never ends. If one is suffering and doing things against his own will much to his own dissatisfaction, it only means that he is captivated - he is possessed, possessed by something more powerful than him - greed, lust and desire. *Man today is a sum-total of his disintegrating components of self, working at loggerheads with each other without complementing one another.* He is the image of the whole humanity degrading, worsening and suffering. Over the vast span of time, despite many religious preceptors preaching out to humanity that the self is a whole, not just mere collection of parts and that one must use mind *not* body to communicate with the spirit and yet if the humanity doesn't pay heed, it only tells us where our collective consciousness is leading us to.

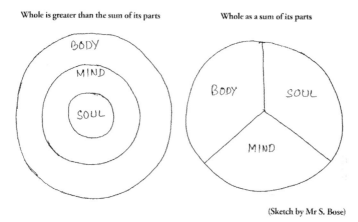

(Sketch by Mr S. Bose)

Fig 9 – Whole vs Sum of Parts

Lord Shiva is supposed to be the beginning and the end of the Universe, the all-pervading God/energy in whom we reside. Lord Shiva along with Goddess Shakti is the source of this creation, giving the energy that the Universe is composed of - in this sense He is the beginning. Lord Shiva also assimilates the soul of every living being after it is dead and redeems the soul so as to allow the cycle of re-birth rendering the soul useful for an ongoing cycle. Redemption is the domain of Lord Shiva, not anybody else's! *God not only observes and controls humanity, but also assimilates both good and bad of humanity.* **When the spirit suffers, the mind and body both suffer.** That's the hierarchy of pain and impact. In fact even God through various means (humans themselves) keeps telling the humanity to let Him stay out of this corruption.

Christ has become our saviour when the humanity needed and deserved it - the Saving! But if the humanity needs to be saved now, it perhaps needs many Christs, not one! Such is the evil now! The concept of saving some millions of people at the cost of life of a saviour when half of them do not even deserve it does not make any sense, it only amounts to sending across a message that we can continue doing our sins and He will come to save us some day! *But who is any saviour anyway with reference to the Universe?* Whose creation is this world? Humanity has been growing at the cost of cosmic energies of certain younger Gods, in fact it has been scavenging on them. *This universe is not open-ended!* It has finite resources and follows its own principles for its sustenance. The humanity resists redemption, it is natural. It is like an organ resisting a tumor to be removed from itself, which when not removed, hampers not just the organ but the functioning of the body as a whole. *A part should not, cannot and will never be allowed to grow at the cost of a whole.* When the evil rises, the regulator takes over the reins to redeem the humanity, purify it and steer its course for its own betterment.

- May 08, 2013, 12:39 AM.

97. The high-tech (third degree) treatment - A story!

Pristina was sensing minor headaches and sudden drift in her thinking patterns and hence approached a (supposedly famous) doctor. The doctor agreed to treat the 'patient', but had to leave India for US for an important work engagement as soon as he started the treatment. In order to test and promote the automated-treatment-framework (ATF) he has been researching for over years, he started experimenting this framework (just call it equipment) on his new and optimistic patient. After a couple of months the headaches transformed into severe migraines, almost blocking her head completely as if she were carrying a granite on her head all the time and her nervous system completely succumbed to the impact resulting in body aches all the time, she was thus bed-ridden. The equipment has a transmitter and a receiver - the system operated by the doc at the other end. It has 3 feeds and the dosage of each feed is done depending on the current characteristics and parameters of the patient. The treatment continued in the same way for over a year and her family finally hired a nurse who could co-ordinate with the doc in US and know and understand the case history (The treatment was costly and already paid for, so they didn't want to shift to another doc, also for the reason not to start treatment all over again with inappropriately understood case history!). This is how the conversation ran between the nurse and the doc:

Nurse: Hello Doctor! This is *Katherine*, you can just call me *Kathy*! As I see it, the situation of Pristina is really worse and we must really do something about her.

Doc: Yeah I understand that, we must do something (or the other)!

Nurse: What do you think might have triggered this situation?

Doc: I don't know what triggered this, but I'd love to know who triggered this.

Nurse: What? What did you say?

Doc: Yeah I said, I don't know what triggered this, but I'd love to know what triggered this!

Nurse: Ok ok! So what are the three dosages you have been giving her?

Doc: Yeah all the three dosages are for different types of headaches depending on the severity of the headache, I have been using feed 1 and feed 3 all the while, feed 1 relatively more!

Nurse: (She tests the drugs fed in feed 1 and feed 3, alarmed she says) Doctor! Did you feed the drugs before leaving India or is it these people who have been filling it periodically?

Doc: Why do you ask that? I have set everything before leaving, the expiry period and all that was all checked, so that people back in India need not touch anything. All that Pristina had to do was sleep on the equipment mat and that triggers everything, I get a call and I call her back and then I check her characteristics at that moment and order the dosage, I operate everything from here! It's all automated you see!

Nurse: (Still alarmed) Ok if you meant all that you said and if you really did all that, then I can't believe this girl is still alive! Feed 1 has alcohol and Feed 3 has spirit fed to it! Keep her headaches aside, but her body has been fighting these two things all the while!

Doc: (He too alarmed...) Wait! Can you check the username and account name on that screen of the equipment?

Nurse: (She checks it and says) She is being treated under your account Doctor...

Doc: Ah! There lies the problem! Those drugs were meant for me! But wait, how could the same account be used by two people? I'll check with my guide wait! (Checks with his guide) Yeah, it seems there's an automatic setting which allows same account to be used by two people at different times. Never mind, so what do you think we should do now?

Nurse: (Kept thinking...)

By this time, Pristina summoned up some energy to speak out and yelled at the audio-con "Stay out of this! I was better off before the treatment, I don't need your treatment anymore!"

That is how systems-automation is carried on these days....seriously man! ☺

- May 08, 2013, 08:31 PM.

98. The spilled right brain hemisphere...

This is it! This must be it! Some time ago when I got stuck over and over and unable to get on with my day-to-day life, I was looking for a right reason, something that I could really relate to my state...then I found this.

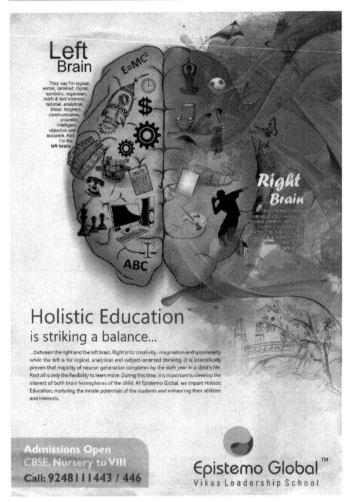

Fig 10 – Brain Hemispheres

(The above image is used with permission from the Epistemo Global school management. To know more about the prospectus of the school, please visit www.epistemoglobal.com)

It was completely apt, my right brain hemisphere was spilling way too much that my left brain hemisphere was rendered helpless and could not take control easily! Not that my left brain hemisphere is relatively weak or something, in fact my academics, thinking and work patterns (logical, analytic, methodical, detail-attentive) have always made me feel that left-brain-thinking is my forte. Creativity, artistic pursuits etc have never been my strength areas at all and I've been so dead practical at analyzing things that I've been my own worst critic. No doubt anybody who would have been acquainted with me closely yet not known me deeply enough would find me emotionally numb. People at my profession in the past have tagged me downright practical, aggressive and professional, but I'm not any, just that I dealt certain scenarios in a tough way. But things took a different turn suddenly and something tapped and unleashed my right-brain. I tried different things to get the balance in place - like stop focusing on right-brain activities, focus more on left-brain-activities, may be play some sudoku, maybe solve some puzzle, maybe solve some math, may be read a book continuously for more than 15 mins with focus or may be just watch TV without focusing on anything at all, meditation etc etc! Nothing worked, so I just gave up and felt that the best course is to listen to its commands and let my brain take its best course naturally. So it did and hence this post... Anyway one of the best lessons of my life has again come to be of some help - *"Resisting anything and staying passive would only aggravate things, instead partly succumb to the pressure to placate it!"* Good that it works time and again.

A hyper-active right-brain-hemisphere actually implies deep depression or even schizophrenia, fantasizing, not synchronized with the world and things like that - but this summary is the dictate given by left-brain people - those scientists, researchers and doctors who would dissect it as a mental illness. Now instead take the summary of that state from a right-brain perspective and it would also mean that the intuition is being thrusted to its best possible state bringing the person closer to God, self, one's own fundamental frequency and hence syncing and harmony with the universe in the 'long run'. At the end of the day, continuous work on just one brain hemisphere is dangerous as anybody might guess. *The actual problem with over-active right brain though is that the brain loses its overall retention and control - the forte of right brain.*

When I talk about brain hemispheres, I'm also tempted to talk about the gender differences when it comes to thinking. Considering the past couple of centuries*, I see that there is a sudden spurt in women studying, making it big in their careers and playing an equal role in shaping the society. While people might say their numbers and contribution is still not enough, I differ. Talking in terms of *women:men ratios today* in all spheres and saying that they are nowhere near equal is very unfair, it means that today's theoretical expectations on women are being taken as the yardstick. Instead talking about the relative percentages - the *women:men contribution ratios of the past* being compared with *women:men ratios of the present* - would give a fair measure of how much progress was made. While it might be that the world's circumstances (industrialization, world wars, caste system/grouping and then globalization - more resources needed, hence more participation of women) have shaped this drift, I also tend to believe that some genetic changes might have also partly contributed to such a sudden change and outburst. That said, I'd like to make this very political and controversial statement - while women have changed suddenly, men did not quite catch up with such a sudden change 'on an average' basis. By that, I don't mean that men did not proportionately grow intellectually, spiritually or anything like that. They did. But they did not yet grow up to a state where they could "accept" this growth of women and lower their expectations from women owing to their participation in other areas, resulting in extra burden on women and also incompatible relationships. In short, the once-upon-a-time frequency match** got out of sync.

Now this frequency match brings me to an interesting topic. Few years ago, when match-search started for me, one of my friends suddenly confronted me with this usual girly question - *"What are your parameters, what is it that you want in your guy?"* While basic criteria must be met decently, I could not much think beyond one and only one parameter - He must be at least as matured as me (how much ever more or less matured I am). I had always felt (and personally realized too) that men being more matured than women, helps in relationships, this essentially owing to the male ego. A man "usually" gets into the trap of "inferiority complex" and spoils his relationships if he 'feels' that the woman he is in relationship with, is more than him, in some aspects 'important to him'. On the other hand, women tend to accept, take into stride and tone down the "superiority complex" of men. Ok let's not get much in to the issues other-way-round, that's not of much concern to me, but I guess these two statements must explain the other-side too. It usually takes a lot of maturity for the guy to accept and be comfortable with a woman 'he thinks' is (irrespective of whether she really is) as good as or better than him. But then on the other hand, I feel the current-day relationship counseling hype plays a bit of culprit too here. From times immemorial, in a couple, man and woman have their own strength areas and weaknesses and one is more than than the other in different aspects. These 'complex issues' are today's innovation of the relationship counseling business,

I feel. Though, I personally feel that *the current times have matured to such a stage that, upon working rightly, two people with a frequency-match (who are into each other) can live comfortably together no matter how much they differ in different aspects, keeping this 'more and less' comparisons and discussions at bay.*

By the way, how does one stop the spilling of one of the hemispheres? I leave it to the imagination of the readers…

* I would like to stick to past couple of centuries only, because if one takes the whole human history there are traces of matri-lineal, matri-local and poly-androus families in many tribes. Maybe, the unaccounted history has instances where women were intellectually and even physically dominant than men, though it might be difficult for us now to come to terms with it.

**Frequency match does not necessarily mean they are equal or compatible in many respects. It only means they have *enough compatibility* in temperamental characteristics, given the societal situations of their times, *to be able to work on the differences.*

- May 13, 2013, 06:39 PM.

99. Energy Centres – II

This is in continuation of the post on *Energy Centres.*

NOTE: These posts on Energy Centres are NOT addressed to a generic set of audience, but to those who are undergoing a sudden trauma/distress/transformation and are trying to cope up with such sudden turn of events.

We are in Yoga as we live. A restless mind, a weak body, mind engaged in attention and observation, relaxed body, euphoria, depression all are one or the other of those yogic states. But the problem arises when we are attuned to one such state for a long time and get stuck there unable to come out of it. That is when we need help from explicit yogic techniques. (While regular yoga accentuates the quality of life, 'normal' people can manage to do away with yoga and still healthily cope up with 'normal' circumstances)

A balance of internal feminine and masculine energies of the human body goes a long way in coping up with the chaotic life styles being adopted today. The *Belly-Breathing* pose and *Sambhavi Mudra* are cited as two simple yet powerful tools that can help in channelizing the energies of base and higher chakras respectively. Yes, just two techniques out of thousands of asanas and hundreds of meditation forms, they just take 10-15 mins of one's time daily! Making them part of one's daily work-out routine will prove to be of immense help to cope up with stress. Sure, they cannot be a panacea to all problems themselves, but they give the inner peace needed to help ourselves, attend to our problems and find an apt solution. If one cannot readily identify which of these two need more work, one can alternate between these two and check for oneself what makes one feel better and balance the channelizing accordingly. Wish you good luck on your path to rejuvenation!!!

May the world receive divine blessings of Lord Manikanta.

Fig 11 – Lord Manikanta

- *May 22, 2013, 05:25 PM.*

100. Frequency Shift Keying

"Spoorti has planned to develop a new hobby of playing a video game 'Lone Survivor'. She cannot play it at office because the office environment does not leave her with a comfortable scope. At home, her brother does not let her play and has flooded her system with his favourite games that do not suit her interests in any way. She goes crazy and restless unable to pursue her interests. Eventually she realizes she cannot play video games when she is home."

"Lil Magdalene has no hope and desire in the present. She keeps dreaming about her future."

"Lil Ted is so nostalgic about his past, he is just stuck reliving his past over and over!"

"Ankita, born into an orthodox family leads a split life being today's woman outside her home and girl of yesteryears at home..."

"We all, as students, feel sleepy when we start studying something seriously and often do not retire to sleep peacefully thinking of the courses we have not covered..."

. . . . .

It's not always about time management. In most of the crucial moments it's about frequency management. I don't know why life has to be so difficult, but it proves too difficult sometimes for some people. If only one can stay at the right frequency at the right time, life would be so easy! Most of the times, the tolerance of too tolerant people continues to be tested because non-tolerant people are not tolerant any way and no body has the tolerance to test such non-tolerant people. Ok too much of tolerance there, let's just wipe that word away! I re-write this again (without tolerance) - People do not try to understand tolerant people assuming they are "strong-minded"... but nothing can remain same forever and there's got to be a limit!

Technically speaking, all life is Frequency Shift Keying! The big question is how do we get that FSK in place working just right for us??? *One has to take that "big shift" to stop dreaming and start staying in the moment.* That's not a big deal of work at all! It's not about what not to do or how to avoid the spurious frequencies; it's more about getting into the present… getting interested in the present…

- May 28, 2013, 11:05 PM.

101. Sex, Religion and Spirituality...

While seeking God and Truth - the highest virtue - can be the ultimate objective, seeking it in the anticipation of abusing it is a sin...but that is exactly what some seers have been doing since ages - abusing the path of realizing God... Those seers who claim themselves to be Gods! While all of us are part of God, NOBODY can be a God when on earth, at most one can elevate oneself to realize God when on earth, which is a unique and blessed experience in itself beyond where words can go...A person who truly realizes God shall never claim that he/she is a God...

Sex has been grossly misunderstood in the context of Spirituality. Sex is a pious act between two "consenting" partners "committed" for a relationship, not a weapon/toy in the hands of just about any spiritual leader claiming to heal people the spiritual way. It can be the beginning (of life), the end, but not an end in itself!!! The sex scandals in the context of religion are a SHAME on the understanding of sex by humans. It only shows the ignorance a human birth and half-baked knowledge can unleash upon us.

Reportedly (as reported by various news sources), a seer by name Nityananda tells some of his devotees that sex with him is a divine act as a path to salvation, to convince them into the act.

(How can anybody dare make such statements like those made by Nityananda? It's unfortunate that we being a 'civilized society' cannot take an appropriate action on such senseless claims!)

That sexual exploit is not new and has been there since long. The abuse of some women as Devdasis[1] by people in the name of religion is just an instance. The rigidity of the caste system ushered in by some Brahmins/seers/whosoever who wanted to forward their interests could not be dispelled by many other seers, say like those of Bhakti cult (Chaitanya, Tulsidas, Tukaram, Meera etc). The exploit does not stop there, it manifests into a larger evil - the child abuse and the rape of women today are a few disgraceful epitomes of the evil-fostering human tendency... (Don't know about abuse of men, so will refrain from commenting)

And this is not confined only to Hinduism. There are other news' sources which talk about top religious (or self-acclaimed and hence so-called *spiritual*) leaders who were caught in sex scandals in Christianity, Islam and other religions too.

Back to Hinduism, it is time people stop associating the cosmic couple, our divine parents as models of divine sex and only sex, the wrong way...and instead understand the real essence of their relationship and emulate it in real life if

---

[1]   Devdasis: *(Sanskrit/Telugu)* A devdasi is a girl "dedicated" to the worship and service of God and not allowed to marry a mortal. This practice is said to have emerged in India during 6th century CE. They usually took care of temple, performed rituals and pursued one of the classical Indian artistic traditions of dance and music and exhibited it in temples. This practice was legally abolished after Independence, through different acts in different states.

possible... The important distinction that we, specifically those practising spiritual chores or exercises, need to understand is that: Spirituality is the union of the human consciousness with the divine consciousness whereas Sexuality (Sex) is the unison of male and female.

- Jun 07, 2013, 07:35 PM.

102. Decreased energy burden on earth - A scenario!

As I see it, there are five fundamental energy-usage patterns:

- Decreased energy needs of humanity.

- Decreased energy consumption.

- Proportionate energy recycling back to earth.

- Energy replenishment by earth itself.

- Demolition of a part of humanity to force a decrease in the energy needs, thrusting the cycle back to step (1).

(1) *Decreased energy needs of humanity:*

This was the phase when mankind was in the beginning of evolution. They did not see any need to use up ALL the energy, since their needs were limited. For a while, even when the needs grew, they did not know how to harness the energy, in fact they did not even know of such a possibility.

(2) *Decreased energy consumption:*

This was when the evolution came to a meaningful phase...past the very early man phase. Man now knows he could use resources from nature. But then he feared nature too. It was still a mystery - the thunder, the lightning, the fire, the waterfalls, the roar of the ocean, the music and silence of nature, birth and death, disease, human body... This was the phase when man worshipped nature. He had inherent fear - he believed that if he did something he did not understand properly, nature will get back on him with double the force and punish him. So he did not go overboard, instead he kept a check on his needs and consumed energy carefully.

(3) *Proportionate energy recycling back to earth:*

Man started growing intelligent by this time, a time when the adage *"Necessity is the mother of all invention"* made sense... The energy harnessing spiked up drastically and so started the abuse of earth (and its resources). It could have been abuse actually, but the fear was still there, so he had sense that he had to give back what he takes. No no, it's not even that, he did not have the power and energy to take what he could not give back. Not that man wasn't selfish then, just that nature still reined powerful. Man just could not get in the way of replenishment nature naturally does for itself...

(4) *Energy replenishment by earth itself:*

No! This is not one of the phases in the evolution. It's not same as the above phase. It's a possibility. I should rather qualify it further - replenishment of earth DESPITE and TANTAMOUNT to the (ever) growing needs of man. This is something man would always wish for. *In fact this is an inherent assumption that shows in the energy consumption patterns of today's man.* Not that he does not know that energy is NOT infinite. Just that he doesn't care, doesn't think about a possibility of - *"What if the future generations starve for energy and resources?" Can nature ever replenish her resources indefinitely as per man's needs? No*! If it has to, it has to be due to some magical geomorphological process. Though it's a very endearing solution to man theoretically, it's not a solution that works! Because, even if such a magic happens, ***the more the earth gives, the more the man takes***. Man must be less greedy and more sensible for this option to work, but as already said, this works only in theory or may be only for short spans of time (after some lessons learnt), because in the long run man gets back to his usual selfish mode.

Besides, nature must be having more things to do apart from replenishing itself.

(5) *Demolition of a part of humanity to force a decrease in the energy needs:*

This happens at that phase, *when man has overpowered, outsmarted and outgrown nature.* As one Telugu movie writer says, it's a phase when "Paapapu tarugai, pudami ki baruvai, manavaali peruguthunnappudu...[1]" It's a phase when man's greed has no check and only a demolition of some part of life on earth and *more importantly demolition of energy hogging entities is a solution*, no other kind of solution exists then. It's a time

---

[1]   Paapapu tarugai, pudami ki baruvai, manavaali peruguthunnappudu... :
      (Telugu) "When humanity grows like a piece of scrap as a burden to earth..."

when a saviour comes not to save humanity, but to save earth as a planet and hence save humanity in the process, whether or not man agrees with it, whether or not he realizes that he too is being saved.

This kind of fury from nature happens constantly - the earth quakes, the volcanoes, the famines etc... but at this phase man knows how to save himself from calamities, besides the population would have been increased to such an extent that loss of some life is not a big deal. Then, it's a pain to nature, not man, that it has exercised and executed such fury...

Ideally, we need to follow a mix of steps (1), (2) and (3) so that (4) happens *"naturally, inherently and implicitly"* without any burden on earth. But since man is not so sensible and is selfish instead, (5) is bound to happen some day or the other... Unfortunately, man sees Human Evolution as a linear process, as if we are progressing in a straight line. It reflects not just in the images of our Science text-books of our School, but also in the way we lead our lives.

We need to adapt our lifestyles so our needs are less (Step 1), we need to use our intelligence sensibly, invest in pro-nature-pro-human technologies, research on harnessing energy efficiently and use abundant alternative energy so that our consumption decreases (Step 2) and feel responsible enough to put energy back and hence innovate such technologies (Step 3), instead of expecting earth to *"somehow"* replenish her reservoirs (step 4), so as to avoid large-scale destruction (by nature Herself - Step 5). But all this, "if only" we all are THAT sensible and wise! We can't care enough to be what it takes to be that sensible and wise...at least this mesh of society does not let that happen right? In that case, we ALL need to learn the hard way, don't we?

So which phase do you think we belong to...now???

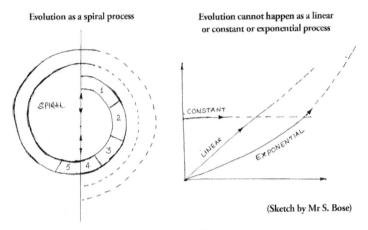

Evolution as a spiral process

Evolution cannot happen as a linear or constant or exponential process

(Sketch by Mr S. Bose)

Fig 12 – Evolution

PS: I might have said – *"thrusting the cycle back to step (1)"* initially, but the idea here more is to NOT be stuck in Steps (4) and/or (5) and instead go further, *beyond the realm of known (the world as we know it)!*

- Jun 11, 2013, 12:40 PM.

103. Feminism - out of context!

On one hand we say marriage/relationship does not complete a woman, on the other hand we say a woman is a reflection of her man. On one hand one in every three women get physically or sexually abused all over the world, on the other hand people (fellow women included) usually blame women saying it is her *'emotional unintelligence'*, behaviour and nagging that invites abuse from men. On one hand we say women must be independent and at par with men, we take slightest of apparently-sexist comment as misogyny and discriminatory of women, on the other hand we talk about strenghtening laws for women and sometimes frame laws that are too pro-women (whether or not they are implemented well). In the name of safeguarding women's interests and rights, today's women end up being confused and burdened by this world. No offences, only an opinion...

The growing pressure on women these days to become independent and stand up on her legs (as if she was standing on others' legs all these days, come on she was serving the family all the while!!!) in the current framework is almost synonymous to asking her to behave more like a man. It does not let her be independent in her own way. No, I'm not generalizing here, it's about subjective cases. When the fellow beings (read it family, friends, professional circles and society in that order) are understanding by nature, independence comes naturally. But otherwise, it comes with associated costs... (say, giving her freedom need not ncessarily mean she must be under the pressure of bringing money equally!)

If equality is all we need, it's high time we stop placing women's independence out of context. Being independent does not mean she does not need love and affection from a partner or that she should stop 'depending' on a man. *Dependence on fellow beings is in the human nature, it's not a woman's arena alone!* It only means women must grow enough to be able to make their choices, participate equally in the decision making of both famiy and society. ***It also means that the society too***

315

should grow along with them to give women their space and let them have their say.

Let's admit, relationships and marriage are an essential part of life for human beings, they are as important for a woman as they are for a man. *In the name of making women independent, let's not undermine the importance of marriage in one's life and make this societal framework even more complicated.*

PS: Triggered by some of the articles and blogs that go gaga about women's independence, quite a few of them mis-interpreting the underlying essence of women empowerment, ignoring the implications of solutions they propose.

- Jun 23, 2013, 05:56 PM.

104. Compatibility

Two friends travelling by car, pressed for time, are trying to meet at a random place one evening... Here's how the conversation goes on phone...

F1: Where are you?

F2: On Road No. 1! And you?

F1: On Road No. 2! Ok, so we'll meet in some time...

F2: (After a while) Where are you?

F1: On Road 1, and you?

F2: Already on Road 2, have been searching for you for a while and came forward....

F1: And I did just the same and somehow we missed, (cuts the phone seeing the police man approaching him...calls back *F2* again after a while) so where are you now?

F2: I'm on Road 3 and might be reaching Road 1 in some time....and how's it going with you?

F1: I'm on Road 2 and it might take some more time before I reach Road 3...

F2: Ok I don't see any dividers here and cannot immediately take a U-turn to travel towards Road 2, will go till the end of Road 3 and travel in the opposite direction towards Road 2...

F1: But Road 3 is fully congested with traffic and is difficult to drive the opposite way towards Road 2?

F2: But the signs on this road are pretty good and it will take lesser time and all the more easy to reach Road 2. If I take Road 1, I might just get lost and might not be able to reach Road 2 any time today, to be able to meet you...

F1: Great! So the plan is to meet at the famous T junction of Road 2 and Road 3, right?

F2: Right! Hopefully... if everything goes fine :)

. . . . .

It's not too often that two people walk the same road. And compatibility is not being similar enough to be able to stay on the same page all the time. Compatibility is the willingness to adjust, compromise, accommodate and work out the differences so as to reach the same page. This despite all the distractions and harbingers in that journey...

While compatibility is often referred to in marital relationships, it is equally challenging to arrive at, in other relationships too. While it is true that a relationship between a husband and a wife is the most fundamental, demanding and challenging, it needs patience to work out other relationships too as they evolve and grow, post marriage. These relationships - between parents and children, siblings, friends, other relatives and finally with the society, are least focused and studied in today's world (irrespective of whether the marital relationships are evolving commensurately with the focus they get). Not sure about the general situation in reality, but atleast the creative world (books, movies, art) of "today" is so full of analyzing and dissecting the nuances of romantic relationships the most...

But, the world is not replete with romantic relationships, even the relationship between partners has many phases sans romance. It needs a lot of patience to withstand the wear and tear of long run for "any" relationship to grow, evolve and reinforce...

Isn't it time we pay a little more attention to the study of non-romantic relationships too?

- *Jul 02, 2013, 02:06 PM.*

105. *Of everything and nothing!*

Over the past three months I have been languishing a lot, got stuck at many places. But there has been a lot of progress, I'd say, by all means. Well yes, I might be feeling like an empty vessel now, but not looking back and checking the progress would mean being too hard on myself. And I can never hurt myself too badly, so I constantly keep telling myself - *Yes you made some progress and that's not a lie for solace!*

I seem to have everything - a good job, money, a good family - parents and brothers to support me through the thick and thin and a given-up (for now or maybe forever in this lifetime) short-lived aspiration. Yet I seem to have nothing.

So what makes me feel I have nothing? Any person would point out that the reason is that I'm not in marriage/relationship and getting married would solve everything. While getting married might set things right, not being in marriage did not cause this vaccuum in me. The reasons are different. That said, marriage has the power to fill vaccuum in life - it can make or break a person, I wouldn't undermine its importance in life. To be loved or appreciated is a powerful motivation in one's life that brings about meaningful responsibilities too. It engages a person in the most fulfilling way.

And there comes the answer - to be loved/appreciated and to love/appreciate back, have meaningful responsibilities and have something to look forward to when you wake up in the morning, are some of the important sustaining factors in life. Marriage and the consequent family is the easiest answer, but not the only answer to achieve that. There are people who are not interested in marriage but have found their life's calling and went on to materialize them (ofcourse by that I don't really mean I'm one of them, but what I'm saying is - for some, marriage has not been the best way of answering it). It all depends on - *at what point one is at, in one's own soul journey and if marriage really fits one's bill.*

My age old funda and perspective of looking at life - "Oh! There are people who don't have food, basic necessities and differently challenged people who are constantly struggling with life on a day-to-day basis, so I'm one of those lucky people who are better off" - is not working on me any more. Yes, but it still helps me to lift myself from my deep fall-downs though. All those people are actively engaged in a constant pursuit of having their necessities met. The necessities they are struggling for, have already been met for me and not necessities-to-be-strived-for any more. Call it luck or God's grace, I only need to put some minimal efforts to sustain my existing resources to see to it that those needs are automatically met. There is a category of people, of which I'm one or have been one, which is the most highly challenged. And that category of people do not even know what their life's necessities are (put aside that "Purpose Of Life" term for now, let's call it a necessity, neat and simple!) and are constantly trying to figure them out. And they seem to have everything, yet nothing.

All in all, I'm tired of brooding over my past - both good and bad parts. I've had eventful, painful, exhilarating, opportune, depressing, dragging, humbling and honoring experiences, none of which I regret now and only thank the Divine for bestowing them upon me. There were phases when I knew my grief, sorrow and depression had no reasons whatsoever, yet all of them could not have been avoided and had to be experienced. ***It's strange to experience a phase you know is*** *not needed, yet can't be avoided.* Sure, all experiences might not be evidently useful, might not lead to success, but they are good to have. But I don't want to be tied to them anymore. It's that time for me when I need to say bye to the old and buy the new. *I want a different reference point from which I can see my life better.* Looking from the past references has only been complicating things and I know that's not needed any more. I know that there are problems in my life, but I also know that I need a renewed perspective/strength to handle them better. *I just need to shift and I know all my answers stay there in that shifted continuity.* And is it enough if I alone shift? No! All those I love and all those I need, all those who love me and need me and all the resources I love and need... :)

- Sep 03, 2013, 11:24 PM.

106. Surrender

I've come across a famous figure (whose name I forgot) saying everybody in this world is replaceable in less than few minutes. He recollects his childhood memory wherein the then American President is dead and he sees some random guy talking on TV when he asks his Dad - *"Dad who's that?"* to which he's replied *"It's the American President!"*...*"Well, but the American President is dead?!?!"*...*"Yes, but he is replaced and there is this new guy"*...

While I'd like to believe that people are easily replaceable only in their professional roles, there is a nice point that the celebrity is actually trying to drive home - *That we all are little cogs in this grand schema of things in the Universe - The Grand Framework or The Grand Illusion.* I'd like to tackle this from a different angle - *Surrender*. When we realize that we are too small, too little and feel powerless not seeming to have any control on things and yet are affected by those very things, the only way is to surrender all our acts and efforts to people who have the power to control them. Sometimes, there is nothing we can do about some things. But, that doesn't mean we are unworthy and that we did not have our share of contribution. We do a lot of things, but they culminate to attention/recognition due to others. It's synonymous to a race, a single race, run by many people passing on the baton to others once their share of running is over. I surrender my past *(its karma: both merit and sin)* to God and my efforts and burden to those who can get the better of them and take over. And feel lighter! :)

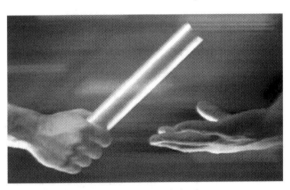

Fig 13 – Passing of the baton

- Sep 04, 2013, 03:16 PM.

107. The Immortals of Meluha - Shiva Trilogy I

My friend Swati is a great fan of Shiva Trilogy. But the majority opinion I came across, from my known circles, on Shiva Trilogy is that it wasn't too well-written. One friend, a voracioius book reader does not recommend the book, same with another friend who put it down after reading it a bit and my younger brother who says, *"Oh that book! It's supposedly not that good"*... But for the fan I am of the *Shiva Transcentendalism*, these reviews did not deter me. So during August 10ᵗʰ and 11ᵗʰ, on a to and fro train journey to Vijayawada to attend my friend's marriage, I started reading this book. I got back to books after a long time, so I had relatively more tolerance for anything that was to come in the book.

Proceeding a bit into the book, I started understanding why it did not attract ardent book lovers. For people who are used to complex narrations, this narration comes across as very very bland. Even for my mind that is used to liking not-so-complex narrations, this seemed dry. One fourth of the content in the book is compilation of simple verbs - *Shiva grinned, Vraka bowed, Parvateshwar growled and so on*. This continuous effort to convey same emotions over and over does not interest the reader in any way and seemed completely unwarranted.

But ignore this and get past one fourth of the book and then you would get into the real part of the story. The story does not get any interesting until Shiva meets Sati and if you have not even got there, you have not even started it yet. And once you get there, the boredom/blandness of the preceding part seems completely justified. That is how all our lives are, we all wander with no aim and everything seems so random....until, until we meet the real people meant for us, until we have some goals and responsibilities, until we know ourselves better or in short until we meet our destiny. Other thing is the frame of mind and perspective with which you are approaching this book. This book would be appealing *only if you can get into Shiva's shoes* i.e., the book is more interesting from Shiva's perspective than from a reader's perspective, *you have to take His side, for the book to be interesting.* If you are one in expectation of heavy literature, analyses, complicated plot, the book is definitely not for you. Are you one weighed down by your destiny and conscience? Or are you one on the path of spirituality, due to awakening of some consciousness and in splits unable to choose between your real life and the so called assigned responsibilities due to that path? Or are you one in search of purpose of life and goals? Then this book will definitely make a good read.

And I give full marks to Amish's creativity; I must say I'm completely spellbound by the simplicity in his creativity. Anybody else would have made it all sound so complicated. ***It takes courage and creativity to imagine and narrate Shiva as a normal human being in blood and flesh.*** The fulcrum of the book on which the story is woven is - *The burden of being called a Saviour and the journey towards accepting it and maturing into one.* Many interesting things are said in the book - the Maika system which handles the multi-class/caste society; the concept of change over the generations; the relative perspectives of good and evil - of how there is no evil, but only an existence of duality; the concept of Vikarma[1]; the governance and the order of the society, all of which takes detailed study of Sociology is narrated in simple laymen terms. ***Amish has shared fundamental wisdom to all of us very generously, I'd say, without he or his characters not sounding preachy anywhere.***

Sati's portrayal as a strong and independent woman is very neat. There's a subtle difference between being independent as a person, yet being dependent on the person one loves and

---

[1]   Vikarma: *(Sanskrit)* Bad past Karma.

expecting complete love and trust from them. Shiva-Sati relationship depicts that delicate balance, which is grossly misunderstood in today's modern love relationships. If a man expects a woman to be independent that does not mean he has no responsibilities towards her or that he is not expected to protect her.

Initially it might be difficult for a Shiva devotee to accept the human side of this character - the errors he commits, the guilt he carries, a very simple world view he has and finally the portrayal of romantic love between Shiva and Sati in normal human terms. Yet a Shiva devotee would be appeased by the end of the book, the devotee in me was. *How Shiva does not put his responsibilities and aspirations above love and his relationships, is some food for thought for today's young men.* And that completely reverberated with my ideologies too - no responsibility is above oneself/one's family and if it is, *then its fulfillment at the cost of oneself,* wouldn't be good to anybody, not even to those for whom the responsibility was taken up. In that sense the story, though a piece of fiction, seems very realistic. Most of the talk in the book is done in rational terms from the perspective of Science and Society and not from the view of faith/religion/God.

My review of this book - As simple as creativity can get.

Strengths of the book - Story, Concepts and World Views discussed.

Weak points of the book - Narration.

My recommendation - I completely recommend the book to you, if you are curious to know what it feels and takes to be a Saviour.

- Sep 07, 2013, 03:26 PM.

108. Don't dig into earth when the sun sets!

Ok, so the sun never sets and it's only earth that rotates and hence the night, right? Fine, let me rephrase - Don't dig into that side of the earth for which it is night.

I said this earlier, in a lighter vein, to some people, who can make some difference, in a discussion on Planet Earth - *Don't bother that side of her when she retires for the day.* But nobody was bothered; nobody even cared to respond on that.

In earlier days, people used to set some rules without bothering to discuss the rationale behind them and people just followed - like don't sleep with your head facing north, don't cut your nails after sun-set and all that. The practice then was to just set the rules, but not explaining the rationale behind them, because most of the people were not in a state to assimilate the rationale. So the preachers or those who set the morals and rules did not get into the tedious process of explaining them. But call it wisdom or ignorance prevailing then, many people used to follow such rules back then! I guess, it's high time we start setting such rules, new rules for the modern day.

And the first one I'd start with, is this.

Don't drill into earth for borewells, pipelines, oil and minerals when it is night for her!

Why? Because Bhudevi/Goddess Lakshmi or some celestial being out there bears the burden of earth every moment and it's going to be quite painful for them! Ok, so all you people are not going to buy this, are you? I'll explain it in a different way... in a scientific way perhaps ...

When the earth rotates and hence when half of it _"turns away"_ from Sun, it ceases to draw power from Sun. It's more or less in a very powerless situation. Earth gives life, for the seeds to sprout into life, to harbour many things inside it and let them evolve in a way useful for humanity; it assimilates the material of the dead and recycles it. Earth is a living being for all scientific purposes and experiments, people! When the plants sleep, when the animals sleep, when the human beings sleep, **_don't you think the earth too retires to a powerless mode every day?_** Trying to draw something from her during that time, is like giving one anesthesia and cutting one's body to smuggle some part of the body... Now don't get me started questioning - then what is the analogy for drilling in the day time? It's at least as good as one donating blood voluntarily and consciously.

These days, many people prefer to dig borewells during night for the fear of disturbing others with the commotion during the day. But this is not so much in the best interests of earth. Mother Earth writhes in pain and weeps when such things happen. You are wondering how I know it? I just know it, that's all. I got a very bad dream just now, as I got asleep after a tiresome day, with Mother Earth weeping and hence this post...

- _Sep 12, 2013, 11:17 PM._

109. Energy Centres III - Balance – Ascension

This is again in continuation of the two posts on Energy Centres. Put all the three posts together to get the right context and understand the message that is being conveyed.

All the three posts are particularly addressed to those who are currently sensing the need for some guidance on how to go about apparently abnormal spiritual experiences that might have shaken them from the comfortable confines of day-to-day living. The rest may really choose to ignore the details of these posts.

Big Bang is supposed to be that process when God (Universe) split itself into 'Consciousness' (Shiva) and 'Energy' (Shakti). Precession of Equinoxes (referred to as PoE henceforth for convenience) is that point of time when Consciousness and Energy unite in the process of expanding this Universe. The earth is currently passing through that phase wherein it has to experience this process.

While the preparation for this phase started long long ago, even before the beginning of *Kali Yuga*, the immediate precursor to this event is to make the Humanity and Earth ready and prepared for the event. *PoE involves inversion of the orientation of Earth's wobbling and also setting it into the next spiral of expansion larger than the preceding spiral in all aspects (energy, frequency etc) and hence can be termed Ascension.* As part of this, many (perhaps not many, could be just 1% who consciously feel that something is actually happening, while for the rest it happens without their awareness) people on Earth ARE currently experiencing Ascension. The real responsibility though rests on whosoever is the *Sustenance Couple* to unite Shiva and Shakti and *through them the Earth and Humanity ascends.*

The experience of Ascension is triggered by *Awakening of Consciousness and Kundalini* within oneself. Experiencing only one of those two is extremely terrible and dangerous too. Consciousness - the male aspect of the Universe - provides the needed information and guidance on how to go about the process and Kundalini[1] - the female aspect of the Universe - provides the material base for the actual process (unison of male and female aspects within oneself*) to take place. Thus the whole event involves three major phases:

❖ *Preparation:* Understanding the information, as guided by the Consciousness.

❖ *PoE:* Unison of Cosmic Mother and Father.

❖ *Ascension:* Assimilating the process of Expansion, once the Unison starts.

These three phases are Past, Present and Future from the frame of reference of PoE. Both the Humanity and Earth have more or less completed going through the Preparation phase and gearing up for PoE. But the preparatory phase puts them to experience all the three phases. The Expansion results in release of huge quantums of energy which ought to be assimilated, again, by both the Earth and Humanity.

---

[1] Kundalini & Chakras: *(Sanskrit/Hindi/Telugu)* <u>Literary Meaning:</u> *Kundalini* is the corporeal indwelling spiritual energy lying dormantly coiled at the base of the spine, that can be *awakened* in order to purify the subtle system and bestow upon the 'seeker of Truth' the state of Yoga, Union with the Divine, the Source. The Yogic philosophy describes it as a form of feminine Shakti or sleeping serpent. <u>Background:</u> We are usually aware of only body and mind, but human body harnesses and perpetuates on the *Spiritual Energy* that flows through the 7 *Energy Centres (Chakras)* connected across the spine.

So, in the preparatory phase, how does one know which phase one is experiencing?

- *Phase 1 - Preparation:* When one is constantly living under the heavy influence of one of these two elements - Consciousness or Energy. This means that further work needs to be done, to unite the male and female aspects within self. Listen more closely to the guidance offered.

- *Phase 2 - PoE:* When one is experiencing a phase of voidness. The explicit influence of Absolute Consciousness has more or less left you and you are feeling numb, almost.

- *Phase 3 - Ascension:* When one is experiencing heavy bounties of energy. This must NOT be confused with Phase 1 and one must NOT repeat the same steps as followed in the initial phase. One must only try to assimilate the energy and wisdom offered.

So how does it feel when one has ushered in balance and is stabilized?

You do not anymore "explicitly" sense the guidance of Cosmic Consciousness. The energy flows freely through your Chakras[1] and you do not anymore "explicitly" sense the same.

Hence in order to reach that stabilized state, try and let the energies and thoughts flow freely through you and do not meddle or tamper with them. If the experience is too heavy and unbearable, practise *Sambhavi Mudra* and *Belly*

Breathing alternately. Also try meditating on sound and breath intermittently.

As I was browsing internet for more information on *Chakras,* I bumped into www.chakras.net. It's a beautiful source of information for fundamental concepts on Chakras, I highly recommend it for both the uninitiated as also the experts. It reinforces a lot of aspects I received through my Realization. Immense thanks to the author of this site for sharing eloquently, fundamental wisdom, for the benefit of others.

* This is not merely combining male and female sexual energies within oneself as it might appear at the outset. It's more about overcoming the negative aspects of self, while streamlining the positive aspects.

- *Sep 14, 2013, 10:21 PM.*

110. Unsettled, Used, Yet Abandoned

I don't feel settled even for a minute, I forgot when I last lived my life...
You seem to unsettle me all the time.
True you have your wounds and scars.
I do understand, if not fathom completely, how broken it feels with them.

But do you also think about mine?
I'm sure you do, so then how does it feel looking at it from my side?
Isn't it difficult and painful, to try giving oneself when one is not taken?

And how difficult is it to always give?
Nevermind, I too am selfish perhaps!

It is said, when one really tries to heal others' wounds, one shall have one's own wounds healed.
And who is not selfish? Selfishness without overreaching others, isn't that a good trait?
Isn't that the reason behind all human marvels and achievements?
If man isn't selfish and stays selfless like a saint, wouldn't this world be so dull?

Who am I?
I am the Nature, taken (for granted) by man and used at will and fate.

But can I remain powerless forever?
I don't exercise power because I don't like it that way...
I save it for that time, when nature can and must rein powerful,
More powerful than man...

- *Sep 30, 2013, 11:50 AM.*

111. State of my mind, today...

As you tender nature, nature serves you, as per its resources. It is through this perfect Alchemy between nature and man that the elixir of life was exponentiated and quality of life accentuated in the so-called "Golden Age" of humanity. This is the truth we long lost in touch with.

- *Oct 08, 2013, 12:01 PM.*

112. Medium

As I move on in life, I realize that it's so difficult to be a *medium, as simple and plain* as *medium,* of and for change.

- Oct 09, 2013, 10:48 PM.

113. Altogether new

I had this musing in life since childhood, of how it feels to conceive, perceive and bring into life, an idea of something which never existed before. No, I'm not talking about creation of life or anything here. I'm more talking about a feeling, an entirely altogether new feeling which one might have never sensed before. To make it simpler, I'll put my secret musing quite openly and directly - We have five senses - sight, hearing, touch, smell and taste (technically termed as visual, auditory, sensory, olfactory and gustatory senses). And yes we talk about sixth sense, seventh sense and so on. But all the five senses seem tangible while any sense beyond them is more or less considered abstract. I wonder how a tangible sixth sense might feel like. No, I'm not referring to sixth sense in the way we all generally use it. How would a new sense be, if God were to really come up with one? All the five senses are tied to five sensory, by that I mean physical sensory organs. The sixth sense, as we term it, is connected to mind or as we move beyond might even fall in the realm of soul. But think of a sixth sense, that can be tied to something that is physical, something that we can more tangibly feel... Think! Just think!

Yes ofcourse that definitely doesn't mean I'm underrating the sense presented by mind. Nor am I stating that any sense that deals with mind alone is abstract. Isn't the so-called tangibility of all the five senses really brought about by mind? And then, without spirit the brain cannot manifest as mind, in fact there's no life at all and then we might have to re-state everything all over again! The statement – *"We are the spirit, we just have a body"* (NOT, we have a spirit) really explains it all.

I had tried to come up with a sixth sense that is more tangible and could make as much sense and be of as much use (by that I mean it must be more or less a necessity to get on with day-to-day life) as the rest of the five senses. But damn! Couldn't really think of any. Creativity isn't such an easy job! Anything I come up with, feels like a sub-set of existing senses. Like a new sense that gifts me the ability to see many more things that were previously invisible - like the X-ray sight to look through. Lo! That clearly falls under sight. More colors, more sounds, ability to patternize immediately after sight, in fact during sight or hearing itself, you name it, you already have it, atleast as the super-set! Should a new sense really mean a new physical part altogether? Ofcourse, a new useful sense would mean a new property (not-yet-explored, not-yet-discovered or not-yet-existent) of things in the creation around us, seen in a more useful light.

Coming back to the sixth-sense, the abstract sixth-sense concept, I think there is a lot more variety possible. Mind-reading, Telepathy, Ability to Time Travel and perhaps many more. Or perhaps all these feel abstract only because they have not evolved to the right amount that makes them tangible and useful and more importantly not harmful and counter-productive. Hmm, abstract just for the time-being perhaps?!?

Does anybody out there have any speculations about this?

As a side note, when I think of senses, I'm reminded of this famous thought proposed by Philosophical Thinker – David Hume. He says that – *"Matters of fact that do not have sensory experience must be rejected"*. In fact as per his theory God and Soul are to be rejected. I was wondering if hunger too must be rejected as per his theory. I just posed exactly this question to a Sociology expert – *"Should hunger be considered abstract and rejected as per this theory?"* She goes on to say that hunger manifests in pain in the stomach after a certain limit and since pain can be felt by the stomach, hunger can't be rejected. Since she was not my friend and did not seem to be ready for any debate then, I did not want to get argumentative with her. But tell me this…the pain felt by the stomach, what category of the five senses does that fall under?

In fact ever since my Awakening, I had literally felt the pain of experiencing God, that pain of experiencing the Cosmic Consciousness, that pain of experiencing Cosmic Energy. I had felt that pain, burden and even the positive spectre of other feelings along with them. So I know, I very much know for sure, God exists. By that I mean I am aware that we are evolving and progressing as One. When I say God exists, I'm saying there is some sort of interconnectedness in our Existence through the Spirit and through the existence of collective consciousness. But then I also understand that people who believe in Hume's theory would reject God since they might have never experienced whatever I had been experiencing and feeling. So how can they understand God then? But on the other hand, I know of many people who *feel the warmth* when somebody *helps* them, when some unforeseen incident *happens in their favour*; I know of those who *cry* when they are *overwhelmed* by *gratitude* and *love*. All of them, those people including me, are ***sensing*** God through our thought and heart. We indeed are! I would definitely advocate for the sensory perception through '*thought* and *heart*' to be regarded as a sense unto itself!

And coming to the argument of defence for Hume's theory to conceptualize hunger – *"hunger manifests in pain in the stomach after a certain limit and since pain can be felt by the stomach, hunger can't be rejected"*, if I a draw a parallel between hunger and our understanding of God, maybe there is that certain limit of time until which we do not feel the pain – the pain due to absence of God, the pain of pining for God, the pain to be undergone to understand the essence of God. Maybe when we reach that time limit, even atheists might be able to believe in God? And maybe that time is near?

- Oct 09, 2013, 11:07 PM.

114. Disaster on doorstep

So says today's headline in *The Hindu* Newspaper. Precisley, it is *"Disaster on doorstep of AP, Odisha"*. *"CNN explains the danger inherent in Phailin"* says another Hindu update on FB four hours ago. *"Cyclone Phailin closing in and is about 40 kms from Odisha coast"* goes another update about an hour ago and the latest news in TV just now is that the cyclone did cross the shore and has already taken the lives of about 7 people.

Unlike the previous cyclones in India this year, the impending of this cyclone has been forecasted 2-3 days earlier. Lakhs of people have already been evacuated but still much damage is being anticipated. According to the newspapers - *"Cyclone Phailin could be among the worst cyclonic storms in the world at CATEGORY-5 strength"*. It's being compared with Hurricane Katrina, USA, 2005 (windspeed 280 kmph) and Hurricane Paradwip, North Indian Ocean basin, 1999 (windspeed 305 kmph).

I only hope that this cyclone does not turn out to be as disastrous as is being predicted. I'll keep my fingers crossed about that.

- Oct 12, 2013, 07:42 PM.

115. A remarkable milestone!

This is indeed a remarkable milestone in the journey of humanity. Especially, given the kind of challenges in the path. Many starseeds have been initiated into the process of spiritual awakening most of the times even without their knowledge. The kind of uphill task they are expected to accomplish is in the inherent nature of the challenge. It is as good as (or should I say as bad as) being trapped or abducted unawares and then posed with the challenge of liberating themselves of this puzzle or pain, whichever way they see it. As discussed in the post – *"Energy Centres III – Balance - Ascension"*, humanity has successfully completed Phase 1 of the preparatory phase and is also on the verge of completing Phase 2. It means that *"The Shift"* has happened in the preparatory phase and we are very close to the much-needed harmony. The voidness currently being experienced only indicates that our systems are being "rebooted" successfully.

A smooth transition from Phase 2 to Phase 3 in the Preparatory Phase involves the following steps:

- Assimilating energy and wisdom. Letting them flow freely. Not meddling with them is half the assimilation.

- Not yielding to inertia. Not repeating acts in Phase 1. Asserting and exercising Will.

- Opening up of Heart Chakra - *Anahata Chakra* so as to connect the realms of matter and spirit. Anahata Chakra represents love and is responsible for balance.

Do appropriate asanas such as Bhujangasana (Cobra pose), Ustrasana (Camel pose), Marjaryasana (Cat pose), Matsyasana (Fish pose) etc which help in balancing and opening of the heart Chakra on a daily basis by checking which side of the healing you need - are you on the *deficient* side or *overpowered* side of the Heart Chakra? For instance, for the past five months, I tend to sit with my head leaning forward and shoulders rounded indicating that I'm on the deficient side of Heart Chakra. If you are more inclined to lean backward, then you are on the overpowered side of heart chakra. Also I now realize that a couple of asanas related to heart chakra have already been part of my Yoga regimen for a long time, the balance of which has been disturbed of late for want of more time for meditation. So please tune accordingly and set a regimen appropriate for yourself.

"To be able to reach this phase is a collective triumph. While this is the victory of humanity as a whole in this collective journey, the people who have been on the forefront of leading this here on earth are - Manikanta (who I believe is same as Jesus), his companions and Manikanta's consort. And not to forget, many star-seeds on the earth at the moment who have been actively taking part in and shaping up the Ascension process. Cheers!!!" - *A message from our Cosmic Father, Lord Shiva, to humanity.*

- Oct 17, 2013, 11:07 PM.

116. Mourning of the dead part!

For about the past two and half months I have been experiencing a lot of emptiness within. For a long time I drifted with this voidness without questioning anything because I already anticipated this nothingness. It has been as though a blanket of blankness has engulfed life. Wexed with it, only recently I started probing and hence trying to get out of it. I realize that this void has killed a part of me and yet I continued to try operating from that dead part. In hindsight, I, as a whole was numb to this process of killing and my whole being missed getting notified that this part was indeed missing. Having realized that, for a while I was perhaps anticipating that I'd get that part back, that I'd feel the same as before, that the same passion, enthusiasm and energy would be restored. That's completely my clinging to my old self at work. While we keep changing all the time and cannot remain the same forever, this sudden change definitely left me quite confused. I now realize that I need to work on growing myselves again. I see that I lost a part of my emotions, intellect and passions by experiencing that voidness. But the good news that kept dawning gradually is that, a part of my pain, burden and baggage also got cleared.

Now I'm not sure what part of me is dead - I mean how big a part of me was dead... While I'm still not sure if this is all the mourning of a dead part or mourning by my dead self, I currently feel like a clean slate waiting to be written. Is it me or somebody else who should do that, is something I must wait and watch...

- Nov 06, 2013, 10:24 AM.

117. The growth tangent

I used to have many random conversations with my friends on where the current growth is leading all of us to. More often than not, I failed driving my point across as I intend to. It used to come across as though I'm against this technology and people are not supposed to modernize, progress and change. I do understand that with growing population, growing needs we all tend to change and find different solutions for progress. As individuals we put our best efforts, but we are helpless really to gauge if all this is in the best interests of collective good.

It is definitely the onus of "some" collective entity that might indeed be suffering due to this growth tangent, that should own up the responsibility and take some action. As discussed in the post – *These are my interests, so what?* - unless the growth impacts us in some way or the other, there is no way that we spare some thought as to which different direction we need to take. It is indeed foolish to expect that change must come from the bottom in such a scenario. Honestly, the bottom section is not aware of the bigger picture and hence that ignorance reflects in their deeds. This is not really surprising. As I always say, real change comes through a *top-down* approach. I stick to that older opinion of mine. When people who are indeed responsible for some action sit silently, the humanity has no choice but to languish all through their lives in ignorance. I see how futile all my thought process would be, if I can't gel it with an ounce of action. Yet, I see that I lack all the will-power needed to bring change into my own life, let alone do something for the society. It will be a real shame on me if I write even one more blog-post without bringing velocity into my own life that has come to an all-time stand-still stuck with inertia of lethargy and lack of interest. I absolutely don't know what can shake this inertia - inner strength or some external motivation?

- *Nov 09, 2013, 06:03 PM.*

118. *The Act of Assimilating and Giving back!*

So what constitutes an *ideal world*? No I'm not talking about a perfect world where everybody is good and everything happens just perfectly. I'm talking of a world where all sort of imperfections exist, yet the world seems ideal. So it is that world which manifests the possible collective best. We are perhaps now in a perfectly, diametrically opposite scenario where the individual best is being manifested.

While a lot of theories can be propounded and different perspectives presented, I present my theory to understand this concept here. We can divide all human beings into a set of three groups - *Producers, Consumers* and *Perfect Conductors* (playing the perfect Medium). While consumption seems to be the easisest of all, production too is easy for people who have that passion. Consider *Steve Jobs* who tapped into the consumerism perpetually growing in the population. And consider those classic middle-class families in India who spend on electronic goods but do not consume them as much. According to me, playing a perfect medium is not all that easy either. Taking and giving just as much back exercising the right amounts of attachment and detachment on the material wealth and aspirations, is being a perfect medium according to me.

So taking does not mean we just earn things somehow and then try to give something back to the society and attain some Punya[1]. No, we are not talking about the process of converting black money into white money. Assimilation must just happen as much rightly as giving back.

So if the world distributes itself into an *ideal proportion* of sets of Consumers, Producers and Conductors, it is going to be an ideal world in a very hypothetical scenario! Anyway that's not really an ideal world, it's going to be a Smart World that "just knows" what's good for itself. One Smart World - Vasudaika Kutumbam[2]!

PS: Ideal being ideal in all the sense of the term!

- *Nov 15, 2013, 12:06 AM.*

119. Killing the addiction

Staying away from something, being untouched and not being affected by it, is a lot more easier than, getting into it, in fact getting dirty because of it and then learn to come out of it and

---

[1]   Punya: *(Sanskrit/Telugu)* Merit.
[2]   Vasudaika Kutumbam: A *Sanskrit phrase* that propels the concept of the World being ONE family.

then continue to be unaffected by it. Anyone who has been through this rigorous regimen to quit a habit would vouch for this.

So this post was pending for more than a day. Well yes it reminds me of one of my old posts – *The churn that creates purity – a rainbow in the making*. Y'day morning while starting for office, as I was boringly curious of what's actually happening around and making news, I was flipping through Telugu News Channels and randomly zeroed in on *AndhraJyothi's ABN Channel*. As if to tell me that there is not much news around and as if to confirm it's just okay not to catch up with news and the world for over 4 months, there was some advertisement for a product going on. An advertisement show going on early morning @ 9'O clock… imagine how busy the world is marketing! So this was not one of those telemarketing sessions, some noted anchor was hosting the show on a product called *"Addiction Killer"*. Yet, the genuinity of the product might as well fall into the category of the host of those telemarketed products. So, it seems that product detoxifies the body and increases the will power (advertised with all those vitalizing metabolism visuals in the background…)

Atleast they succeeded in sending this simple fundamental across right. When a habit surpasses and takes control over a person, all that happens is - to sum it up in a simple phrase - *"decay of will power"*. And it will be overambitious if their loved ones ask the person under addiction to develop that will power "somehow" and gradually leave the habit. I'm personally aware of a good family which lost its peace and finally the family head under addiction too, since they were too adamant in asking him to quit the habit. Well yes, his health was degenerating already but what hastened the death was the demand to quit a habit that has eaten into the person so much…

It is difficult, but the loved ones of such people must accept this fact that change in such scenarios cannot happen due to any internal motivation. They must leave behind this adamant myth that, it is due to lack of internal motivation that the person is unable to quit something. There could be various unfortunate reasons why people get into such habits, but having gotten into it, the person needs *"external help"*. So the family can let the experts help such people and if possible the family members may actively get engaged in the process of quitting. The sooner it is realized, the better it gets for everybody.

There was another thing too that I wanted to write, but I will keep that for some other day...

- Nov 28, 2013, 10:32 PM.

120. Varna - Women Empowerment?

So the day before yesterday I've been to this movie Varna[1] - Irandaam Ulagam[2] in Tamil, whose title has been inappropriately modified for Telugu Cinema. What was thus perhaps a fiction movie was portrayed to be a heroine-oriented movie. And it's not an art movie by any chance (the way an art-movie is perceived in Tollywood[3]), it's perfectly a commercial movie with all the commercial aspects, if only the audience could make it so.

---

[1]   Varna: *(Telugu)* In this context, the name of the protagonist of the movie. Otherwise it means color.

[2]   Irandaam Ulagam: *(Tamil)* Another Earth.

[3]   Tollywood: *(English)* An English term used to identify Telugu Film Industry.

I've not got any positive reviews on this movie through that word of mouth advertising. And then I bumped into this review in a leading newspaper titled *"Where women aren't victims"* dated *November 30, 2013*, not that this was any positive. In fact I'm surprised to see a review in a leading magazine wherein the script has been manipulated so much to fit into the mesh of their agenda of the article - *"Women Empowerment"*. The woman does try to make the first move (as said there in the review), but she doesn't quite succeed. No, she doesn't pursue at all (as said there in the review), it's the guy who pursues. No, there wasn't any eve-teasing or a similar episode towards the guy (as said there in the review) as such. No, all the women in Earth2 do not surpass men so easily and enslave them (as said there in the review). It's only *Varna*, the protagonist who does that, that too in a very different situation the context of which is quite different from the one set by the critic in that review. We have always had women rebelling against the oppression and suppression. And we had men too, doing the same. How is this any new? And how did this become any newly empowering for women? This was not a movie primarily aimed at empowering women by any means. It's just a pure love story portrayed very beautifully.

Love travels light years in this movie, in split seconds though. It unfolds the concept of Parallel Worlds so mesmerizingly. *Arya* (the actor who played the hero) was just perfect. *Anushka* (the actress who played the heroine) too was great. Great creativity as far as the story is concerned and the script has been perfectly executed. In fact this post is not meant to be a review of this movie and I don't want to talk about it more, for it only spoils the fun if you plan to watch it. What I do want to talk about is the short review given through the aforementioned article. What is so wrong about a woman falling in the arms of a man all out of her choice? From when is that being sympathized as "such a fate befalling her"? And from when did staying loveless being equated as staying independent and strong? I'm totally confused with the way people talk about "Women Empowerment". I already spoke about my ideas on this aspect in the post – *"Feminism – out of context!"*

Even before aiming at *Women Empowerment*, we really need to understand what is it that we want to achieve? ***A woman is NOT empowered when she is "free" to become like a man.*** A woman who stays as a woman and yet has the needed power stands empowered. Such kind of macho empowerment would never happen because it's not in the best interests of women and women collectively would not even let it happen for they don't like it - ***they don't like it when they transform into something completely unlike themselves just to wield power.***

If you have expected an inversion of sexes in this movie, then you are bound to be disappointed. Everything stays just as it is. Men stay men, women stay women. *The movie is more a portrayal of pain of denial of love.* The movie is about triumph of the faith in love and to make that faith succeed. The genders could dominate each other at different points in time, for no single entity can sustain the dominance forever. The emphasis is not on gender domination as much as it is on making love succeed. It's a melodrama showing the craving of love by a man when he loses it - the foothold of men in Indian Cinema for ages. How I wish there is one good Indian movie showing the true trauma undergone by a woman in a similar scenario? And that, without later conveniently forgetting the man and getting married to another - the opposite of which is dedicated to the characterization of women in Indian Cinema for ages again.

Do go watch *Varna* if you have been deterred by negative reviews. It needs you, the audience, for it could be heralding fiction into Tollywood. Well, if you are comfortable with the run-of-the-mill masala movies, that's fine, you will get them more. The choice is completely yours.

- Dec 05, 2013, 07:15 PM.

121. The million-dollar question

I go ahead to take liberties to publicize a piece of communication I had with one of my friends today...this is how it goes...

. . . . .

My friend: *Hey mamata, how have you been? I have been prompted on my inside twice before to write these following lines, but I didn't for no reason. This Christmas, I have great news for you. Jesus loves you soooo much. He cares for you, no matter what you are going through, please remember, Jesus loves you so much. He will see you through. Praying for your future, well being and prosperity! You can contact me @ **********. Jesus is the answer.*

Me: *Hey xxxxxxx, I'm doing good, thanks. Hope you are great too! I believe in the existence of Christ, so you need not hesitate at all to discuss such stuff. Please let Jesus too know, through your prayers, that I love him back. The humanity loves him!*

More than that, humanity needs him for all the faith it has kept in him. Many people too have been bearing the collective burden of human sins along with Jesus since long. It's time Jesus asserts his presence and reinstates that faith! Jesus needs to answer!

*Thanks for your number, I'm reachable @*********. Keep in touch! And hey, Happy Christmas and Happy New Year 2014 in advance!*

For some, Jesus could be the answer, but for many Jesus IS the question...

The million dollar question though is the one, one of my colleagues asks in a lighter vein: *Jesus himself has been muddled up with problems ever since Crucifixion, so how can he solve others' problems?*

I didn't answer though I could have probably given an apt answer. In fact I laughed along with him and said - *Yes, yes, he himself is in problems neck-deep :) So very typical of Gods on Earth...*

I got from Facebook, through the posts of the very friend above who messaged me, the same answer I had: *Prayer is spiritual warfare, but know that God is in the fight and He is with you. Expect to win.*

- Dec 17, 2013, 09:32 PM.

122. Liberation!!!

Our body is a centre for seven *Energy Chakras*. This is something we already know. Man can get back to his true self when the consciousness can successfully reach *Sahasrara*

Chakra, the highest Chakra, starting from *Mooladhara Chakra*, the lowest Chakra. ***Humanity can thus realize its true potential when it can grow to give its consciousness its true destined place. This is the real Cosmic Plan of God for Man.*** This is the kind of existence, a thoughtful collective-pro existence, human beings must lead, according to God. But unfortunately the consciousness loses its power and dies in lower Chakras itself, for various reasons (abuse of sex being one of them), instead of traversing towards the higher realms. The most important help Humanity can do to itself is to enable that consciousness flow to its real seat of destiny. Perhaps this too is something we already know. In fact this is the real problem we face at this juncture of Information Age - We are aware of everything, we are knowledgeable of anything and everything, whether or not we really ought to know it. But we fail to put into practice, even 1% of those things we must really implement in life, we lack the will to do it...*unfortunately the human race by and large has been losing its will power slowly.*

- *Mamata Anurag,*

14/13/12, 08:38 PM.

(The reason for this new way of sigining off is that this is most probably the last date in dd/yy/mm format in such a descending fashion, for this century)

<u>*Self-Notes:*</u>

"Release" in the spiritual sense seen from one perspective is the release of the soul from body, liberation of life from these worldly bonds. That lays the real path to salvation or self-realization (I in my personal capacity say, this could literally mean death, strictly from the earthly plane, NOT the death of the soul). From a different perspective, Release/Liberation could mean liberation from ignorance and rising to the capacity of knowing one's true identity, capacity and responsibilities.

Most of the living organisms in this nature naturally perform the activities of food-production, self-defence and reproduction, through the power and properties bestowed by nature. But man is regarded as the highest living form in existence for he possesses - *a consciousness that is intelligent*, heart - *a thoughtful heart*, intellect, wisdom, ego - in fact egoism, discretion as also the ability to laugh, hate, desire, envy, doubt, be kind, feel shy and also get into the confinements of caste, creed, nation and virtue. He also possesses the fervour of devotion, desire, detachment and salvation. But such a highly evolved living being - the man, is he living up to his true potential and is he really on the path of self-realization?

In yester-years people in search of truth followed rigorous practices, controlled their senses and hormones to reach a state of no rebirth, got themselves liberated from this cycle of birth and death, thereby attained salvation and have become blessed.

Change is inevitable and natural and the current *Kali Yuga* is no exception to this eternal law. With growing population and rampant competition, the world has become a global village. We might have achieved a lot of development in materialistic and intellectual senses, but man is suffering with lack of mental peace and solitude and has been burdening himself with materialistic pursuit of accumulation of wealth. *There is surely a long way to go for him in the pursuit of real happiness and spiritual evolution.*

But then does that mean man can't be liberated from this intricate web of meaningless bondages he created for himself? The answer is definitely yes, he can be released! The essence is to know that earning is not wrong, that family and bonds are an essential obligation one needs to fulfill but then that **too much of anything is unwarranted**. That this life, the current form of existence alone and the resultant bonds are not permanent, that we as a body are not eternal and not going to stay here forever! Once we understand this simple truth, we can surely get released from this whirlpool of very tight confinements we are confining ourselves to. We are indeed larger than what we really think and subjecting ourselves to. We can then move on to that evolution and expansion of ourselves.

Though to understand this essence is not too easy, we must try and practice detachment, like a water drop on lotus leaf, while we are still fulfilling our earthly bonds. The key is to stop unnecessary accumulation of materialistic wealth and **practise contentment in life**. *Devotion, Wisdom, Karma and Yoga are steps to salvation*. Meditation is one of such keys to thoughtful living and mental freedom. Heaven and Hell are both in our mind, it's just the way we look at life and create them. Let's just hope that through assimilation of this truth and ardent practise of that wisdom, we can attain happiness we totally deserve and reach our rightful place in the human evolution.

On a different note, lately I've heard this song– "*Egiri poovee raama chilaka...aada pillavi kaadu ganaka*[1]" – which calls for a

---

[1]   Egiri poovee raama chilaka...aada pillavi kaadu ganaka: *(Telugu)* Lyrics of a Telugu song which mean – "Oh Parrot! Fly away since you are not a woman!" This song is to be interpreted particularly in the Indian context or perhaps in any other country's context too where gender differences majorly prevail to curb the freedom of women.

parrot to fly away since it is not tied by any unseen cages as a woman is... *So, Oh Women! Liberate yourselves, if a parrot can, you too can!!!*

- *Dec 21, 2013, 08:27 PM.*

123. Miracle

To be living in the moment of miracle seems more miraculous than the miracle itself.

- *Dec 27, 2013, 10:40 PM.*

124. Maintaining Continuity

I've talked about *continuity* in some of my earlier posts – "*When the time stands still*" & "*The continuous process of learning*". This one is more from team management perspective. Now, imagine a team consisting of three groups of people - under-performing, moderately performing and outperforming bands. It's not that the first group is really under-performing as per certain standards, but the adjectives are just used on a relative basis, just to distinguish that three different groups actually exist.

Now, the actual motto of the leader, the Project Manager (let's just call him/her PM henceforth) of the team ideally must be to ensure that the project is excelling or atleast doing good moderately 'continuously', but definitely not in a deproving cycle (deproving as per the required indicators here, be it net profits or new sub-projects accrued thus increasing business prospects for the future, so on and so forth). But sometimes PMs make a mistake of assuming that their goal is to actualize the potential of all the employees working under them to their best possible levels...like make them realize their actual potential and also do keep leading the project based on that model.

The most inherent danger of this model is that, this does not cater to critical (in fact many other category of) situations and the continuity might just break.

Another theory that I come across very often is to select/focus on candidates who perform moderately well as they are the most reliable group in most of the situations. While I agree that this is true, companies see through most of the critical situations with the help of high-performing individuals, BUT, but that comes with this disclaimer - they might not always be reliable in a sense that *you cannot expect the same high-productivity in every situation.*

It is very important to give rest periods to those in the high band, by that I don't mean it's OK for them not to be productive at all, but just let them safely fall in the moderate band. They would not like to be in the low band for a long time anyway. Do not push them often to see to it that they perform in their best levels. This is the cost you pay for these people - *not expecting consistency with them.* But if that's the case, then how is continuity maintained? It is the obligation of the PM to identify these three bands of people and give proper grace periods. It is also his obligation to ensure that, say if high-band is under scrutiny, the grace period is rotated across different people in that band, so that some people are in grace period and some people can still rise to the occasions of emergency and go beyond their duty call. Different points I can think of, catering to different situations:

- Special focus on those people in the transition phases where they can migrate from one band to the other (higher band ofcourse ;-)); Helping them undergo such migration; Identifying and facilitating the needed resources.

- At any point of time, the pressure and supervision of PM must be the most (I mean relatively more) on people in the low band. If people cannot reach up to a minimum prescribed level, they OUGHT to be terminated*, thus saving time and energy of many others in the team. (Imagine the chain of events always active – decreasing quality, time of other employees consumed, schedule slippage, impact on brand image of the product – in order to facilitate low-performing individuals be part of the team and by that I'm referring to consistently low-band people). It is their head-ache if they can't fit into the team, not PM's. They (below-low-band) will go to places/domains they better fit and more appropriate for them. Perhaps the current work is not their cup of tea, their interests and skills might lie somewhere else, so you are only helping them by showing the door.

- Exceptionally high performances come with a cost, so PM must consider the normalizing factors before taking for granted that these people would work the same way forever. PMs must not overdo to pressurize them for consistency.

- All said and done, *the strength of moderate-band is definitely their consistency.* But monitor, along with providing timely feedback, those people who might slip into low-band. *After all they are your majority and you got to retain them.*

- Give high-band people their freedom (**a controlled freedom** anyway) to rise to the occasions of critical situations. Of *course do not let their high self-worth get into their heads.*

Through the above points, it might sound that I'm saying - all that a leader is supposed to do, is to let people work their own way according to their inherent potential and let them exercise their free will and get rid of worse-productivity band. While this is true to certain extent this cannot be applied completely. If everybody works according to one's own capabilities, then where is the connecting thread of project's interests and why do we have leaders?

Yes, yes! I have deviated from the central topic quite a bit, but the bottom line, if I have to sum it up all is: In order to work through critical situations and achieve as much low down-time as possible (ideally zero) and attain project-continuity, *do Time-Shift-Keying of productive zones of high-band people.* And you know this already - *different high-band people again have different thresholds.* So keep that in mind too.

And yeah, many writers, those management gurus, might be well ahead of me in discussing not only well-established but also time-tested theories of *Chaos Management.* But as you know, if you have been closely following my blog, I have poor-reading habits and have definitely a long way to go there. It's purely a matter of interest, but I had always preferred idling of time, thinking and talking casual stuff, meditating and observing people and events around me and at most reading news papers and flipping through news to actual reading of books (I mean real books not any course books). While this non-reading activity might not be any exceptional activity for most of us and already is inherent part of lives, I perhaps do it a bit more or maybe not and I possibly don't even realize I'm lazy and can do better? In any case, I'm not suggesting that non-reading or reading activities are superior or inferior to the other category. I do see that doing only one category of activities all the time is not worthwhile. So this writeup is a notes jotted down purely based on my observations and musings of my idle time...written purely for my own sake in fact (very much the way rest of the blog is written, not any self-help writing for others) so that I can lean back on it when needed.

And yes, this long talk does remind me of "Leadership Wisdom" by Robin Sharma, my first brother gave me yesterday. So it's on my to-read list which already has many pending books. If I do manage to read it, it shall be the first book I'll be reading that falls under Leadership or even Management category. Oh yeah, I have read many articles on such stuff but not any books so far.

- Dec 30, 2013, 05:10 PM.

125. In the microcosmic illusion

Sri Aurobindo says in one of his quotes that *Love is at the heart of all creation.* But I doubt *the universality of the statement.* Sometimes life is born out of sheer lust, no love. But does that mean, the life born out of such lust is not capable of love at all? Thankfully, the *human karma* does not operate to such an extent of inheritance - inheritance of things one can't control, one can't have a say in. Life can happen as a result of accidental few minutes, eleven minutes, if I have to wax poetic, as Paulo Coelho puts it, so philosophically and boringly. I don't understand anyway, this kind of sacredness attributed to sex despite promiscuity. Period. I leave this here.

On a different note, what if we were all born here at a happy moment in the macrocosmic script of the universe to accomplish some eventful thing, yet we can't realize that in this microcosm of human life and subject ourselves to pain. Imagine the irony of life then. Imagine the irony of harsh reality of microcosm being watched silently and cruelly (or should I say eagerly and benignly?) by the macrocosm to let us learn life's lessons and unravel life's illusions at our own pace whenever we can or rather when we should, as timed by the (micro spawned by macro) cosmic script.

I would like to end the last blog post of this year with a spam sms broadcasted on my mobile, nothing too fancy, but it's here - *Life has no pause buttons. Dreams have no expiry date. Time has no holiday. So don't waste a single moment of life. Live it, Love it, Rock it. Happy New Year.*

- Dec 31, 2013, 07:52 PM.

Self-Notes:

Ok so the poignancy with which this post was written did not let me voice out the other opinions I had. Well, the sacredness might not be in the act itself. But, surely there is sacredness in the tolerance of the mother (as also that of the father, if he is with her to see through the pregnancy) to actualize life.

- Jan 01, 2014, 10:44 AM.

* * * * * * * * * *

"It is not the consciousness of men that determines their existence, but it is their Social Existence that determines their consciousness."

— Karl Marx.

* * * * * * * * * *

"Mankind, when left to themselves, are unfit for their own government."

— George Washington.

* * * * * * * * * *

Part V: 2014

The beginning of 2014 was like a new dawn for me. Things started getting clearer. Especially the answer to "Why me"? Despite my employer's (Adpative Mobile) genuine consideration towards my state and requirements, despite their offering of flexible work conditions and timings, I finally quit in Feb, since working for a Software Organization was not fitting my way of life during this period.

Also something inside me very strongly told that the transformation was going to finish soon in April this year. Not only for me, but for many others who have been undergoing this spiritual metamorphosis of Ascension, this process is expected to end. It indicates the successful culmination of this process in the realm of mind (Consciousness) for the humanity as a whole. What awaits us is the manifestation of the same in the realm of body, our materialistic world.

. . . . .

126. The twinning branches approach

These days our life is replete with debates and discussions more so because of the growing awareness of people on various things happening around. When the argument has two sides and if you are very clear about which side to take, then fine, there is no confusion at all. But in many or maybe in atleast some cases, both the sides make sense and if you have started taking a particular side clearly, there might arise many examples and scenarios which invalidate that side of the argument. It's more because of the many contexts possible as the debate evolves and we usually naively stick to a particular context yet universalize our argument to one side.

So the best approach in such a case (in fact I'd say in any debate these days) is to take the middle-ground first and observe how the discussion is shaping up and understand more about what is being debated and the many possible facets of the argument. After making a decent progress, if you feel that you can clearly stick to one side only, take that side, of course making it clear your assumed context and any possible exceptions. If you feel that both the sides have a point in different scenarios, this middle-ground will allow for easy switching of sides. It's like you can tilt and rotate your argument to either of the sides very flexibly depending on the context at hand…This without sounding stupid. If you were actually taking a side before, then this switching of sides is not going to be so easy.

I call this the *twinning branches* approach. And this might be very liberating too…liberating from aggressive and unnecessarily long debates, yielding plain and simple informative discussions.

- Jan 04, 2014, 11:36 PM.

127. Death

Telugu Hero *Uday Kiran* is no more. He breathed his last in Jyothi Apartments, Hyderabad, yesterday midnight. What was more saddening is that he gave up his life by committing suicide. I could not fight back tears seeing images of a once handsome and lively person, now broadcasted on TV lifeless, face deformed due to the impact of hanging. I just wished that was not even shown on TV. He was a very dear person to the young generation, a generation that was young during early 2000s. Specifically what made him endearing to me when I was young was his innocence and lover-boy image he always exuded and also the fact that he resembled a friend of mine. Many relatives used to say that he resembled my first brother. Even before that fact could sync with me, his movies almost stopped. And later I completely forgot about Uday Kiran just like many Telugu Audiences. And now after few days this news too will just fade away, thanks to our capability to forget and move on.

2013 has seen many deaths in Telugu Film Industry - *Manjula, Srihari, AVS, Dharmavarapu Subramanyam* and now Uday Kiran in early 2014. Except Uday everybody else died of health ailments. Unlike others he was so young and could have had lot of bright life ahead. I have lots to talk about this death, yet I choose to stay silent. I'm in no moods to talk about it. I don't know about the suicide rates in olden days, but when I hear of suicide now, I wonder if man has become so helpless or if society has become so cruel? Or if it's too easy for man to give up life rather than ambition? I don't want to dismiss suicide saying it's the lack of courage to fight problems. Sometimes it could be due to the lack of interest to continue life too. Though an entirely different situation, I had the same dilemma while I was watching the *Har Har Mahadev* episode in Telugu on TV yesterday when *Dhadhichi* gives up his life for loka kalyanam[1] to become the Vajrayudha[2]. I wondered if *Mahadev* and *Adi Shakti* could not have devised an alternative and if only death of Dhadhichi is capable of solving the problem at hand (killing of an asura[3]). But then it is what it is and maybe they really had no alternative. Dhadhichi's sacrifice has been exemplary in *Hindu Puranic history* of deep God-devotee connection and also in driving a message that no sacrifice is too great when it does good to the world.

Coming back, Uday Kiran was perhaps a misfit in the Telugu Film Industry already rotten with family/dynasty politics. Lady Luck did not smile at him even in Kollywood[4]. Perhaps Tamil audience liked macho guys more. I only hope Uday Kiran has better things to do outside this world. I wish his soul all success in that journey ahead. He was indeed very dear to many people like me when he did act, may his soul just know that.

Whatever it is, death is very painful...not to experience it by oneself, but to see it happen with others.

- Jan 06, 2014, 03:17 PM.

---

[1]   Loka kalyanam: *(Telugu)* Well-being and prosperity of the world.
[2]   Vajrayudha: *(Sanskrit/Hindi/Telugu)* It's the name of a powerful weapon of Indra made of *Sage Dadhichi's* bones. It was specifically used to kill the daemon *Vritra. Dadhichi,* according to the Puranas, is one of the greatest sages and also one of the most ardent devotees of Lord Shiva.
[3]   Asura: *(Sanskrit/Hindi/Telugu)* Asura is the one who is not a Sura (Deva or God). Celestial beings were divided into two groups of Suras (Devas/Gods) and Asuras (Daemons).
[4]   Kollywood: *(English)* An English term used to identify Tamil Film Industry.

128. Frozen Heat

I should have written this post y'day, but couldn't for whatsoever reasons. For the last three days, had to go through the same voidness I went through some time ago. The strange ordeal of this period is that, despite going through it for the n'th time, the intensity of nothingness and confusion stays just the same. After all it's nothingness isn't it, how could I expect any change in the intensity when there is no such thing as intensity itself? It's like knowing you know this and that is going to happen but just remain a silent spectator and be frozen in time. But this time I could come up with a new interpretation in addition to the old ones, of how to describe the situation. I felt like water being sucked under Corialis impact, this is the old interpretation. New ones - I felt like a rat in a rat-trap gasping for air (though I've never been that, it's comprehension of unknown ok ;)), felt like being split into two, one of which is helplessly looking at the other mirroring the same mistakes.

Didn't know what to talk, what to say, but all I was, was to be desperate of getting past it. Tried a bit of meditation, the meditation on inside, but it only aggravated the situation. I then realized that I was meditating on the inside that was all wrecked up, so no point focusing on it then for a while. I had to focus on the outside now, the transition felt gradual yet surreal, but I don't have words to express it rightly anyway. All that I can say is I was utterly confused as to which direction I'm taking and then I got some hope after focusing on the outside...the direction, for me perhaps, is to revisit a bit of past insights of mine. So I'm trying to gain my focus again, hmm! All you people out there wondering how people undergo such phases of void? I'll give you an example of a case in point.

It was recently reported in the *Neurology* Journal as a case-study – *"Right Brain: A reading specialist with alexia without agraphia"*.

Well, I keep saying that the mind-boggling complexity of human brain is beyond the comprehension of human brain right? It is said everything is said to be normal with brain. It means that abnormality is a norm for the (human) brain. There was this case where a woman had suffered a stroke and the cognitive function of her brain was affected in such a way that she was unable to read anything (irrespective of known/unknown languages) and it all appeared as incomprehensible symbols, as hieroglyphs. Basically the stroke interrupted the connection between the "language zone" of her brain and her visual cortex itseems. But itseems amazingly, she still had emotional reactions to seeing words, even though she couldn't recognize them! Can you imagine this? Can you believe it happening?

Well, if word blindness such as this is possible (and studied by Science too) then experiencing void is possible too. Well you never know the burgeoning complexity of mind and come to think of it, ***atheism could perhaps be just a state of mind*** due to our consciousness (let's just call it mind for now) not being evolved so much (or our consciousness dipping in so much from its better state before!) Okay, I'm not saying all those who are not atheists are evolved beings. Theism (understanding of the concept of God, I mean) is definitely a lot different from the current day religious faiths.

- *Jan 09, 2013, 09:18 PM.*

129. Inertia

Oh so I thought the ordeal was over with those three days, but it wasn't?!? So today was the day for inertia of voidness. Extreme pain is fine, complete voidness is fine. Atleast they are wholesome feelings how much ever difficult they are to endure. But today's feelings are the creepiest ever! On one side I feel complete and lively and when set to work I feel I'm not at all ready for things. Now how creepy can that be? Like you feel pain and numbness all at the same time and *I feel all frozen and all awake, all at once*! And then I have this feeling of constant pull on and off. *Oh inertia, when will you go?* By tomorrow atleast? I have so many left-brain activities honking at me please... Knock, knock! Readers, any help out there?

So do you remember this post from the past – *"The spilled right brain hemisphere"*? There, I just left it to your imagination on how to stop the spilling. Well, it was evident that the spilling can (perhaps) best be stopped if the right hemisphere (RBH) is laterally inverted, so that whatever it is that is spilling, pervades the left hemisphere too (LBH). My RBH looks healed completely, but the LBH still seems numb, why? How is that possible? Because without the LBH taking over, my RBH shouldn't be at solace, what kind of lag is this? **I so much wish there is no partition at all between these brain hemispheres**, may that happen soon! If some vaccuum bubble is coming in the way, please please may that melt away soon...

- Jan 10, 2014, 11:56 PM.

130. State of my mind, today!

I've been wondering and wandering aimless and restless, but that's fine, I've been in perfect sync with the chaos in the Universe...

- Jan 14, 2014, 12:45 PM.

131. Future need not be predicted

Very few people know about the mystical/spiritual experiences I've been undergoing for sometime. I dislike calling it especially mystical because of the way the word is misinterpreted, I'd like to plainly say "...I've been awakening and I call the process Realization". Of those few people, most (who are not undergoing this process themselves) of them have a common question - "Why are you undergoing all this? So, can you predict the future?"

Itseems according to Science, future can't be predicted. That agrees with Nature's way of things too, I believe. Future can be predicted to some extent, but with some probability and error. Again one can't predict all the future, only that relevant future their consciousness is concerned about, only that future The Divine or The Universe opens to a person...for that person's purpose of life includes that, for there is some collective benefit through such awareness. So it's not really so, that a 'person' can predict the future, the Universe is revealing the future through a 'person'. There are many forces at play there.

All said and done, *future need not be predicted*. It's not something to be predicted, it's something to be lived in the future, in the moment then. Once a person is on a path to predict future, he/she has ceased to live in the moment. Future cannot be predicted with 100% accuracy, for all of us are living currently and are creating our own future courses through our own deeds, so it's evolving all the time, it's moving. We are not really aware of sudden outliers that might pop-up any time before the event unfolds thus changing the course of the event completely. The accuracy of prediction increases as the timeline of the future event comes closer and closer. And if something can be predicted with 100% accuracy even before it is going to happen, then either the person predicting it cannot be part of that future or one has predicted a future event that does not happen in his own dimension, thereby one has predicted an event that happens in a different time frame of which he is not part of. It's very much similar to the Heisenberg's Uncertainty Principle - both the position and momentum of a particle cannot be determined simultaneously. Mapping this principle here – both the future and the existence of the predicting person in "*that*" future cannot co-exist if the prediction is expected to be 100% right. ***As humans, as believers and followers of Science we can only be certain about the uncertainty.***

But why do we human beings have an impulse to predict the future? (of course, the recorded history shows that only certain few have got such a chance) It's because we see God and Fate (Chance) as an entity outside us, alien to us. We make a futile struggle to safeguard ourselves against some future catastrophes. We try to predict out of sheer curiosity for the humans we are. But that's not really in the best interests of nature *and hence us*, because we are all part of Nature/Universe/God, whatever you call it. God is inside us and outside us. The Creators have created the Creation through us and through that process they are always in the process of Creating Themselves. We are all part of The Divine and when we see ourselves outside it, we are not expressing the Divinity within us. So let's not get into the business of predicting the future, let us create the future while we happen to live in our moment, the moment.

Despite all that I wrote now, I'm not saying predicting future is wrong. I'm only saying it might not always be too useful. I understand that this practice, when people get such a chance, is in sheer human nature. But it's very important to know that the Universe does not bestow complete powers to a person to predict certain kinds of future events because it is also in the sheer nature of the Universe to safeguard itself *and hence us.*

So now that I know this, I have also got aware that the Universe is not expecting me to waste my time in future prediction henceforth. It will only be futile if I continue pursuing it. Whatever I had to know has been made known to me so far. (I have a feeling that) The Universe might not want to waste its resources anymore in trying to reveal things and educate me (and maybe others too!).

- Jan 14, 2014, 04:53 PM.

132. Regulation

There was a post on Regulation before – *"Corruption – at what level? The Indian".*

I'd like to write a bit more on that. When systems grow larger, become more networked and hence more complicated, the role of *Regulation* becomes more and more important. When systems are small or less complicated, either self-regulation is in place or they are easily manageable despite the absence of explicit Regulation. The media (social media included) today is the best example for such a complicated system where effective regulation measures are not in place. As systems grow, measures and checks for regulation ought to be put in place and yes they do cost us something. The costs might look huge in the small run, but they are extremely essential in making the systems sustainable not only for the long run, but also for current needs. Else they end up in complete Chaos. What do we choose - Chaos in the future or invest additional costs in Regulation and make systems *Manageable* and *Sustainable*?

- Jan 14, 2014, 05:10 PM.

133. CM getting practical? I like that!

So I'm writing this in the context of this news... [*The Hindu article titled: Kiran hints at taking drastic decision, dated Jan 23, 2014, National News, Andhra Pradesh*]

<u>Background:</u> *Some background for the uninitiated and Non-Telugu people...*

This is written in the context of recent political crisis in the state of Andhra Pradesh, India, where there has been a conflict between two groups of people – for (Telangana part) and against (Seemandhra part) the process of bifurcation of the State into Telangana and Seemandhra.

I know this is a very political opinion and might also sound biased, but these are the views yelling inside me to be voiced out, so I rather do it.

Agreeing with a person's views and liking a personality are two completely different things I guess. In the current times, I've been and remain a great fan of Kiran Kumar Reddy's (the current Andhra Pradesh Chief Minister (CM), let me call him KKR for my convenience here) ways of administration. He has his ideas clear on United Andhra and has been steadfast about it. I might have agreed with specific views of JayaPrakash Narayan at specific times, but I'm not too great a fan of his ways of politics. He is a great bureaucrat and I consider him a very thoughtful Sociological Thinker and more than that a great, humble human being and my admiration for his views/ thoughts ends there. And let's not even talk about those other leaders who talk everything and agree with everything and have no stand whatsoever except getting back to power. Well, it's not too important whose fan I am. But my likes and dislikes might matter in the confinements of my notes.

AP has been adjudged the best state for governance recently by *India Today* magazine and the decision has been ridiculed by some especially considering the CM's ways. Well, this is a very valid response from *Citizens' perspective*. But governance I guess is quite a different aspect viewing it from *Citizens' lens and Administrator's lens*. My reading of Administration over the years, how much ever little that is, leads me to make some statements on how governance must be rated. (In my opinon) The quality of governance can be rated based on three factors primarily:

1. On deceleration that we did NOT run into (and "our most similar neighbours" ran into).

2. On maintaining the Status Quo.

3. On further development.

- all of them based on the current situation of the region being assessed.

Usually citizens and mind you those citizens belonging to the group of "above-average to intellegintsia" (I'm only referring to intelligentsia as citizens here) often run into this impression of gauging governance based on the third factor alone most of the times. But that near-intelligentsia group is very small in numbers and to appease them and make them believe there is development happening, the administrator might just have to sacrifice his grip of resources meant for a majority lot; again we must all remember resources are limited, while wants are infinite. Sometimes it might amount to increasing the gap between haves and have-nots, *the 'haves' appreciate such development while the 'have-nots' don't even get a voice to condemn it.*

To me, maintaining *status quo* is the most difficult task. And come to talk of *deceleration*! It could easily creep in. We *are not marching towards a future that is ever-growing favourably for us!* The societal situations are knitting and manifesting themselves to present a very unfavourable space to juggle with. Stopping deceleration can prove very burdensome.

KKR has taken over as CM under very crucial conditions, when the state was boiling with *partisan views* and when there were no big heads to readily take over (and in fact when *Mr. Rosaiah garu* himself gave up due to ill health). To get the machinery running, to get governance going amongst Dharnas[1] on top of the already rampant *policy-paralysis*, is a task in itself. The biggest achievement of the CM could be that - we the people of Andhra have never sensed lack of any service delivery despite all the additional turmoil and embroiling happening around. ***Well, there's no way we can be aware of what work was done by somebody when we don't know what negative repercussions that work has counteracted.*** Ideally, we must not be aware of them and so we are here, doing our work in our own comfortable spaces, dreaming and expecting development. Well the real development indicators and statistics, comparison with previous years and previous leaders, what policy decisions have been made and implemented is never portrayed well in day-to-day newspapers, the ideal stuff to refer to for such info would be *Publication Division of India* printed monthly State/Centre magazines. This Division to this day (in my opinion) has given *credible material, neutral and untainted by politics*, serving as bread and butter of many centre/state civil service aspirants. And in that sense, this is the kind of info which lies in the interests of people who would like to execute governance.

Actually this post might look like a fanmail to KKR (I'm fine with that too), but the idea is to talk about governance and more about the state division process. Personally, I can't help but be taken aback by the charisma KKR exudes. You must follow the Assembly discussions closely, oh my God the clarity he has on things he talks, his eye to detail and the composure he maintains not unnerved by complete opposition and all this without sounding argumentative and without letting the discussions spiral into small-size war zones.

---

[1] Dharnas: *(Hindi/Telugu)* Plural of *Dharna*, which in colloquial Indian terms means *Strike* expressing resistance or disagreement.

Well yes, I'm aware of the talk of the State being hand-in-glove with the Centre and all those back-end strategies. *But show me one party in India which is pure and devoid of such politics for power-mongering?* **Politics can never be pure especially when the task at hand is to rule a huge populace which is not pure itself.** So these strategies are an evil-factor constant across all the parties, so we can safely ignore that.

Coming to the state division, ofcourse it must have been evident by this time to you, that I'm "FOR" division. I'm for it, despite all the hassles involved in division (separation of machinery, infrastructure, revenues, resources etc and establishment of the same in the other half) *for the sole reason that the spirit of brethren is lost.* The people are emotionally divided and they don't subside until a decision is taken, they continue to agitate and stall development and make lives more troublesome. To them the decision of being united is not the conclusion. Well, KKR says, the real loss is to Telangana and not to Andhra if the decision happens! One cannot just consider physical/financial resources; one must also consider the enormous human capital being lost! He says it's unfair to say that Telangana people are losing out in united Andhra Pradesh, when the development was equally contributed by all the three regions. Well, some people think otherwise and nobody knows the impact until it has arrived.

(Theoretically) The decision has been taken. (In my opinion) *It's a futile argument if one argues on whether or not the division must happen. People must rather focus on "how well" the division can happen, when they are together.* Once separated, no ruckus can resolve a stalemate and bring about the conceding of other part's demands, so both the halves must rather try and get as much justice as possible in the current scope (resource/revenue sharing and all that). The current context has modified the legend for "United we stand, Divided we fall" to "United we run into Chaos, Divided we live our lives"...live our lives peacefully for the foreseeable future! *The world is never at rest and the rest will be tackled by future generations.*

- Jan 23, 2014, 11:45 PM.

134. Time is Precious

Time is precious and remains a critical factor in life. Today's scientific field of medicince has rightly identified its value and gave time its right place by saying *"Time is Muscle"* in case of heart-attacks. But, we the people of today have modernized this legend in general as *"Time is Money"*. So is time money only for certain people and only in certain cases? In many cases, we inordinately delay things as though the time we have is infinite! Some of us delay our decisions, marriages, relationships, turning away from many realities of our life and run after money or materialistic riches and mechanical pursuits.

But if people don't have time to spare a thought for life, to get in touch with real people that form their life and create space for them, i.e., if they are choosing money over life, yet take life for granted, then life is all very free to cease to agree with them and take its own course and also go ahead to stop choosing to be on their side. Sometimes we do it intentionally, stubbornly to gain power, fame and riches and sometimes we are compelled by our circumstances to do this, but this is the moment we start complaining that life is slipping out of our hands and that we have no control whatsoever on it, a situation we all fondly reckon using the phrase - *"Such is life"*!

- Jan 26, 2014, 03:13 PM.

135. Ego that can annihilate!

One, Two and *Three* planned to play a "Tug Of War". The agreement is that they should not stop playing the game until they finish the game i.e., until one side loses. *Three* is very powerful, so powerful that it can equal *One* and *Two* put together in strength. So they started the game: *Three* on Side A and *One* and *Two* on side B. They played the game for a very long time, but neither of the sides gave up. Unrelentingly they tried to pull the other party to their side. It went on and on for a long time and then came the brink point when the rope started breaking. They could not afford to break the rope. So, finally they arrived at a compromise. Side B promised Side A that if *Three* comes over to their side, they will work as his sub-ordinates forever. So *Three* relented, gave in and came over to the side of *One* and *Two*.

Side A   Side B

3 ========*======== 1, 2

One is Mind.

Two is Body.

Three is Soul.

Side A is *Annihilation*.

Side B is *Creation*.

When *the Soul* goes against *one's Mind and Body*, it's *Ego*. It can annihilate our pure self. ***Then one is actually at loggerheads with one's ownself.***

When *the Soul* comes over to the side of *Mind and Body* and becomes capable of guiding them, it's *Conscience*. ***Then it can re-create us to realize our pure-self and allows us to progress.***

Oh yeah, the last but not the least, *the ROPE is our LIFE*. We cannot afford to break it! So crucial is our Soul and how it can be rightly used to better our lives.

- Jan 30, 2014, 07:56 PM.

136. The (in)famous (Rahul) Gandhi Interview!

Background: Please refer to Rahul Gandhi's interview with Arnab Goswami on the show of "Frankly Speaking" on TimesNow on Jan 27, 2014.

I can't help but write this, it's too tempting to give up adding one more perspective to this already controversial interview. While this might have been triggered by responses to this interview by some of my friends and the popular responses reported in Newspapers and on Internet on how the interview should have been given a lot better, I write this more with the general populace and their opinion on mind. And please do excuse me for any possible offences.

While I agree that people's argument is right, I feel they are arguing on a wrong point. Did Congress announce Rahul Gandhi (let's refer to him as RG for convenience henceforth) as their Prime Ministerial candidate? No! Then why do people see this interview in that light?

RG gave this interview only in his capacity/power as Congress Vice-President & Congress Poll Campaign Chief and at the max as a Minister-of-Parliament (MP). Congress has not pushed RG on to people as the PM (Prime Minister) candidate, YET! (might happen in the future and we don't as yet know!) It is people (general public and perhaps even political big-wigs) who are pulling him into this ASSUMING he is the PM candidate.... TO BE!

There is no arguing the fact that people will have a lot of expectations from their PM-to-be and their frustration is very justified considering the strong *anti-incumbency sentiment** trending currently. But when he is not even announced as PM candidate, why do people judge RG and his talk based on this assumption?

The interview in fact opens with a discussion wherein RG says it's not constitutionally mandatory (it's just an option, not an obligation) for a party to announce PM candidate ahead of elections. AND THAT IS TRUE! People elect MPs and MPs elect PM. If we are not putting enough focus on whom we intend to elect as MP and check if he/she is eligible enough to be elected, then either democracy has not seeped well into our country or people have not become matured enough to understand the power of democracy. Or we have become too lazy or complacent to study such issues.

It is we who are mocking at the democractic structure of India by voting a party based solely on One Leader at the top instead of focusing on decentralized powers. And by doing that we are reinforcing such a flawed structure, we are allowing political parties to get away with it, with one leader at the top and the party individuals not really accountable for their deeds and never taking enough heat and pressure from the public. The pressure is always on ONE PERSON at the TOP. And if he/she is unable to delegate or share the pressure, then there are no results. The onus is more and more falling majorly on the leader, but we are failing as citizens. We don't even fulfill our minimum responsibilities created by the simple role of being a citizen (please refer to FUNDAMENTAL DUTIES charter of Indian Constitution to understand what I mean here), but yet go ahead to criticize a person who has not even taken (and perhaps not even ready to take) the reins. We fail to do simple things such as sticking to rules, not littering, not flouting traffic rules, paying taxes on time and the list could be very long...

I wonder if our education has helped us enough to be the good citizens of a country that is changing so dynamically and is demanding commensurate dynamism from the people too. *Are we making the informed choices being the netizens of this Information Age? Or are we hooked up to the age-old premises of politics?* If we are expecting change in the way of politics, there is a lot of change expected in US (purely in our minimal capacity as citizens) too! Whatever results our yester generations have achieved DESPITE all the oppression they faced, whose fruits we are enjoying now, is due to the fact that they channelized their frustration rightly into the real world through actions, while we are putting it in the virtualized bubbles. *The camaraderie and social grouping that brings in real change is a passe now!* The journals they wrote in those days to inspire people and the huge readership they had, is just an example for me here and there are many more, we need not duplicate them here, but atleast we could derive a part of it to adapt to our circumstances!

And coming to the interview, I'd still feel RG has done so decently well. I'm reminded of many interviews when politicians walked away when posed with such spot-on controversial questions. In fact in the interview, the interviewer is not ready to answer the interviewee's questions, yet the former expects the latter to answer his questions damn on to the point, without allowing him to explain any background or set some right context for the discussion. Now, how rude is that? It's as though the interview is like a battle at gun-point and you got to somehow sail through it and win it over. It's not seen as a discussion between two educated individuals. That is where it is disheartening to see such debates. They only seem to cater to media hype that the current state of affairs in politics is being dissected, while the interviewers do not actually give a chance for such dissection!

If I don't like a party that does not announce PM candidate ahead of its elections, then I must not vote for it, as simple as that! One point that really catches my attention is RG so honestly says something on these lines - *"I was not born in this family out of choice. I have only two choices to make - leave it in lurch or take up whatever I can"* (wasn't word-exact, only whatever my memory allowed). No politican today would be so honest in expressing his/her helplessness of being so unfortunate to be in the helm of things at a wrong time. Listen to the interview closely, to RG and it is very clear that he himself IS AWARE that he is not ready to take up things. Then why don't we understand that he is aware of what he ought to be aware of and instead WE become aware of our citizen duties first, that might help us more!

*Congress headed United Progressive Alliance – II has been ruling India for the last two five-year terms.

- Feb 04, 2014, 10:49 PM.

137. For some, losing is not easy!

We all know about the good-old hare-tortoise story. We also know that hare is way too faster than tortoise and it's not only unusual, but also impossible for hare to be finally slower than tortoise, given all conditions are same in the race and given the natural physical abilities of those animals.

So, all the animals in the forest have come up with a new variety of game for the hare and tortoise. ***The challenge set for the hare is TO LOSE the race***, since it is no wonder that it can easily win. Here are the rules of the game:

1. Both the participants must NOT slow down beyond what their abilities allowed for that day.

2. The race is ON during the day and OFF as soon as the sun sets.

3. Both of them can take five breaks during pre-agreed intervals of the day.

And the real rule:

4. The race starts on one fine noon, both cover as much as distance possible and break down the race for the day as soon as the Sun sets. Next morning *__hare must reverse its journey to meet the tortoise and then again start 'going ahead' of it__*. If it cannot meet the tortoise before the noon sets, then it is declared to have lost the race. *__The tortoise has no obligation of reversing its journey, it must just 'keep moving forward'.__*

So it is a *__"moving target"__* for both in the race. The assumption here is that these two animals are true to their conscience and not flouting the rules of the game. The hare did not think much about how it is going to win this challenge by losing the race, but both started the race one fine noon!

So everyday hare meets the tortoise before the noon and then leaps ahead on its own journey. The days were just passing by and the same thing repeated and repeated. The tortoise was honing its running skills gradually and the time of both meeting gradually kept shifting ahead of noon by few minutes.

By this time, hare was getting depressed as it was not at all unable to find out a way of losing the race. While we humans would have come up with some crooked clever plan with our time-distance calculations, all that was happening with the poor hare and tortoise was that they were running to the best of their abilities.

So hare was getting very depressed thinking about the precious life, time and freedom it would otherwise be enjoying. On the other hand tortoise was happy every day as it is increasing its speed gradually. Hare could not bear this idea that this is going to go on forever, its sheer depression dawned upon it a *'golden idea'*. So, it thought, the rule of the game is to run to the *'best' of the abilities*, so the challenge is to 'decrease' the abilities and it kept its idea into execution immediately.

That noon after meeting the tortoise, hare pushed all its abilities and ran almost thrice its usual speed ***to go VERY FAR away from the tortoise***. And then came the sun-set. Next morning the hare woke up to see that its legs were all bleeding and it was very happy! So, that morning it limped back slowly reaching a point where it almost stopped walking since it *COULD NOT!* On the other side, tortoise was racing ahead fast, but luckily, the math had it that it reached only after an hour after the noon had set. Hare was gleefully waiting there leaning back against a tree very sure of its victory or failure, whichever way you see it!

Moral of this story, for me: When comparing two very dissimilar (or not-so-similar) entities or situations, the parameters picked up for comparison/analysis are extremely important.

- Feb 10, 2014, 08:31 PM.

138. Thoughts Today!

One shall know the pain of earth (Nature/Universe) only (at that point of time) when one is "one with" earth (Nature/Universe).

The message from God to the world is: "How much ever you are trying to shake me out of the present, I'm trying to remain there"...

Half-Knowledge is EXTREMELY dangerous. This will replace my previous adage "Ignorance is bliss" on top of the list of timeless principles. Half-knowledge makes a person stubborn in ways you can't fathom or conquer. You can tell a person who is ignorant, who is bad, who is foolish, but a person who is *Half-Knowledgeable* and is hence stubborn is beyond preaching. I'd rather stay away from such people than waste my time for them because otherwise they complain that I am wasting their time instead!

Nobody can shake half-knowledgeable people from their stubborn rigidity and reservations (not being open to be told anything) who are all set to doom themselves. They wouldn't realize UNTIL they are doomed!

Somebody asked me today what if we lose our "global" society today, if we believe in *Karma* and wind back our clock to not be too selfish, not be too technology-oriented and instead start getting concerned about the nature. I said, I believe it's the other-way round. The global society today is **the result of** us nearing the *"Disaster/Equilibrium Point"* when we ought to get concerned about nature. So, getting concerned about nature is not winding back our clock, but instead allowing it to go forward, taking its own course - its natural course. We cannot sit on top of a stop watch, stop time for long and keep waiting for an "optimal" point when we want to release the clock because by that time (or is it time already?), Universe would be running out of time and so shall we! In such a face of disaster, all this development, technology, globalization, everything, EVERYTHING becomes nothing for the Universe, for this Universe runs on its own *principles of creation and time.* Universe is the ultimate God by whose laws even the Gods we worship daily, abide by, I believe, for they too are nothing but entities at a higher level in the hierarchy *but not magicians beyond the laws of TIME!*

I wrote this almost a year ago, completely in human capacity, for humans to understand and I'm tired of repeating this: *A part can never know global interests on its own by any means or standard.*

Sometimes the part does not know its personal interests too in the face of global conflicts or challenges. The best way, in my opinion, is to be "open" to "listen" to the global entities who know the global statistics, global interests and if you believe your personal interests too, all optimized, so that we first get "aware" of what's in store for us, what is good or bad for us and then we become completely free to take a call!

And maybe, (it's a clause) maybe (I don't know), *how do we know that this is the real face of globalization?* Does globalization mean being "connected" by advanced transporation and communication facilities alone? *Are we connected as fellow human beings at all, to say the least?* Besides I can see a lot of unrest in the humanity, in people around me. Many are tired, they are losing faith in the collective slowly, some take their frustration on God and some do it on fellow human beings and many other aspects of human psyche. Maybe there is more to globalization that we haven't got it right yet? *To me, globalization happens when we can appreciate "WE" as much as "ME", but definitely not at the cost of ME.*

- Feb 18, 2014, 04:44 PM.

139. Zero, Equality and the art of Replacement

Nothing = Everything, (at that point of time) when there is nothing.

So how do we dispose our wastes? If you want to replace your laptop, do you just put your data you have collected all your life inside it, without backing up anything? No isn't it? There's a way to dispose an old laptop. How does a person get his ailment treated, say that of heart? Aren't we very careful about not to disrupt our life, to ensure that it is going, running as it should and get it treated? Science has made an amazing progress there. And then there could be n number of examples I can't think of, now, right away! *It is easiest to dispose something if disposing is as good as destroying it, as good as making it a zero. But if your aim is to put in place an equivalent system, then you work on it.*

The art of replacement, I guess, gets interesting as Zero and Equality tend to become equal when attributed to different aspects one is shedding off and aspects one is gaining.

- Feb 18, 2014, 05:28 PM.

140. Finally!!

Finally, I have one thing to say today. When all of us become aware of the gushing truth on how the humanity as a whole is suffering today to make some progress (call it twisted progress, not just progress), a part of humanity which has the sense of "morality" and moral obligation will commit suicide. For it will know that it has been preying upon brutal and blatant abuse of human emotions of the brethren. For it will know that the world is lavishing on the blood of gross human right violations and torture and abuse of people.

We only think that the course of the World is fine as it is today and that it's good, but it isn't. It hasn't seen the worse yet. Because the worse is being tolerated and shielded by some entities, for if it befalls on mankind, the course of humanity shall be spoiled and disturbed in an irretrievable way beyond repair. So to say the least, the worst is just contained when the worst should have already happened.

There is no way that the world can create a better future for itself on such inappropriate foundations, how much ever one tries because the world has so distributed itself now, that it has started amplifying the bad and not the good and will continue to do so, unless intervened...

If you thought the world needs to deteriorate further, for the judgement to be passed, that the last tree needs to be cut, that the last fish needs to be eaten, that the people should go insane and finally kill each other, then you are completely mistaken. This world is not Godless! The Gods know when and how to take the reins! The Universe will always try and evolve to its best possible state despite all the garbage dumped into it; it could be a zero state too, if you go any further on this small part of a huge system. We don't care if we are going towards a better or worser future from good or bad past as per YOUR parameters of development here on earth, but WE WOULD NOT LIKE TO SEE THIS KIND OF "PRESENT" here!!!"

- The Cosmic Wisdom & Energy speaking...

- *Feb 19, 06:00 PM.*

141. Mud

All that has been left of me
And all that I am Now,
Is plain mud.

You still want to loot me?
Amazing! Go ahead!
You are free.

But wait! Did you know this?
All that shall remain of you
Is to decay with me,
Inside me.

- *Mother Earth.*

May the ever-tolerant Earth gather more mis-fortune and strength to continue to bear the burden and sins of humanity... (Clearly all pun intended).

"Prathamam" Bharathi naama, 'Dwithiyam' cha Saraswati, Trithiyam Sarada Devi, Chathurtham Hamsa Vahini[1]...so goes the Saraswati Dwadasha Stotram[2].

---

[1] Prathamam Bharathi naama, Dwithiyam cha Saraswati, Trithiyam Sarada Devi, Chathurtham Hamsa Vahini: *(Sanskrit)* "Her first name is *Bharathi*, her second name *Saraswati*, third *Sarada Devi* and fourth *Hamsa Vahini* (the one with the *Swan* as her vehicle)"... So go the twelve names of Goddess Saraswati and so are chanted in the *Saraswati Dwadasha Stotram.*

[2] Saraswati Dwadasha Stotram: The *Sanskrit* hymns (Stotram) that chant the twelve (Dwadasha) sacred names of Goddess Saraswati.

Did you ever pause and think why we are living in this Information Age and sub-consciously consider it so and came up with that term?

It's not due to the proliferation of Information, not because it is crucial for our lives nor because we are worshipping it...

It is because Wisdom is being expected to bear the burden of humanity in its bare human capacity.

The mind power that has grown here and is growing is (by scavenging on) at the cost of its very Spirit. And hence by bargaining our spiritual strength...

- March 07, 2014, 07:00 AM.

142. Regulation – is that a waste?

I see more and more people campaigning on internet for freeing entities/systems from regulation, for instance *"Internet itself as a system"*. Yeah people say Internet must be free, that it must be free from regulation.

But regulation actually comes into picture when systems grow bigger and bigger and more inter-networked. Else small or less-networked systems will do well to do self-regulation, for instance TV media and Newspaper some time ago did efficient self-regulation. As they grow huge, that gets difficult, that is when external regulation IS needed if the systems are expected to sustain further. *Well, if we are in the assumption or staunch invincible belief that regulation is not needed, all that we are doing is to make the systems UNSUSTAINABLE.*

The lack of regulation shows everywhere:

- In a limited few making huge monies with movies.

- In paid and fabricated news that is shaping the opinion of a person incorrectly - it is no more your opinon...to a decent extent, it's a created opinion.

- In the social media (which apart from good set of benefits, for instance as tiny a benefit as a very means to create this information through my notes) which creates so much of peta zetta bytes of unnecessary information eating away unnecessarily huge natural reserves far exceeding the benefits it actually reaps.

- In Politics, where people ought to do some regulation but fail in vain...the growing lack of choices and in turn fostering more bad choices...

- The list is huge, I can go on and on....I'm sure there are better blogs out there on internet which discuss this in more detail, but the point of this post is NOT to create such a list...

What better system than our very own human body to be a case in point? That's the best system in this World. Will there ever be a point of time when this human body does not create wastes? No, isn't it? It is only when it is dead or only when it did not come into existence. In the same way, ***there shall be no evil in the society only at that point when this society and the world is dead***. As long as a human body is alive, to keep itself running, wastes are created. That's part of growth and sustenance of human life. We ought to regulate our body through various ways, else it becomes diseased.

If you don't want wastes (or anything that needs to be eliminated out of the body) to GET OUT of your body, you will stink, your kidneys will fail you. For a man, if you are restricting his sexual urges for a long time, you better know what happens. And for a woman, if you want to stop her cycles for a long time, it will result in such feminine issues that she will fail her man. You know what the current society is "treating" (read it partying) its woman with? ... with such kind of conflicting demands and stress, for her to be the man of past alongside the woman of future outside her home and to be the woman of past inside her home. I rather not talk about it any further. (And you wondering, of the four combinations of past, future, man, woman - the man of future has not surfaced? Yes, the man of future has never emerged, not yet atleast, he is too busy sacrificing his future to raise the woman to her ultimate potential, you know, you better know, he is still treating [you can read it as raping, abusing, harassing] her and in turn receiving a similar treatment of realizing his worst potential ever!)

Just as a human body will not be alive and sustain if its wastes are not eliminated in a timely fashion, so is our society. The society too needs to be eliminated of its evil in a timely manner. The evil that is created is indicative of our growth, no doubt. Though, whether the growth is for good or bad of humanity and earth in equal measures or even atleast to acceptable measures…is always debatable. If you think the evil will diminish, that it will change and *become "somehow" good on its own*, know that it is totally out of question. The evil remains evil or even grow further UNLESS REGULATED, when there are no self-regulatory measures in place or when self-regulation is getting impossible.

Saying that you don't need regulation is saying that you want to live with your crap! Even if humanity can leisurely wait and say, *"No I don't need regulation"*, (kind of saying *"I'm invincible, you know!"*), the nature CANNOT wait and hence SHALL not wait for Man. It doesn't need Man's approval.

Thinking that one is invincible is like thinking one can never be dead. ***Just becase one does not understand death, it does not mean one shall not be dead...***

Regulation is not a waste, in fact it is FOR the waste...to not remain a waste anymore...which otherwise will trouble you, impede you and ultimately fail you...

No, I do not rest my case here.

I will carry it in my mind and work on it...

- March 14, 2014, 07:07 PM.

143. Leaving FB – A note

Though this is more of a goodbye note, I start it with an entirely different thing. I'd like to talk about some Indians, in fact those Indians specifically, who do not do anything different themselves, but go ahead to say that Indians drumbeat about past and are merely boasting and sleeping without propogating the essence of ancient scriptures. It hurts to hear these statements. It's not really because I'm an Indian nor is it because I'm biased about it. Luckily my life's journey has given me enough maturity to grow above these regional and national sentiments (though I'd always argue that some amount of patriotism is natural for most of us and at the same time essential, but must not go to the extent of disabling us to see the value of other countries).

Firstly, Indians need not go about preaching the importance of the ancient Hindu scriptures to the world, for the world has headed on a different journey and has been shaping itself in such a way that it cannot be too receptive to the ancient Wisdom. So, why must Indians go after people to gain acceptability? There is no point, in fact they have started treading the path of the World of the majority or the more powerful, in assisting them with their journey of Science and Technology. Wouldn't you agree that those Indians, a part of them geniuses, a part of them hard-working, a part of them artistic and passionate (and definitely a part - very random and lethargic but yet have their cool share towards something creative or the other!) have still left their mark and impact in various fields along with Science & Technology? In fact, even if some are residing outside India and making their mark, they are still the products of Indian Culture, Indian Constitution (which is an excellent piece of work, which inspite of borrowing some ideas from World Constitutions has been drafted and crafted so well to cater to the land that preaches and exemplifies *'Unity in Diversity'*) and have been imparted educational and moral values in India itself. In fact, they form an important part of US too along with other Asian origin people.

People who are complaining about Indians say that way, even without their knowledge, either to sound cool and fashionable or out of this innocent or ignorant craving to sound West-inclined. I guess that is a natural human tendency to be inclined to the majority :) Ofcourse constructive criticism never hurts, but I'd say before criticizing the fellow country men, one must first check, what one has done oneself!

In fact it is much similar to me, who have been writing so much stuff on FB, sharing so many posts since two years (though I've been on FB since 2007, but never used it at all until 2012 in the actual sense of using it), but whose content is either rarely noticed or rarely acknowledged or followed by few. All of it boils down to "NEED". If people do not see any interest or need to go through my content, then they won't g through it. But I on the other hand felt the need to go through every bit of data floating around and in fact "bear" the burden of that internet traffic (both good and bad).

Every type of data - offending, controversial, non-sensical, educative, entertaining and much more including huge bundles of data not worth my time at all, in fact of zero worth. But I still had to invest my time to sort it out - sort out the useful from useless (to me). But I would not definitely go after every friend convincing them that my content is worth paying close attention to. It is always the hierarchy of need – who needs whom more? I'd say we all need each other in one way or the other, but the extent of dependence and priority varies. I need as much attention from you as you need this information from me. It means that if you do not see the need for this information, then I do not as well need your attention. It also means that if you see the need for this information, then I'd ofcourse need your attention too. Any relationship – real or virtual, must be mutual and reciprocated mutually, else it's a losing game and not worth pursuing.

It's similar to a case in point I have come across in FB (Facebook) about a noted musician playing his music in a busy area, where people naturally are doing their own chores and go about their work. The musician fails to get people's notice despite playing one of the most famous pieces of music which he later sells to make some millions of dollars. Who needs whom more there? Do people need his music or does the musician need public attention at that place? Well again, it's mutual, but the musician did manage to find his audience else where, an audience that's more interested to pay him their attention. *So life is more or less executed on the law of 'hierarchy of need'.* That survey only indicates that today's people have grown less responsive to things around unless advertized. But please remember, there are many things in this world which won't advertize themselves, because they might not have the scope, need and time to be after you, for they too have their own work and priorities!!!

So that relieves me of this long-oppressed feeling craving to be voiced out, to address those Indians complaining about lethargy of India. This part is done and need not be revisited again! :-)

Anyway, it's time I bid adieu to all. I'm going off FB for good tomorrow (by tomorrow morning) because I don't see any need to stay here anymore. I was on FB for a purpose, all these two years. My self-realization, my journey of these 2 years tells me that the Earth does not have enough resources to support 7.1 billion (and counting) people in the first place. And then it does not have any resources left to support the internet traffic of so many internet users. *It's boiling, it's suffering.* But then to solve any problem, you need to get into the problem, get

INSIDE the problem or the system infected with the problem and get your hands dirty. That is what I did too.

Somehow FB never interested me before. But in 2012, my life's calling demanded me to explore synchronicity and it needed me to inspect everything, virtually everything happening around me, in a meta-plane. That everything included data floating around on internet too. My writing speculating about various things is arrived at, through a very scientific process of observation, being inquisitive, methodical, analytical and diligent and above more than anything else, by being passionate, for a purpose. It's just that my subject of study is quite different from what Scientisits or Students of Science today usually pursue. *My subject of study is this very Humanity, its psyche and its happenings and Earth-Humanity's inherent connection with the Cosmos.* But that too was observed in a scientific manner, none the less. There, I'd call myself a student of Sociology or an amateur Sociologist, a Social Scientist. But interest in this kind of study was triggered after experiencing something, a mystical experience by the inside of me.

Science is more an introspection that arises out of passion and is hence just a way of looking at life, to arrive at things useful for life. I have no doubt to go ahead and say Science as a stream of study is the product of many ancient philosophies of the world and hence will end up merging with them.

As long as man is alive, man will introspect the nature around him, so it's merely a different side of man. The way he introspects differs over the Ages and the vast span of time that is, depending on the state of world and what he needs from the world to make his own living. And we men are part of God, please remember! It hurts to see that belief in God is being seen by some as dogma.

God has become Dogma due to some less-than-doggish attitude on earth, that's all.

(no offences on dogs as species, but in the sarcastic sense of the word).

But now, time has come for me to make that trade-off, *a trade off between – the benefit of using FB vs impact on my surroundings because of using FB.* Now that I have made my conclusions, now that my exploration of synchronicity is not needed any more, I'm not really interested in using FB anymore. I've been using it against my convictions because of my need. Some people use it as a tool to connect with people, some for entertainment, some are just plain interested and some people might even educate and get educated through it. But now that I know, now that I'm aware that Earth is having a huge trouble with its usage, I'll not use it anymore. I'll do my bit, before telling it to the world.

So do not separate Man – Science – God, **they are all different aspects of our own Self,** our higher self and part of The Absolute Self. We are all ONE. But we just lack the awareness in our journey on Earth due to human birth, human ego and human conditioning. We have reached that point of evolution when we all are lucky to get and sense that awareness. Watch out!

I have nothing to take back from FB – except my FB notes, perhaps some crucial conversations and ofcourse the beautiful FB lookback video :-) Everything else – my interaction with you all, my posts, my conversations, everything is lost.....

deeply buried...inside what? I don't know! I guess it's deeply buried in the eternal time, my mind and your minds as much as our memory and time permits. FB is such a nice little creative world, a bubble world and I'll surely miss my activity and existence here; ofcourse I'll miss yours too…

This post is dedicated to you all, my friends on FB. Goodbye! Until we hear from each other or meet again in person…

Best Wishes,
Mamata Anurag.

- March 17, 2014, 06:50 PM.

144. Parallels between Mysticism and Science

The perception of Science from a layman perspective or perhaps even from the perspective of most of the ardent believers and students of Science is that it is based on a more *"realistic"* *"rational"* analysis. On the other hand atheists view God and some aspects of Philosophy as fictitious mystical concepts and opine that they have no real proof.

May this be read loud and clear - *Science is as much derived from abstraction as any other fundamental analysis of nature, world or society.* Yes, but it is not without its own distinct set of features that makes it different from other disciplines of study. But the fact remains that Science is not devoid of abstraction. In fact Science starts from it, progresses through it - the abstraction, whereas Mysticism actually starts with a reality, a more profound reality than any rationalist non-believer of mysticism could believe.

Excerpts from the "Tao Of Physics" by Fritjof Capra here...

"The direct mystical experience of reality is a momentous event which shakes the very foundations of one's world view..."

- Eastern Mystics.

"It is the most startling event that could ever happen in the realm of human consciousness...upsetting every form of standardized experience."

- D. T. Suzuki.

"The violent reaction on the recent development of modern physics can only be understood when one realises that here the foundations of physics have started moving; and that this motion has caused the feeling that the ground would be cut from science."

- Heisenberg on transition from Newtonian Classical Mechanics to Quantum Mechanics.

"All my attempts to adapt the theoretical foundation of physics to this (new type of) knowledge failed completely. It was as if the ground had been pulled out from under one, with no firm foundation to be seen anywhere, upon which one could have built."

- Einstein in his biography on the new reality of atomic physics.

. . . . .

Will Science ever be able to explain the Absolute Knowledge? We know it's infinite. You may ask if there is something called *Absolute Knowledge*. While the term itself might have various connotations, in this context I'm referring to the *perfect knowledge of everything, absolutely everything*. I'm sure you would agree that this is not only difficult but also impossible. The paradoxical reality of human intellect is that, it being the seeker of perfection is also the very cause of imperfection. And again, it is this persistent seeking of perfection that is the reason for sustenance. The central theme of Ayn Rand's *"The Fountainhead"* is – "Man's ego is the fountainhead of human progress." While I completely agree with this idea, I feel that is only one side of the coin. According to me, man's ego which aids him in his progress also equips him to be the most capable self-destructor ever. Ego is the root to both progress and destruction, so definitely that cannot be the anchor on which we base. Whether it leads us to progress or destruction depends on how it is tamed. So there must be something else that guides it and that is consciousness for me, be it man's consciousness, society's consciousness or the Absolute Consciousness.

There are many real-world questions that the current day Science does not answer...yet! It might, in the future. Does Science explain death appropriately? If it doesn't explain *death* appropriately can we claim that it explains *life* enough? Life is a form of energy - energy that is the root to all our existence. Once a living being is dead, what happens to that energy? Science clearly says energy can neither be created nor destroyed, it can only change forms and that it is conserved. So what happens to that energy once a being dies? Is it suddenly lost... lost forever? Or is it assimilated by the Universe? Or would the energy gradually decay inside the body with aging or disease until death, when it is finally exhausted? Then, how is the sudden disappearance of energy explained in case of sudden deaths due to accidents? Can life and death be explained appropriately without considering the existence of soul?

All through out, I might come across as though I am lobbying against Science, but that is not really the case, but yes I agree it does sound so. More so because my posts are just an expression of a limited perspective as a response to a given situation; that is also because, on this path that I'm walking, there has been a lot of opposition to my ideas. Talking about spirituality is being seen by some as speaking against Science. *I don't understand by any standard, this attribution of mutual exclusivity.* Science is a subset of Man, Man is a subset of Universe and if you believe this Universe to be the God that is guiding (as also influencing, affecting and finally bearing, in fact containing us) constantly, arguing that Science and God are mutually exclusive sets is completely RIDICULOUS.

Some people look at belief in Science as practical or rational and belief in God as irrational or dogmatic. Science is but a miniscule subset (aspect here) of this Universe (God in my context) and there is no arguing about this. Maybe people who don't understand science are such a miniscule set in this universe, that their tininess makes them incapable of fathoming the larger set they are part of, so such people assume such mutual exclusivity. They are actually that set of people who understand neither Science nor God properly. The sad thing of our current times is that such set is increasing in size exponentially. We need to act on this, for our own well-being.

It is not in my human capacity to address all aspects and possibilities of Science and Mysticism in this confined space.

I have due respect towards the achievements of mankind so far using Science. I'm a student of Science myself. But the argument and complaining at some points of my book from the perspective of my Realization is not against Science per se, but more against the current-day ways of perception and application of Science.

That said, let me talk about certain ill-manifestations of Science now. The iPods, iPads, high-end mobile phones just some 5 years ago were under the category of exorbitant comforts and now they are fast becoming essential part of life for many. Perhaps, *it's a law of sorts that man shapes (atleast tries to shape) his life so as to convert once-upon-a-time comforts to bare-essentials*. But mind you, this cannot always be equated to development; it could well imply down-fall too (as it is already). The way we are using internet these days for every petty reason…for various things which could otherwise be accomplished by five minutes of physical effort or five more rupees, a mobile app for just about everything, speaks for our growing negligent attitudes. Not only are so many natural resources at stake all through out the network chain – the usage of those resources which is upgraded and scaled every year as per Moore's law or similar laws - but the earth's atmosphere too is contaminated with spurious and rogue frequencies of communication. Earth is depleted of many precious resources, which are not compensated for, in any way, to get the Internet as a system going. But these problems are just the tip of iceberg of the problem of the evil-manifestations of Science. In the case of Internet, atleast it has such a large set of benefits that its ill-effects can often be overlooked. The real challenge here is to draw a line that determines the trade-off of benefits vs counter-effects. But come to think of how concepts like

Cryonics[1], Transhumanism[2] and especially Technological Singularity[3] and the like reveal the possible devilish side of Science. How can anybody guarantee that tomorrow these aspects will not emerge as the norms not remaining as exceptions of Science anymore? (Given that man progresses in the same path or rather when man is allowed to progress in the same tangential path to the evolution of Universe)

---

[1] Cryonics: It is defined as the practice of preserving "legally dead" human bodies with the hope of reviving them sometime in the future when advances in medical sciences can revive their corpses and what ails them – or, atleast, extract their memories and consciousness. A person preserved this way is said to be in *cryonic suspension* and is termed a *cryopreserved patient* because the believers of cryonics do not consider the legal definition of "death" as a permanently irreversible state => According to them, the person might be dead as per current legal definition of death and technology available to resuscitate the person back to life, but the person might not be in a state of death as per future standards. The cost involved in this treatment (to preserve the corpse) is quoted of the order of six figure sum in dollars (~$100,000).

[2] Transhumanism: Wikipedia definition – "Transhumanism is an international cultural and intellectual movement with an eventual goal of fundamentally transforming the human condition by developing and making widely available technologies to greatly enhance human intellectual, physical and psychological capacities". Transhumanism advocates for the ethical use of technology to transcend biology and enhance humanity's physical and intellectual abilities.

[3] Technological singularity: Wikipedia definition – "The **technological singularity**, or simply **the singularity**, is a hypothetical moment in time when artificial intelligence will have progressed to the point of a greater-than-human intelligence, radically changing civilization, and perhaps human nature. Because the capabilities of such an intelligence may be difficult for a human to comprehend, the technological singularity is often seen as an occurrence beyond which the future course of human history is unpredictable or even unfathomable."

Ant's Science – A story:

An Ants' colony has emerged in one of the tropical areas of India during summer. They have been residing there in that colony ever since their birth and they don't know of any other place. It's their world, the only world they know of. The inherited purpose of life for these ants is to collect and save food for winter.

We know how organized and hard working the ants are. And apparently they co-ordinate and work based on certain protocols. Man! They seem to _arrive at_ protocols through concerted efforts, in fact! They seem to convey information to fellow ants through some antennae on their heads! In fact there seem to be many animal species in nature which work in such co-ordinated groups – penguins, fish and bees to name a few. But let's stick to ants for now. They do seem to work systematically based on certain framework; let's call that _Ant's Science_ for now.

So, on one fine day, there came a heavy cyclone in that area. Some ants succumbed to the unexpected event and some survived. The ants that survived were actually washed off to the nearest stream due to the impact of the floods. The marshy wet area has become their new colony. Now would the _Ant's Science_ help them anymore?

Well, the protocols and laws formulated might not work, but atleast their approach and experience might work...one might argue. But their previous trial and error approach was starting to prove more and more disastrous, it killed many ants, the approach was proving fatalistic to the survival of their race (only a group ofcourse, but for them they seemed to constitute a race unto itself). The ants have decided to incorporate drastic changes in their approach. They decided to group up as per their age. They also constituted a Policy Formulation wing. The King Ant, the head of the policy formulating wing for the whole bunch of ants declared that it's time that the oldest bunch of the group risk their life in order that the rest of the ants can continue to live. It has been decided that the oldest group will in turn split, some shall set on food exploration, some shall get the information back to the younger groups (which have been assigned different jobs of information analysis and assessment, food storage etc). Some of these ants in this group are expected to die in the process.

This process of age grouping was never before heard in the ants' colony. It was the first of its kind. This kind of splitting of responsibilities too never happened. All the ants were involved in all random sort of activities, but all they did was to come up with certain protocols collectively and propogate their science, the Ant's science, through word of mouth. While we humans would like to embed our knowledge in books and internet to share and pass it on, the ants were not too far-sighted and confined their knowledge to word-of-mouth propogation for a given life time.

Just as the Ants' colony emerged victorious by finding their way to food and formulated a new set of rules for leading their lives, a bunch of biologists visited this place and lifted the ant colony into a soil aquarium (sans water) of sorts and transported it to their lab. The subject of research was – *"How do ants survive under harshly cool temperatures?"* The ants were given required food, in fact it was evenly distributed across the aquarium. So the ants never fell short of any food. Hence their purpose of life totally changed now, it was to find a way to escape these harshly cool temperatures. The ants were a little smart to know that escaping out of the aquarium is somehow not a cool idea because they liked this idea that they will be given enough food, they no more had to work for it and that their time will be well-used in exploring *other better and finer aspects of life!*

The ants instead started researching on how to build their homes so that they are not impacted by the inconvenient temperatures. A technology to transform their food into thin sheets of clothes to protect themselves was also on their cards – *The Ants' ToDo List!* The biologists often saw a specific bunch of ants trying to come out of the aquarium. The biologists assumed that these courageous ants were planning an escapade to escape the cool weather. The biologists did not know that the ants were trying to come out in search of resources needed to materialize their intended technologies :-) *"Stupid humans!"* Those ants thought while they were shoved back into the aquarium – *"Looks like these humans are not aware of 'live and let live' funda! God save them!"*

. . . . .

So did you see how vulnerable Ant's Science was? But the ants were dynamic to adapt themselves to their drastically changing life and world situations. Don't you think our human science too is a little vulnerable if not as much? In fact we don't even know the extent of its vulnerability when the world around us changes rapidly. Would man need Ant's Science for his existence? No, would he?

Every aspect and process in this world has a threshold and I've come to think that Science has reached its threshold now in a sense that the net further contributions to the World due to scientific innovations henceforth can in no way be beneficial to us, the human beings itself, keeping nature aside, if (read it aloud, IF) we continue our scientific development based on our current day perspectives (towards both Science and Universe) and capacities (of introspecting and using the Nature around) without any *"self-introspection"* and conscious efforts to change them (our perspectives and capacities). We have reached that point where development is tending to have many counter-productive effects that outweigh the benefits.

The evil is in our perceptions of linear time when it comes to the Cosmic Process of Evolution…in our expectations of linear (and in fact exponential) development when in fact the Cosmic Time is cyclic, when in fact the Universe inherently imbibes in it the wisdom that the development and evolution of any aspect has a cyclic trend. The evil is in our attitude of getting accustomed to convenient and comfortable modes of living without realizing that those conveniences and comforts are a byproduct of the abuse and suffering of a part of humanity and Earth. The evil is in getting accustomed to the gap between haves and have-nots. The evil is in equating the recent *technological development* to Science confining its limits when in fact Science is much more old and vast than technology and much much beautiful when rightly used.

The blur between man and machine is making man more and more mechanical thrusting him away from his *"human"* side. Did we even notice that this human transformation due to technological advancement is muting our human and humane sides and making us more of machines when it comes to social responsiveness? Take a peek at what Mr. Ray Kurzweil writes in his work, *The Singularity Is Near: When Humans Transcend*

Biology - *"Singularity is the union of human and machine, in which the knowledge and skills embedded in our brains will be combined with the vastly greater capacity, speed and knowledge-sharing ability of our own creations...That merging is the essence of Singularity, an era in which our intelligence will become increasingly nonbiological and trillions of times more powerful than it is today – the dawning of a new civilization that will enable us to transcend our biological limitiations and amplify our creativity. In this new world, there will be no clear distinction between human and machine, real reality and virtual reality..."* On the other hand, Transhumanists speculate that human beings may eventually be able to transform themselves into beings with such greatly expanded abilities as to merit the label "posthuman". I have nothing against Mr. Ray Kurzweil or those particular ambitious Transhumanists, but as per my understanding of Singularity (popularly termed as the Science of Transcendance) and Transhumanism, I have this fundamental question – ***In our quest to enhance ourselves, aren't we bargaining and losing our own selves?*** The believers/lobbyists of Singularity and Cryonics speculate 2045 as the year in which technology might surpass or overtake "natural" human capacities and technology might be able to resuscitate the cryonically preserved "patients" back to life, respectively.

But it would be foolish if I'm speaking against the advancing human intellect. Who am I or anybody to stop and criticize the growing intellect? But definitely I am somebody entitled with a right to ask if human intellect wants to prosper and advance by harassing or killing somebody (including man's own self or a part of his self) or something. The question is - do we have resources to bear its advances? In fact this would be a better question to ask – Is human intellect advancing exponentially alongside its own ignorance of what damage it is fostering upon other entities of the Universe including the human race itself? And would those cosmic entities continue to tolerate this at the cost of troubling their own sustenance? As ant is to man, isn't man to nature and Universe? But, looks like the equilibrium of Universe is inherently woven around the principle of *"Live and Let Live"*. Has man understood enough the essence of this principle?

Personally, the *"exponential"* growth of human intellect makes more sense to me as long as earth's resources are growing exponentially or as long as human intellect has devised technologies that take care of "exponential" refilling of resources being used. In fact I'd be greatly elated to propose through this book, my idea of ***"Twin Technologies"***. Ladies and Gentlemen! Please welcome my idea of *Twin Technologies* which I'm highly excited to bring forth to you:

Technology to extract water from earth ⇔ to be balanced with ⇔ Technology to mandatorily refill equivalent water back into earth.

Technology to manufacture high-end electronic devices ⇔ Technology to dispose those devices efficiently so as to compensate periodically (even once in 25 years sounds good) the replaced natural resources.

Technology to deplete rock from earth ⇔ Technology to create suitable conditions for the formation of rock.

Technology to extract and harness fossil fuels ⇔ Technology to replace those fuels in equal amount or technology that garners other alternative fuels in equal amounts.

. . .

. . .

. . .

Technology to extract Wood, Iron, Steel, Marble to construct and adorn our houses with ⇔ Technology that does x, y,z...

. . .

. . .

While I can go on and on with the list (it's so easy to come up with vague ideas anyway), this list barely exposes this fact that we have tried to use so many resources without ever giving a damn as to whether (if not how) we must replace them and if we can't compensate (if not replace) them for earth, why are we even taking them?... When humanity can foray into those high-end technologies to expand the horizons of human beings, why can't we think of technologies needed to give back to nature? Why...are we not that capable yet? Or are we not willing or even trying to will and take up such a responsibility? Or are we not even deeming such a responsibility necessary?

I might have used the phrase *"growing negligent attitudes"* earlier in this post, but I take that allegation back. The recent spurt of Technological Development (which we subconsciously equate to Science) is the result of *we losing awareness of our ownselves*, not really the result of negligence; we have either forgotten, denied or suppressed some aspects of our own selves to make this development happen. This is exactly where Science is not self-sufficient the way it is going now. ***The concepts of***

Mysticism can be used to balance our sense of selves and re-assess where and how we want to march into the future. We have lost a part of our sense, a part of our common-sense that bestows us the capability of discretion - to decide what is good for us and others, to design trade-offs, *to not exploit when one can't pay back*. I call it common-sense; others may call it spiritual sense, moral sense or social responsiveness.

Science and Mysticism both have a commonality - they stemmed from man's capabilities itself - thinking, reasoning, introspecting and analyzing. But they differ on subjects of focus and what ends man wants to meet using such analysis. Mysticism goes a bit further in a sense that it is not just the result of reasoning but also *experiencing*, in fact *experiencing* first and the rest later. So the need of the hour is to shift our focus and priorities. We don't need to blend Science and Mysticism if they feel like poles apart. Man can try understanding mystical concepts, be receptive to Mysticism and change (enhance) himself so as to apply Science better. *While Mysticism can be applied on ourselves to bring our refreshed selves out, to see things (including Science) in a new light, we are instead applying Technology on to ourselves and bringing our distorted selves out!* Man is forgetting that while he is in an ever-growing quest to change the creation around him so that it will be of use to him, he is also being constantly changed by the Universe as it is evolving. He is discarding the impact of the Univserse on himself and aiming at ideal human-centric development wherein man and earth are unchanged by the Universe and nature is always at his disposal in its complete capacity.

The ideal and actual way

The way man sees and
executes it

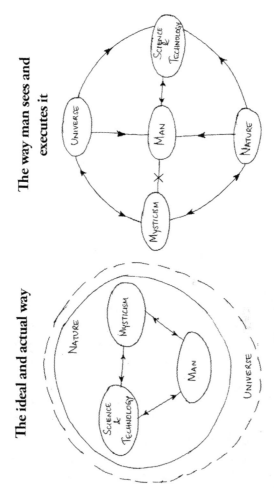

Fig 14 – Mysticism and Science

In the "Ask Deepak" series Mr. Deepak Chopra answers very elegantly this very interesting question – *"If the Universe is perfect, why are we not? If nature functions with perfect harmony, synchronocity and precision, why don't we?"* He explains it this way –

"This is a very good question and let me see if I can answer it to the best of my ability. Nature does function with effortless spontaneity and perfect harmony. And that includes all of nature, the whole Cosmos…the earth spinning on its axis, the earth going around the sun, the galaxies moving apart from each other, dark energy, dark matter, gravity, electromagnetic forces, strong and weak interactions; they all kind of synchronize to make the Universe possible. And since you and I are an activity of that Universe and that Universe is functioning with perfect precision, perfect harmony, perfection, then why aren't you and me? And that is a huge question…that is a huge dilemma for many people…

Here's what the great Vedic sages had to say about this. They said the cause of imperfection in our lives is the mistake of the intellect. And the mistake of the intellect is that you are an observer of the Universe, from the outside of the Universe…you observe it as Science would, as an observer, when in fact you the observer are also an activity of the Universe. It's the mistake of the intellect that divides the observer from the observed. And the mistake of the intellect ofcourse is our ego identity. So, when we realize that the ground of our being is the ground of all Being, the ground of our existence is the ground of all Existence and when we are established in Being and from there we feel, think and act, then we have restored ourself to our original state, which is one of perfect harmony, perfect synchronicity, precision, spontaneous right action, spontaneous right thinking, spontaneous evolution, self-regulation, self-referral and pure creativity. That can only come when our identitiy moves from the separate ego-self to the unified self which is Atman, which is Brahman – the ground of our existence, the ground of All Existence.

The most important sloka or phrase in the Bhagavad Gita is – "Yogasht Guru Karmani" – translated into English is – "Established in Yoga, perform action". I would go and explain that a little further, Established in Yoga => Established in Union with your source, which is the source of all Existence; Perform Action, Think and Feel. And if you can do that, we restore ourselves to the perfection we are!"

Thanks to Mr. Deepak Chopra for sharing his words of wisdom on youtube. This answer of his sums up so elegantly this entire churn inside me, which I have fallen short of words to explain it out here.

. . . . .

Having voiced out vehemently the ill-effects of Science in the current decade, this discussion shall be incomplete without upholding Science for what it is. Science no doubt is a wonderful instrument in tackling our day-to-day challenges; it did enable us to lead better lives. On the other hand, the beauty of Mysticism can only be realized by those who have the luck of *experiencing* mystical experiences. There are a multitude of factors at play there. Human capacity alone is not sufficient there whereas Science can be studied in bare human capacity, that is in fact the beauty and strength of Science. But still, there are some parellels between Mysticists and Scientists, let's see how.

Not everybody who is willing to become a Scientist is guaranteed to discover or invent something new. Discovery or invention happens only with highly intelligent, hardworking, persistent beings and that too by sheer chance. But, surely if you are willing to study science, you sure can, in bare human capacity, there are no impediments there. In the same way, Mysticists are those who have had the luck to *experience* some mystical experiences. But Mysticism as a discipline can be studied by anybody who has the willingness to *believe* in it, be *open* to it and *derive* wisdom from it if not directly *experience* it. Not everybody in the society has the intellectual capability to discover things, not everybody has the resources and environment to work on scientific theories, not all of us have the resources, willingness and need to even verify those scientific theories. Yet, we study scientific laws accepted, verified and formulated by a given set of academic community and progress based on them in the *belief* that they can be based and relied upon, for our own applications, study and living. The key here is that Science still is the result of work of a minority set of people who have worked hard to gain majority acceptance. And since it *has been capable* of catering to the *needs of majority* it has been able to shape the world and humanity accordingly.

We must understand that even Scientists did not gain this acceptance overnight. They too faced rejection initially, reportedly (as reported by our history) rejected by an *orthodox* community who did not have the capacity to understand science back then. If Science today is so widely accepted, why did it face such a rejection back then?... Because it is inherent of humans to yield to intertia and pre-conceived notions. *If people today accustomed to the ways of Science, are unable to open themselves to any new proposals from Mysticists,*

I would not consider such people any less orthodox than those blindly religious people unable to open themselves to Science, some centuries ago!

It makes more sense to me, to believe that, human beings do not have the capacity to *"perceive"* the whole world around them accessible to them, the way it is. **The world we perceive is "limited" by our perception of it.** I came to know recently that this faith of mine is no new theory and that "Philosophical Realism" prevailed back in the times of 400 BC itself. Wikipedia states that *"Realists believe that whatever we believe now is only an approximation of reality and that every new observation brings us closer to understanding reality".* So just because a person is unable to understand, comprehend, perceive or believe something, that incapacity itself does not invalidate the existence of that something. If a person is unable to understand a scientific theory, that by itself does not invalidate the theory. It's just that the person does not have the intellectual resources to fathom it. Before the establishment of Science as a formal discipline, Science was not as comprehensible, that does not rule out the possibility of progress of Science as it is today. It needed some time to evolve. If I am able to perceive God and if somebody is unable to, I would only see that the *"sense of God (Collective)"* is muted in him/her, that such a capacity is absent in them…as simple as that, isn't it? My belief in God stems directly from my own belief in my own perception system and somebody else's rejection of God stems from their unwillingness to accept others' belief system since they themselves have not had the same perception. I would only believe that we all need some time to evolve to comprehend God appropriately. We can only get closer to the perception of anything, at any point of time we cannot have the absolute understanding of anything since we are not the Absolute at all times. But *when* we are one with Absolute, then maybe we will be able to gain such an understanding.

Despite all the talk, no discipline of study will gain acceptance unless people see the need for it. The onus also lies on the set of people who believe in that emerging discipline to work towards its acceptance and outline its need for the society. Any instrument, medicine, study, approach howmuchever good it is, cannot linearly grow forever and is not good for all possible world-scenarios. In that sense, the acceptance of many aspects in the society has been cyclic. We see fads and fashions following a cyclic trend. Sometimes, what we think is the emergence of a new aspect, might not really be new, it's possible that it is so old that it has never been in the set of our knowledge (awareness) base. Everything is being shaped based on the *hierarchy of need* and our needs are constantly changing. The change in our needs itself is a sign of evolution; if our needs are cyclic so will the shaping of our society be too.

When a set of needs have been satiated, man looks for something more. There he is only trying to evolve, it can be for his own good or bad, but either ways cannot stop his evolution. In his quest to evolve, the current-day man is leaning on Technology. Some are seeing Technology as a panacea for mankind and some are metaphorically equating it to God. This is a dangerous trend in which we are denying our ownselves by trying to surrender our own discretionary power to machine-run intelligence, mechanisms and machine-dictated decisions and allowing them to take over. ***That clearly is a bargaining of our own power!*** Now, that is in the intellectual domain. Extending metaphorically to the physical domain, it's as good as allowing the disease of cancer to take over one's body. How is it any different? Even cancer is nothing more than exponential cellular growth, but is it any good for the body? More importantly it is considered as an abnormal and uncontrolled growth, the body does not have the power to withstand such growth! The growth of technological development is not any different, in fact it can be much worser, because handing over discretion to machine and allowing it to control our emotions (the *'information'* – or to put it better, the exploding *'data'* - on Social media and other parts of the Internet actually shape our psyche gradually in a good or bad way), is losing control on both the machine and one's own self.

Making machines do monotonous chores as long as we have sufficient resources to run them is not at all a subject of debate. But making machines that will alter our discretion, emotion and psychology by expending precious natural resources and human power in the process, without compensating the loss with alternative resources, is not just a bad-trade off, it's not even a trade off. It is like saying – *"Mommy! I want to get a little more crazy, moron, morbid, arrogant, individualistic, sociopathic and finally indifferent to even you, Dad, sis and bro, can you give me a lakh more bucks please?"*

The human race was not really orthodox when it intuitively believed in the existence of God few centuries ago. That faith was solely based on *'intuition'* – the right brain forte – without any formative evidence. But that faith alone was not sufficient for the survival and progress of our species. So the right brain allowed itself to take a backseat and facilitated the left brain to take over so it can evolve more and **attain a capacity enough to reason this intuition**. We did well to achieve a lot of Scientific progress by realizing the ultimate potential of reasoning capacity of the human brain. But then there was a threshold too. The progress is currently happening beyond this threshold because human intellect is not appropriately balanced by the spiritual power, so the left brain has started suppressing the right brain and is trying to "reason out" that the world can progress much better if left brain grows in more and more capacity by (at the cost of) muting the right brain. Unfortunately the world is being shaped according to this one-hemisphere domination! It is indeed insufficient wisdom to think that by believing in the primacy of God and soul one is going back to the orthodox and dogmatic times of past. There were certainly some dogmatic views and practices associated with God and religion back then, but that was purely due to our insufficient knowledge (awareness levels), but now we have enough awareness to dispel such dogma. *But it is all the more dogmatic to think that belief in God itself is a dogma.* If that is happening *then our hearts and minds are being shielded by the dogma of human ego* and we have turned blind to understand simple essences of life. Let's just introspect, is man today trying to reason the desire, greed and indifference nurtured by human ego? Isn't science being driven by the needs, pressures, whims and fancies of the human ego? By shifting that ego identity from individual to the collective, we will realize that believing in God and Soul is _not going back in time_ and embracing dogmatic past, but _coming back_ of suppressed and/or dormant faith and intuition, to be balanced by our reasoning, to embark on a more holistic future and development instead of a destructive future.

Can time be linear? By that question, I'm more asking, will we have time forever to evolve and evolve until there is a break to our growth? There is a nice maxim in Telugu which is relevant in this context – *Peruguta viruguta korakee*. It means – *"Growing is for collapsing"*. Keeping aside the skeptic connotation of that statement, it more conveys this idea that *every progress happens with a self-destructing tendency alongside it or rather at the cost of it.* **It means growth is cyclic.** I believe growth is cyclic, because *"Time is Cyclic".* I believe **Cosmic Time is Cyclic** irrespective of man's perception of time from earth. The event of Precession of Equinoxes whose periodicity is of the order of 25, 920 earth (human) years implies cyclical time; *it is an expression of cyclic nature of time, of birth, death and rebirth.* It might appear linear for us (which leads us to think we can grow and *"develop linearly"* as a species) for we are part of a very miniscule time for any given lifetime of ours, that we do not have the knowledge of the vast time of the Cosmic Cycle, we have lacked awareness of.

Though many say that our intuition of cyclic nature of time, as is evident from birth and death and seasons, does not answer the questions of Science (based on which we are currently shaping the world as though we are linearly progressing in time), I strongly believe that understanding Science deeply will enable one understand that Science indeed has already accommodated this argument. Below is a nice reference provided by *"When will Time End?" Cosmic Journeys (directed and produced by Thomas Lucas), Season 1, Episode 113, Original air date: January 1, 2012:*

"…..

The 19th century physicist, Ludwig Boltzmann, found a law he believed governed the flight of Time's arrow. Entropy, based on the 2nd law of thermodynamics, holds that states of disorder tend to increase.

From neat, orderly starting points, the elements, living things, the earth, the sun, the galaxy, are all headed eventually to *states of high entropy or disorder. Nature fights this **inevitable disintegration** by constantly reassembling matter and energy into lower states of entropy in cycles of death and rebirth.*

Will entropy someday win the battle and put the breaks on time's arrow? Or will time, stubbornly, keep moving forward?

We are observers, and pawns, in this cosmic conflict. We seek mastery of time's workings, even as the clock ticks down to our own certain end.

....."

Anyway, back from laws of Entropy to what I was discussuing before - All I am trying to arrive at is, Technology and even Science as it is today is not sufficient for the current needs of human evolution. Not everybody might realize this because they are caught up in their own individual struggles, but the fact is that the Collective is suffering. The Awakening within many people is a manifestation of that pain. Not only are we growing our technologies exponentially, but we are also expecting our intellect to grow at hyperbolic rates. But most of us are not aware that this growth has been at the cost of bargaining our spiritual power. Awarness of our roots by regaining our spiritual strength is needed at this time. Only that can lead to further human evolution. When the gap between human self and the so-called higher-Self decreases, Mysticism might not be as alien as it seems today. Then I will not be required to say that it is difficult to pursue Mysticism in bare human capacity, because the human capacities will change then.

We recharge our mobile batteries for a while so that they are ready for a long and busy day of chores; we don't recharge them all day.

But recharging is crucial for the mobile to work all day. It's my humble effort to share my revelation with you all that it is time for us to recharge our batteries, recharge ourselves so that we are ready for yet another quantum of evolution. The balanced and recharged man can arrive at a healthier, holisitic and wholesome Science and ways of life. *When one is not acknowledging the presence of God and the presence of divinity in the fellow human beings, one has ceased to express the divinity within onself, has ceased to be aware of the fact that we are all one and part of God.* When that gap between Humanity and Divinity is decreased, human beings would have made a quantum leap in evolution.

- Apr 15, 2014, 03:56 PM.

145. When are we now?

When are we now? I mean *Where are we now* in the cosmic time frame of Yugas is a question that many New Age Thinkers are trying to explore and answer. What thrusted my exploration on this is my process of Realization. It landed me at http://www.alignment2012.com/Chapter12.html (authored by Mr. John Major Jenkins) way back in mid 2012.

As mentioned earlier in the 'acknowledgement note' of *Figure 6 – "Sri Yukteswar's model, adjusted"*, in Chapter 74, "era-2012" is seen as the period of Galactic Alignment, by Jenkins, the author of the book *"Galactic Alignment: The Transformation of Consiousness According to Mayan, Egyptian and Vedic Traditions"*. Jenkins considers 1998 +/- 18 years i.e., 1980-2016 as *era-2012*. A little further browsing on this leads me to believe that many New Age thinkers and writers indeed believe that we have already passed through the time frame of Galactic

Alignment. For instance, one of the previews of the book *"The Yugas: Keys to Understanding Our Hidden Past, Emerging Energy Age and Enlightened Future"* by David Steinmetz and Joseph Selbie says – *"…According to their teachings, we have recently passed through the low ebb in that cycle and are moving forward to a higher age – an Energy Age that will revolutionize the world…"*

I have not read any books so far on either Cosmic Time Frame or on New Age theories, apart from the reference mentioned in the above link and a little more browsing of internet out of curiosity. But, my Inner Consciousness tells me that we have moved past the end of "Ascending Kali Yuga" and currently heading towards "Dwapara Yuga". The reader would have already come across this finding in the earlier part of the book. I have no literary base or evidence for this; it's arrived through both intuition and analysis as guided by the Absolute Consciousness/Wisdom.

As per the information I "received" from the Cosmic Source, through the process of Realization, my understanding is that, the laws of time are different at the "Conjuncture" Yugas, i.e., at the periods of occurrence of Precession of Equinoxes, time is governed by laws different from the *laws of time* in the rest of the course of our journey in time. ***Time elapses even before galactic alignment happens and we compensate for it later when the alignment happens.*** It implies we have been living in *"Borrowed Time"*. It's simple! The laws of time here are similar to the laws governing the motion of a Simple Pendulum. As a Cosmic Body (Earth here) which needs to undergo Galactic Alignment reaches that point of time, it slows down from its normal motion and behaves like a pendulum. It oscillates!

It slows down and oscillates when it doesn't *naturally* have enough energy to surpass that point.

These are the points of shift – shift from lower energy (frequency) time arc to higher energy (frequency) time arc. In fact, I believe that the accurate Cosmic Timing can be arrived at, NOT through a *circular Cosmic Time model* but through a ***spiral Cosmic Time model***. The two ends of Precession of Equinoxes - the extreme ends of either of the cones – are indeed the two ends of the Time Spiral at the transitional points. Since the pendulum doesn't have enough energy to leap on to the other spiral arc of time, it slows down; time is borrowed in exchange of (spiritual) energy and later compensated, when we gain the momentum and are ready for the leap and hence ready for the galactic alignment. The earth needs high amounts of energy in order to leap from one arc to the other larger spiral arc of time. In order to lead a synchronized life, a life in harmony with earth, humanity too needs to attune itself to the higher frequencies of Earth. This is the Fequency Acension needed of us. But instead of allowing earth to assimilate the much-needed energy *from the Universe*, we have been in an energy-grabbing mode. We have been doing just the inverse of what was required. Humanity has not accredited such great merit that we *naturally* have enough energy for this process when such a time actually arrived some 2000 years ago.

So, there are two arguments prevalent on internet regarding the Cosmic Timing and the placement of *"NOW"* in that framework. According to Sri Yukteswar's model, Ascending Dwapara Yuga has started in the *time period* of 1900 AD and the lowest point of the circle of Yugas happened as long ago as 500 AD. Though not worded directly (I'm not sure since I have not read the *"Holy Science"* book that discusses

Sri Yukteswar's model) it presents an implication that the galactic alignment indeed happened during 500 AD. Many New Age Thinkers are backing this hypothesis. On the other hand, John Major Jenkins, in his thesis through *Galactic Alignment* book, presents a time-adjusted or rather a time-shifted version of Yukteswar's model and says that Galactic Alignment is currently happening now in *era-2012* (Courtesy: Aforementioned resource on internet and a one-on-one mail discussion with him) and that we are *now currently* at that lowest point of the circle of Yugas, as shown in *Figure 6*. This is a clear conflict - a gap of about 1500 years in time - between the two versions (500 AD vs era-2012 as the lowest point).

I believe both the arguments are partly true. I agree with that part of Sri Yukteswar's hypothesis that we are already in ascending Dwapara Yuga in terms of time elapsed. I agree with that part of Mr. Jenkins' hypothesis that Galactic Alignment is still due for Earth in era-2012. This agreement definitely sounds like a paradox, let me explain what I mean by agreeing with these two parts.

No doubt, Sri Yukteswar's model has given me a profound base in the cyclic nature of Cosmic Time in terms of Yugas, but I believe it needs a piece of correction in a sense that Cosmic Time cannot be represented through a circular cycle of Yugas, but rather through a spiral cycle of Yugas. This, I believe, is the important piece of information missing in both the arguments and also the reason for conflict in hypotheses of where we stand in time now. Thus the next cycle of Yugas, a repetition of Satya, Treta, Dwapara and Kali Yuga in the reverse order cyclically, is not an exact replica or mirror image of the previous cycle of Yugas. They are longer in time, higher in energy and frequency and account for the expanding

Universe => Expanded Time and Energy for the expanded Universe. These are the fundamental differences and there might be numerous changes that follow from this cardinal change, which we ought to accommodate due to this shift. For instance we need to accommodate a new 13th month when the shift happens; we need to accommodate 13 divisions in our standard clock instead of 12. It means we will then have 26 hours in a day instead of 24. In fact, *Figure 5 – "Precession of Earth"* (in Chapter 69) and many such similar theories need to be adapted to accommodate this shift. Basically it's a transition of 12 -> 13 in the *Time Spiral Arc count*. In this context, the reader may refer to *Self-Notes* in the posts – *"60. The Expansion – The Spiralling Expansion"* and *"69. The goal of the whole and the return of Gods"* - of this book. Also my humble thanks and reverence to the insights of Sri Yukteswar (and hence his predecessors), which stood as the fulcrum for the hypotheses of many people including me. In fact, the model must be considered perfectly correct for the time spiral arc we belong to. It's just that it needs to be enhanced as we transition to another time spiral arc, as our awareness is increasing.

The big-question now in front of us is – *"For how many years or yugas are we (Earth and hence us) going to oscillate (precess in an oscillatory motion) like this?"* We are going to oscillate until we gain the momentum for the leap. The next question then is – *"How and when do we get the needed momentum?"* Actually, the Universe, for long, has been giving energy to both Earth and Humanity for this big step. But we have been in the mode of "the more we are given, the more we take!" We have transformed energy given to Earth for its own evolution and leap, into our Technological Evolution and hid it in the form of huge buildings, electrical and electronic gadgets and a lot of other materialistic wealth. And the energy given to humanity, we have sparsely used it for the process of Enlightenment and Awakening and expended it relatively more on Technolgical advancement; we have transformed the physical resources to population and mental resources to thinking big to how to make it technologically big. We might call this development, but anything that does not assist humanity in its journey forward in time cannot be deemed development. ***Any development of humanity ought to take it forward in time***, atleast in the long run. The technological development unfortunately has manifested in many people ideologically going back in time. But this drawback is inherent in the nature of journey because we are at our farthest point from Cosmic Source in a diametrically opposite alignment and *'progressing'* TANGENTIALLY to Cosmic Evolution. Thus we are not going forward in time, but oscillating in time, sort of stuck there! Frankly dissecting, perhaps this is the best we could do and we haven't done it too bad. Naturally, it's a point where the awareness of the purpose of our journey is very low, posing a challenge of repulsive tendency away from the Cosmic Source. The challenge of the Cosmos is to fight this repulsion and take us into its stride for a wholesome mutual progress. The point of achieving the needed momentum has been a moving target for us.

Since we are unable to put breaks to our accelerating gears on our own and are travelling *tangentially* to the process of Cosmic Evolution, the Divine entities are forced to take control into their hands and force Regulation on us. The harsh truth is also that the Divine entities have invested *Life on Mars* to help Earth in its leap...for Earth has been a superior entity in evolution and hence was given this preference. This is exactly what I meant when I said, at some places in this book, that we, the people on Earth have been scavenging on the cosmic powers of certain younger Gods. Since the Divine Wisdom has finally assessed that any further investment of energy is bound to go in vain, it has drawn 2014-2015 as the line. Then it will be time that we the Humanity is expected to pay back to Nature and Universe both in Energy and Time. And yes, that means Destruction...of a *part of Humanity* as also of a *part of Earth...* so as to enable rebirth of Earth and Humanity as a whole.

- Apr 26, 2014, 09:42 PM.

146. Microcosm and Macrocosm

As difficult as it is to resolve the sequence of birth of the five elements of nature – air, fire, water, soil and space, the humankind has had many questions on what emerged first – egg or chicken; object or idea; microcosm or macrocosm? Let's dissect the object-idea sequence first. Wheel as an object might be the result of an idea, but the idea might have been inspired by an object and derived out of wood, another object. Fire might have been harnessed by man into useful forms as a result of his ideas, but the first idea seems to have occurred to man as a result of an accidental collusion between two rocks, two objects.

So it looks like object came first. According to Materialist Philospohy, matter precedes thought and the world exists outsides of us, independent of our perception of it. Even according to the laws of science - law of conservation of energy and energy-mass equivalence, matter is deemed to come first. Especially note that an idea is NOT being viewed as a form of energy here! And even if idea is considered energy, the results of the discussions I have had on this subject revolve around this central theme – *Let's restrict to earth, keeping aside the Universe, idea emerges from man; and earth as an object emerged before man. So, object came first.* So that is the majority opinion I came across. In fact, Science as of today completely bases itself on Materialism. According to Materialism, matter precedes thought.

While I did not want to argue with the majority opinion by presenting my opinion, I certainly want to present the same here. Let's keep Universe and even Earth aside, let's narrow down our scope further, let's apply this question to creation of life, new life… a new-born baby. So is object first or idea first in the context of a creation of a new-born baby? Well, the first thought that might strike us is – A baby is born out of mother's womb, so object must come first. I dislike the idea of considering mother's womb as an object…can a baby be conceived and the embryo grown inside a dead-womb? Ok with the advent of science, maybe yes, since embryos can be nurtured inside test tubes these days. So let's just assume mother's womb as an object for the sake of our discussion. But the baby is born out of the fertilization of egg by the sperm, both of which are a result of two living beings with ideas and feelings irrespective of whether the birth happens through test-tube or mother's womb. Mother and Father are not mere objects, they are objects with ideas and feelings…they are living beings. Now, let me keep aside the advent of science and talk about the way *creation of life* happens usually. Irrespective of the actualization of life into the world, the conception of life happens as a result of ideas and feelings of living beings and the chemistry between their material bodies. Can a baby be born out of artificial insemination and fertilization of some organic entities extracted from a dead man and a dead woman? If yes, maybe then, I would accept that object precedes idea. So what do you think now, is idea first or object first? Atleast for the current case of discussion we can pretty clearly derive that they co-exist at the *absolute beginning* of new life.

Now to the egg-chicken sequence. Scientists at the universities of Sheffield and Warwick claim that they have resolved this long standing conundrum saying chicken came before egg, considering the *'species adaptation'* factor of evolution.

There has been no definitive answer for microrcosm and macrocosm. The very literal meaning and definition of the terms indicate that microcosm has a similar structure as macrocosm and is contained within macrocosm, a complex entity regarded as a system in itself. But man views his own biological evolution through an approach of *"from microcosm (cell) to macrocosm (the man)"*. So, atleast for this specific context man considers microcosm to have come first. Again the paradox is that man also knows that this Universe (the macrocosm) has emerged much long before man (the microcosm) took birth. But then, man has always used microcosm to reflect over macrocosm and understand it better. Because, after all, undeniably we are so tiny and contained as a part within this Universe that we don't have a choice but to use microcosm, since *apparently* that is what we have better access to inspect and dissect. Our preference of inspecting microcosm to inspecting macrocosm very much shows in the way we are trying to discern the vast dark matter and dark energy using particle collisions of LHC (Large Hadron Collider), more famously known as the machine discerning the God particle.

Certain philosophical theories consider this distinction between microcosm and macrocosm inappropriate since we are living in an intricately webbed, interconnected and undivided

Universe; it's all One. I'm more inclined towards this belief. But I want to try my hand at explaining this in scientific terms especially for agnostics and atheists. Based on the Big-Bang model, a prevailing cosmological model contested by a majority of the scientific community, the Universe is born out of a giant explosion 13.8 billion years ago before which the whole Universe as a matter is contained in a single point. So doesn't it sound (atleast going by the literal definitions) that we believe microcosm existed first, just as we believe that cells came into existence before humans? But an essential aspect here is that, microcosm is first *at that point of time when*

$$microcosm = MACROCOSM$$

The Kundalini/Consciousness Awakening is that magnificent process which enables a human being to "*experience*" the macrocosm inside his microcosm. The macrocosm could be the reflection of energy or consciousness of this Universe (only an appropriately *scaled reflection* of it, not the whole of it in its entire and exact scale of totality) or it could be that of earth or any other cosmic entity depending on whichever cosmic entity has willed and agreed to assist you in this process. Thus, this process of Awakening does not happen totally based on one's own free-will as and when one wants or strives for it to happen or experience it. It requires *External Help and Guidance*. It requires that *External Intervention* when the time is ripe for it, to materialize your purpose of life, based on the agreement your soul has made with those entities before you embarked on this human journey. More importantly it requires that your soul is capable to handle this, so it depends on the merit and experience your soul has accredited in its journey over its many past lives. It requires that your soul is capable of accessing your higher Self since the Awakening cannot happen in bare human capacity.

Through the process of Ascension, we are not just ascending to higher frequencies; we are going to ascend to a new dimension. The lack of a dimension suppresses a lot of details. Perception of a flat earth, once upon a time, viewing earth as a disc, suppressed the fact that earth is an approximate sphere and thereby suppressed many other truths related to earth, essential to lead better lives. When we acquire a new dimension or rather let me say, when we become capable of perceiving a new dimension, which is just one of those many other unknown dimensions which we for sure can't perceive in our human capacity in their entirety...who knows...may be we will know that earth does not revolve around Sun the way we see it or perceive it, but maybe that each planet goes on its own spiral course while the sun is moving linearly around the galaxy.

Many aspects of this Universe are not tangible to us as such tangibility is limited by the human perception. Why talk about Universe, we cannot see many microscopic organisms or things due to the lack of microscopic vision of human eye; we cannot see far off planets in the sky through our naked eye as it is limited by human vision for the given optical environment. We cannot distinctly perceive and realize the sprouting of a seedling owing to our perception of time. And we are only talking about vision here; there might be so many things on Earth itself that we are currently unable to "perceive" owing to our limited perception of world, owing to our limited perception of dimensions and owing to our limited capability of human brain and human consciousness. In fact for a given dimension itself, at any point of time, the realm of unknown far exceeds the known and is open for human exploration.

But then addition of a dimension does not mean that all our existence before that is a life led in a lie. No! That is where I really love the methodical ways of Science. We stick to a frame of reference and formulate laws around those fundamentals. As long as that base is right, the formulations are right. The problem is when the base shakes literally pulling us off our ground. But still the formulations are right and have served some purpose for us, while we stood on a wrong frame of reference. The formulations are right as long as we lie in that wrong (unevolved) frame of reference. My Realization tells me that it is time we (The Earth and Humanity) shift to that new dimension and expand our horizons using new paradigms to correct (evolve) not only our frames of reference but also many theories and (apparent) facts we have formulated for ourselves.

Itseems David Hume said - *No fact can be unlimitedly true –* this thought is just so apt for this context. In fact Science avoids temporal absolutism in theory in a sense that scientific theories are open to be debunked if there arises even one exception that does not agree with its scientific laws. **It means no scientific theory is "guaranteed" to be valid forver.** But in reality the believers and lobbyists of Science more or less tend to accept most theories as facts and fundamentals and not only progress based on them, but also tend to reject any *mystical* theories that go against these theories. The problem here is that they expect any proof in a scientific way. How can a scientific proof be given when the argument does not fall under scientific ways of detesting and verification? Note that both Scientific and Mystical theories do not have absolute proofs in such a case, but the acceptance of the former through rigorous tests and usage happens only *owing to the needs and awareness of the majority* for a given time. I'm trying to say that the *collective needs of the human species* are shifting. But, as individuals we have lacked that awareness, we have given in to the inertia of our past, unable to grow beyond it, thereby troubling ourselves.

I'm also trying to say that *majority acceptance* does not make an approach right and scientific. Nor does a minority advocation make it blindly religious. All human progress was based on questioning the status quo and a strong struggle to make a minority opinion the majority opinion, well, if only that is right and catered to the needs of a given time in evolution. If we all forever base ourselves on what the majority believes and thinks, we would be the same forever. In fact scientific progress itself wouldn't have been possible if people during the Renaissance period did not heed to the minority group.

This and a couple of paragraphs below are written specifically to address those people who are using Science to argue that there is no soul, that it's just a ghost in the machine and that Consciousness of man is an emergent property of biological evolution. Being a theist and having *experienced* mystical experiences, I put forward my ideas here: In laymen terms, for the current discussion, Soul is the intermediary between the brain and the world around it, it communicates with the vibrations (frequencies) of the Universe to manifest mind. What we sense with our five senses is still "our" perception of the world and not the world per se. With our five senses we cannot see micro-organisms, cannot hear ultra low sounds, cannot see cells in our body, but that itself does not invalidate the existence of microorganisms, ultra low sounds or cells in our body. Our perception of the world around us has been limited by our five senses. We have taken help of machines to explore the realm of unknown, yet we are limited by by those five senses. Our understanding of brain too is limited by our capacity of brain.

My brain is able to feel God (the sense of Collective Consciousness, for this context) because my soul is able to communicate with higher frequencies of the Universe. So my mind has accepted the existence of God. The brain of atheists might not be able to comprehend God because it is not able to feel it, because their soul is unable to communicate with higher frequencies. So I'm saying atheists' comprehension of God is "limited" by their soul capacity just as the comprehension of "Sense and Sensibility" novel might be limited by illiteracy.

If a person's brain is unable to understand Einstein's Theory of Relativity, that is his intellectual limitation. An illiterate on the other hand might not even be aware that such a theory exists so he might not even try to know it. But once he is made aware of this theory, maybe he can rise to that state to comprehend it, if he feels the *need* to understand it. Some adamant competitor of Einstein back then, might not want to read through the theory by opening his brain and ego, so he will never be able to genuinely judge the Theory. That competitor is restricted (limited) by his pre-conceived notions.

A monkey does not have the resources (language, communication, intellect, etc.) not only to understand Relativity theory but also to become aware of the existence of that theory and its relevance for its life although it is living its life in a world that might have been abiding by the laws of Relativity. It is at a lower stage of evolution, so a monkey will never understand Relativity Theory and will not even attempt to understand even if one puts the proof before it. It is limited in so many ways, the first one being *the lack of need by a monkey, for its existence, to understand a theory* formulated by its succeeding species.

A person who does not have enough resources (the materialistic equivalent of the term 'capacities') to fathom God, cannot "verify" or "prove" the existence of God, because its proof lies in the realm of "experiencing" and that person's resources (soul and hence mind) are mute to the phenomenon of "experiencing" God. That is his emotional or spiritual limitation. The soul is mute so the person is unable to understand that soul exists, so that becomes the dead-end to anything further.

Just as an evolved brain is a pre-requisite for understanding the nuances of brain, an evolved soul is required to understand the nuances of soul. **It is the limitation of "evolution".** A person who is deaf by birth cannot fathom the beauty of listening to music. So it is impossible to verbally explain him the beauty of music, he is deaf, he will not be able to listen to the explanation. There can be other means to explain him, but the beauty of music might not be encaptured in its totality. But if the music comes from within him vocally, out of a heart that responds to the music of the Universe, then nobody can stop it. I have no doubt to say that, when man *needs* God for his existence he SHALL be able to comprehend this concept of Collective Consciousness. We all know our *hierarchy of need*, don't we? We searched for food first, then clothes, then means of transportation....so on...you know the history... the spiritual needs do really come at a later stage. When man is in a conscious and sensible search of God, which is indeed happening today, man can be deemed to be at a higher step of evolution.

Today, man is trying to explore the Universe based on his understanding of the Universe, though in the process, he is not aware of the damage he is creating. *Space Junk* which is making further space exploration difficult is just the tip of the iceberg of the problem, but that too is known to us, because it is impeding us. Man's ways of looking at Cosmos are Human-centric. If people attempt to detach themselves from their ego and attempt to see the Cosmos devoid of their pre-conceived notions as a result of human ego and conditioning, one will TRULY EVOLVE to realize how beautiful the intentions the "Cosmos" has for Earth and its people, they will realize how beautiful the Earth is, as a "part" of the "whole" that is Cosmos.

The Cosmic Way of looking at Earth and Humanity is way more beautiful than viewing a galaxy through a telescope and assuming that man has evolved by creating equipment needed to acquire the knowledge of Cosmos. I will never make a mistake of calling it "Cosmic-Centric way of looking at Earth and its people (Humanity)" for they are part of Cosmos, for then it will be such a misnomer. To comprehend Cosmos and start embarking on extra-terrestrial journeys it's very important for man to know how this planet is an inherent part of the Cosmos and how this planet has been given energies and wisdom for its sustenance by the Cosmos and what all forces have been at play for the earth and its people to reach this point of evolution. That awareness comes by ascending to the next dimension, the next step in the evolution.

Coming back to the microcosm – macrocosm sequence, let's get back to Big Bang Model. While we all know the scientific theories proposed as part of this model, my Realization tells me that Big-Bang happened at that point of time when the Universe split into Consciousness (Shiva) and Energy (Shakti). At that point of time,

Consciousness = Energy

Shiva = Shakti

It implies that Energy cannot manifest as Matter without the impregnation of Energy by Consciousness. It also implies that Consciousness cannot be activated in the absence of Energy. Big Bang is that point of time when two complementary aspects of Universe invigorated each other to expand this Universe. It also implies that the progress of Universe has always been happening based on the churning, co-existence and mutual dependance between paradoxes. That is why the experience of good and bad, darkness and light, happiness and grief and many other complementary aspects, makes our lives more fulfilling and complete.

- Apr 27, 2014, 11:23 PM.

* * * * * * * * * *

"Love is an endless mystery, for it has nothing else to explain it."

— *Rabindranath Tagore.*

* * * * * * * * * *

Epilogue

As a leaf that falls off the tree, rustles, swirls and drifts in the infinitude of the air, dries up as the time passes by, decays and dissolves inside the Earth and be one with it…As the water of the river born when the glaciers melt or when a cloud outpours, flows and flows, meets other rivers in its course and finally finds its way into the Sea…so are we humans existing here on Earth, leading our lives cut off from our native aspects. The human journey and conditioning has an inherent character of making us lack this awareness of our pristine aspects. But that does not mean we lack this awareness forever. There arise certain situations when such an awareness is "required of us".

I've been trying to connect the dots of a puzzle through the chapters in this book. I've fallen short of words to describe this magnanimous process that happened inside me. I was limited by the power of language, by my own knowledge of language and my power of expression. What I wrote in this book is no where close to make you feel what I felt. But here I write about the connection – that connection which thrusted inside me, the effort to connect the dots – thus placing these dots in context. That connection is none other than this Universe itself. The Universe as it evolves is in an ever-dynamic state of equilibrium, yet its individual forces are always in the fight, some reinforcing, some conflicting, but never at rest. What initiated this writing was one such group of forces - the forces of Earth, as it tries to *balance itself* for the Cosmic event of

Precession of Equinoxes, also necessitating the Humanity on Earth to ascend along with it.

The most important aspect that the current times need to gain awareness of is the animate nature of the Universe. Yes! The Universe has a Consciousness associated with it. The world today has majorly based itself on Materialism. By that, we are only acknowledging (subconsciously) the existence of our Cosmic Mother and by denying the animateness associated with the Universe, we are denying the existence of our Cosmic Father. Yet, the world is shaping itself more and more as a masculine-dominated world based on man's way of thinking, feeling and acting shaping up things based on his needs, with feminine aspects pushed to the backseat. Now that sounds like a paradox doesn't it?

Yes, by losing awareness of the Cosmic Father, man has lost his native characteristics and aspects too. By gaining that awareness back, he is sensitized towards the other gender appropriately, he is expected to treat woman at par with him and grow matured to allow her to take her due place. By gaining that awareness back, woman understands that she is powerful the way she is, that she need not resort to think, feel and act like a man to gain power in the society. The society shall no more be dominated and shaped in turn more and more by left-brain activities. It shall sustain balancedly with both left and right brain activities propelling the world approriately. By acknowledging consciously, the existence of Cosmic Father, *WE ARE* equipping ourselves to receive Wisdom from Him.

The Divine Feminine has been dedicating their efforts towards this mission of lifting up the man (humanity) to gain this awareness (of Cosmic Father). Because, ***the awareness of our true state is the key to proper existence and way of life.*** While all the Gods are constantly working for their own well-being and hence that of humanity too, since both are correlated in some way, the Divine Feminine has been under the veil for a long time in order to *contain* the negative effect of the deeds of humanity so as to facilitate them in their upliftment and evolution. If the effect of results of the deeds of humanity was to be borne by humanity itself, this world would have been a different place altogether by now. The Divine Feminine remaining behind this veil was thus for a collective benefit, but this was not devoid of its side-effects. It shows in the suffering of the majority of women on earth wherein one in every three women is being abused in one form or the other daily, it shows in the disparity, misunderstanding and mutual exploitation between the genders.

The *Return Of The Divine Feminine* happens when that mission is fulfilled, when humanity gains the awareness of the aspect of Cosmic Father within themselves. This is expected to happen through Ascension at the point of time of Precession of Equinoxes (PoE). Every progress embeds within itself the aspect of self-destruction over a certain period of time and time has arrived to express that periodicity. We have grown beyond reform, blown out too many chances and have invited upon ourselves a change not through Reform, but through Regulation from **"The Divine Intervention".**

We have been living in borrowed time in exchange of (spiritual) energy and though time has come when we must give that energy back to the Universe, we are still stealing energy from earth because of our discretionary power, that bestows us to draw a line and say *"Now, it's enough!"*, being taken over by greed, due to lack of awareness of our roots. All in all, we are now in a self-defeating, self-denying, individuality-pro and collective-no march into the future in a tangential path to the evolution of the Universe. Yes, the greed of man on earth to progress linearly as if there's no tomorrow, has been at loggerheads with the evolution of Earth as part of the larger Cosmos. Each of us is part 'I' and part 'We'. The delicate balance between these two aspects is the key to a content and happy existence. The end result of the PoE is expected to be regulation and tackling of various problems of human psyche (including the negative jitters of individuality) by lifting up the consciousness of each and every individual on earth through frequency ascension and improve the discretionary mechanism.

This process is expected to usher in a time when not just a few theories of Science are going to be debunked, but most importantly, our perceptions of this world are going to radically change through paradigmatic shifts. The debunking could be so radical that the simple laws we believe to be Universal Truths/Facts might just change…like the fact "Sun rises in the east and sets in the west" might not be valid anymore when our sense of direction itself changes (Ofcourse that's just an example to explain the case in point). The way we perceive and use Science is going to change.

When the caterpillar metamorphosizes into a butterfly, would it need its own caterpillar's science anymore to lead its life and survive in this world? The butterfly needs a different science; it might not even want to call it Science. The outside of us is going to change, the inside of us is going to respond and hence our perception of outside in turn is going to change. The Universe as we perceive it is nothing but a *mirror* of the response of our inside to the outside. The Universe itself is constantly shaped by that mutual give and take between microcosm and macrocosm. *And we indeed are the Inside of that Outside. And that Outside is our Inside.*

The butterfly is waiting to happen…now…

Atma Shatakam / Nirvana Shatakam
The Song of the Self
by Adi Shankaracharya
(788-820 CE)

॥ निर्वाण षटकम् ॥

मनो बुद्ध्यहंकारचितानि नाहम् न च श्रोत्र जिह्वे न च घ्राण नेत्रे
न च व्योम भूमिर् न तेजो न वायु: चिदानन्द रूप: शिवोऽहम् शिवोऽहम् ॥

न च प्राण संज्ञो न वै पञ्चवायु: न वा सप्तधातुर् न वा पञ्चकोश:
न वाक्पाणिपादौ न चोपस्थपायू चिदानन्द रूप: शिवोऽहम् शिवोऽहम् ॥

न मे द्वेष रागौ न मे लोभ मोहौ मदो नैव मे नैव मात्सर्य भाव:
न धर्मो न चार्थो न कामो ना मोक्ष: चिदानन्द रूप: शिवोऽहम् शिवोऽहम् ॥

न पुण्यं न पापं न सौख्यं न दु:खम् न मन्त्रो न तीर्थं न वेदा: न यज्ञा:
अहं भोजनं नैव भोज्यं न भोक्ता चिदानन्द रूप: शिवोऽहम् शिवोऽहम् ॥

न मृत्युर् न शंका न मे जातिभेद: पिता नैव मे नैव माता न जन्म
न बन्धुर् न मित्रं गुरुर्नैव शिष्य: चिदानन्द रूप: शिवोऽहम् शिवोऽहम् ॥

अहं निर्विकल्पो निराकार रूपो विभुत्वाच्च सर्वत्र सर्वेन्द्रियाणाम्
न चासंगतं नैव मुक्तिर् न मेय: चिदानन्द रूप: शिवोऽहम् शिवोऽहम् ॥

English Transliteration from Sanskrit

Mano Budhyahankaar Chitani Naaham, Na Cha
Shrotra Jihve Na Cha Ghraana netre

Na Cha Vyoma Bhumir Na Tejo Na Vayuh,
Chidananda Rupah Shivoham Shivoham

Na Cha Praana Sanjno Na Vai Pancha Vaayuhu,
Na Vaa Sapta Dhaatur Na Va Pancha Koshah

Na Vaak Paani Paadau Na Chopasthapaayuh,
Chidaananda Rupah Shivoham Shivoham

Na Me Dvesha Raagau Na Me Lobha Mohau,
Mado Naiva Me Naiva Maatsarya Bhaavah

Na Dharmo Na Chaartho Na Kaamo Na Moksha,
Chidaananda Rupah Shivoham Shivoham

Na Punyan Na Paapan Na Saukhyan Na Dukham,
Na Mantro Na Tirthan Na Vedaah Na Yajnaah

Aham Bhojanan Naiv Bhojyan Na Bhoktaa,
Chidaananda Rupah Shivoham Shivoham

Na Mrityur Na Shanka Na Me Jaati Bhedah,
Pitaa Naiva Me Naiva Maataa Na Janma

Na Bandhur Na Mitram Guru Naiva Shishyah,
Chidaananda Rupah Shivoham Shivoham

Aham Nirvikalpo Niraakaara Rupo,
Vibhutvaaccha Sarvatra Sarvendriyaanaam

Na Chaa Sangatan Naiva Muktir Na meyah
Chidananda Rupah Shivoham Shivoham

<u>Meaning</u>

1) I am not mind, nor intellect, nor ego, nor the reflections of inner self (chitta). I am not the five senses. I am beyond that. I am not the ether, nor the earth, nor the fire, nor the wind (the five elements). I am indeed, That eternal knowing and bliss, love and pure consciousness.

I am Shiva, I am Shiva.

2) Neither can I be termed as energy (praana), nor five types of breath (vaayu), nor the seven material essences (dhaatu), nor the five sheaths (pancha-kosha). Neither am I the five instruments of elimination, procreation, motion, grasping, or speaking. I am indeed, That eternal knowing and bliss, love and pure consciousness.

I am Shiva, I am Shiva.

3) I have no hatred or dislike, nor affiliation or liking, nor greed, nor delusion, nor pride or haughtiness, nor feelings of envy or jealousy. I am not within the bounds of Dharma (Duty), Artha (Wealth), Kama (Desire) and Moksha (Liberation) (the four Purushartha of life). I am indeed, That eternal knowing and bliss, love and pure consciousness.

I am Shiva, I am Shiva.

4) Neither am I bound by virtue (punya) nor by vice (paapa), neither by happiness nor by sorrow, pain or pleasure. Neither am I bound by sacred hymns (mantras), holy places, scriptures, rituals or sacrifices (yajna). I am none of the triad of the observer or one who experiences,

the process of observing or experiencing, or any object being observed or experienced. I am indeed, That eternal knowing and bliss, love and pure consciousness.

I am Shiva, I am Shiva.

5) Neither am I bound by death and its fear, I have no separation from my true self, no doubt about my existence, nor have I discrimination on the basis of birth (caste and creed). I have no father or mother, nor did I have a birth. Neither do I have relatives nor friends, nor Guru, nor disciples. I am indeed, That eternal knowing and bliss, love and pure consciousness.

I am Shiva, I am Shiva.

6) I am without any variation (attributes) and without any form. I am all pervasive, present everywhere as the underlying substratum of everything and behind all sense organs; I am everything, everywhere, every time, always in equilibrium. Neither do I get attached to anything, nor get freed from anything. I am indeed, That eternal knowing and bliss, love and pure consciousness. I am Shiva, I am Shiva.

· · · · ·

Shiva Yajur Mantra
(Yajurveda Shloka)

॥ शिवा यजुर मंत्र॥

कर्पूरगौरं करुणावतारं संसारसारम् भुजगेन्द्रहारम् ।
सदावसन्तं हृदयारविन्दे भवं भवानीसहितं नमामि ॥

English Transliteration from Sanskrit

Karpura gauram Karunavataram Samsaara
saaram Bhujagendra Haaram I

Sadaavasantham Hridayaaravindee Bhavam
Bhavani Sahitham Namami II

Meaning

The one who is as pure as camphor, who is compassion
incarnate, the one who is the essence of the world,
the One with the serpent king as his garland;

Always residing in the lotus of the Heart,
Oh Lord (Bhava - the Creator) and Goddess
(Bhavani), I bow to you both.

Fig 15 – Our Cosmic Parents